Foliage House Plants

THE TIME-LIFE ENCYCLOPEDIA OF GARDENING

Foliage House Plants

by

JAMES UNDERWOOD CROCKETT

and

the Editors of TIME-LIFE BOOKS

An Owl Book

HENRY HOLT AND COMPANY

NEW YORK

THE TIME-LIFE ENCYCLOPEDIA OF GARDENING
SERIES EDITOR: Robert M. Jones
EDITORIAL STAFF FOR FOLIAGE HOUSE PLANTS:
EDITOR: Ogden Tanner
Picture Editor: Kaye Neil
Designer: Leonard Wolfe
Staff Writers: Helen Barer, Marian Gordon Goldman,
Gerry Schremp
Researchers: Gail Cruikshank, Barbara Ensrud,
Helen Fennell, Rhea Finkelstein, Gail Hansberry,
Sandra Streepey, Gretchen Wessels, Penny Zug
Design Assistant: Anne B. Landry

Library of Congress Cataloging-in-Publication Data
Crockett, James Underwood.
Foliage house plants.
(The Time-Life encyclopedia of gardening)
Reprint. Originally published: New York : Time-Life
Books, 1972.
"An Owl book."
Bibliography: p.
Includes index.
1. House plants. 2. Foliage plants. 3. Succulent
plants. 4. Indoor gardening. I. Time-Life Books.
II. Title. III. Series.
[SB419.C69 1986]   635.9'65   86-12061
ISBN 0-8050-0123-9 (pbk.)

First published by Time-Life Books in 1972.
First Owl Book Edition—1986
Printed in the United States of America
10 9 8 7 6 5 4 3 2 1

ISBN 0-8050-0123-9

THE AUTHOR: James Underwood Crockett, a graduate of the University of Massachusetts, received an Honorary Doctor of Science degree from that University and has been cited by the American Association of Nurserymen and the American Horticultural Society. He has worked with plants in California, New York, Texas and New England. He is the author of books on greenhouse, indoor and windowsill gardening, and has written a monthly column for *Horticulture* magazine and a monthly bulletin, *Flowery Talks,* for retail florists. His weekly television program, *Crockett's Victory Garden,* has been seen by millions of viewers on public broadcasting stations throughout the United States.

GENERAL CONSULTANTS: Russell C. Mott, Ithaca, New York. Albert P. Nordheden, Morganville, New Jersey. Staff of the Brooklyn Botanic Garden: Elizabeth Scholtz, Director; Robert S. Tomson, Assistant Director; Thomas R. Hofmann, Plant Propagator; George A. Kalmbacher, Plant Taxonomist; Edmund O. Moulin, Horticulturist.

THE COVER: Glowing fresh and lustrous against a backdrop of old barn siding is a sampling of the almost infinite variety of foliage house plants available to the indoor gardener today. Grouped around the large Iron Cross begonia at center are *(clockwise from top left):* a Victorian fern, a vivid red-and-green caladium, a Massange's dracaena, an Emerald Ripple peperomia, a Cretan brake fern, an English ivy and a silver pothos.

CONTENTS

A world of greenery at home 1

On a visit to New York City not long ago, I discovered that one of its most fashionable new stores is not a chic boutique on Fifth Avenue but a full-sized working greenhouse built on top of a four-story loft building near the East River. On almost any day, Sundays included, streams of customers climb the last flight of stairs to the roof and enter a veritable jungle of tropical plants that overgrow the aisles and arch toward the glass ceiling in the warm, humid air. When I was there I saw what must have been close to a hundred different species and varieties on display, each carefully keyed by number to a pamphlet visitors picked up at the door ("No. 60: Nephrolepis; Boston fern. Light recommended: low. Watering: heavy. Temperature preferred: medium"). In this dazzling array of foliage there was something to suit practically every taste and pocketbook, from a 1½-inch-high powder puff cactus for 89 cents to lush banks of 4-foot dracaenas for $50, to a $1,200 *Dizygotheca elegantissima* that had grown a good 20 feet tall and nearly as broad. (Whatever would happen if the nurseryman actually sold this tropical tree I was unable to find out; he would probably have to dismantle the side of his urban greenhouse, lower the tree with a crane to a truck in the street below, then dismantle another building somewhere else to deliver it.)

Only a few years ago such a rooftop rain forest could not have existed, nor could all the other new plant stores that I have noticed in the city. What has brought them into being is the unprecedented boom in the popularity of house plants, particularly those prized for their foliage rather than flowers, for display in every kind of place imaginable, not only in apartments and houses, but in office buildings, banks and stores.

The burgeoning interest in foliage plants for indoor use is by no means limited to New York; it is going on all over the country at a rate that surprises even the commercial growers who supply the plants. More and more people, apparently, have realized that plants make the long hours spent confined indoors a little more

Surrounded by foliage plants, a customer in a Philadelphia greenhouse inspects a hanging basket of rex begonias. In front of her are Norfolk Island pines and Sprenger asparagus ferns; above are Boston ferns.

pleasant. Many may recognize that plants, indoors as well as out, give us vital oxygen in return for the carbon dioxide we exhale, that, particularly in numbers, they help humidify dry indoor air by giving off moisture through their leaves and that, in general, they are not only healthy but pretty things to have around. But most plant lovers grow them simply because they satisfy deep human needs. Not long ago I came across an appraisal of those needs in an unlikely place, the Bulletin of Atomic Scientists: "Unique as we may think we are, it seems likely that we are genetically programmed to a natural habitat of clean air and a varied green landscape. . . . For centuries in the temperate zones we have tried to imitate in our houses not only the climate, but the setting of our evolutionary past: warm, humid air, green plants and even animal companions." The thought was expressed more succinctly by Ross Parmenter in his book *The Plant in My Window:* "Whether he knows it or not, a man needs to be close to growing things."

THE BOOM'S BEGINNINGS   The plant in Parmenter's window—a struggling specimen that was left behind by the apartment's previous inhabitant and nursed back to health by its new owner—was a heart-leaved philodendron, the most widely grown foliage house plant in America today and, in fact, the plant that can be said to have started today's boom in indoor gardening. This appealing little vine, known to botanists as *Philodendron oxycardium,* was first brought from the West Indies to England in 1793 by Captain William Bligh—the Captain Bligh of *Mutiny on the Bounty*—along with several hundred other species of varying interest to the Royal Botanic Gardens. It was half forgotten, however, and does not seem to have played much of a role in the 19th Century fad for greenery that turned proper Victorian parlors into miniature jungles. Its great popularity as a house plant did not begin until 1936, when John Masek, a nurseryman in Orlando, Florida, rediscovered it. Noting that the plant was attractive, virtually pest free, easy to grow indoors and—most important in that Depression year—economically propagated in quantity, Masek decided to pot up heart-leaved philodendrons and sell them not only through florists but in five-and-ten stores. The ready availability of such delightful plants at very low prices brought a quick response from the public. Pots of philodendron appeared everywhere, and before long a sizable house-plant industry was born. By the late 1970s, Florida produced more than $110 million worth of foliage plants a year, over 50 per cent of the total U.S. output, and about half of Florida's 354 commercial shippers were clustered in the Orlando area; of the plants they shipped around the country, one in 10 was a heart-leaved philodendron.

Although the philodendron remains America's favorite, its

popularity has also spurred the search for other, more exotic plants of every type. Today there are hundreds of species for a buyer to choose from, of every size and shape, leaf pattern, color and texture (*pages 14-23*). Not only have the potted palms, ferns and aspidistras of grandmother's day come back into favor once more, but scores of new plants have been brought back from around the world to be propagated and crossbred in commercial greenhouses. Many were unknown only a few years ago, when they were discovered growing wild in the tropical or semitropical regions of such faraway places as South America, Africa, Asia and Australia.

These labors have produced plants that not only provide a fascinating display of exotic greenery but by and large get along with a minimum of care. Not all of them are green. Some of the most popular have leaves that are purple or red or splashed with white or yellow markings, and almost any imaginable color, pattern and color combination can be found. What they have in common is attractive leaves—or in the case of cacti, stems—rather than an abundance of spectacular flowers. They are different enough from flowering plants in character and growing needs to constitute a category of their own. Unlike many flowering house plants, which need bright sun and cool night temperatures to blossom, most can manage under average indoor conditions. And while a flowering plant's moment of glory may only last a week or two, foliage plants keep on giving year-round pleasure, year after year. In my own house I have a shiny-leaved India-rubber tree that is at least five years old and still going strong, a spiky six-year-old *Dracaena marginata*, a 10-year-old Norfolk Island pine, a twisted asparagus fern that has been growing for 10 years in the same pot and a spider plant that has been around for longer than I can recall. Being natives of tropical or semitropical climates, all these species thrive better than most flowering plants in the 70° F. warmth of a heated house. And several of them tolerate lower light levels too, so that I can place them away from the windows in almost any part of a room.

You may have noticed that I said "tolerate" low light. Actually most plants are sun lovers. What we think of as shade-loving plants are so only to a degree; young plants growing in a forest or jungle have developed the ability to survive in the shadow of their elders until they adapt to the shade or became large enough to find their own place in the sun. If kept indoors where light levels are never as great as outdoors, they simply grow more slowly. Similarly most tropical plants will tolerate the dry air of a heated house, which averages between 10 and 30 per cent relative humidity, although they would prefer the 70 to 80 per cent humidity, as well as the 70° to 90° temperatures, of their native habitat.

LONG-LASTING BARGAINS

A 10,000-YEAR-OLD DRACAENA

One of the longest-lived and largest trees on record is the same kind of plant that grows 3 to 4 feet tall in a pot indoors, Dracaena draco. Known as the Dragon Tree of Orotava, it was found growing on Tenerife in the Canary Islands by the Spanish commander Alonso Fernández de Lugo, who conquered the island in 1496. The trunk, 50 feet in circumference at its base, rose 60 feet before dividing into 12 gigantic branches, each up to 18 feet around with leaves 2 to 4 feet long. The tree was so imposing that de Lugo set up a small chapel in a cavity formed by the massive aboveground roots. The naturalist Alexander von Humboldt estimated the tree's age at 10,000 years when he saw it in 1799. Despite all efforts to preserve the ancient specimen, it finally succumbed to the winds of a great tempest in 1867.

It is just as well for most indoor gardeners that they cannot comfortably maintain indoors the high heat, light and humidity levels that tropical species are used to, or even a few plants would soon crowd out their owners. It is a startling experience for a Northerner to visit a semitropical area like Florida for the first time and suddenly realize that the same plants he has had for years in pots indoors grow outdoors as big vines, shrubs and even full-fledged trees. At an amusement center in Florida visitors aboard one of the attractions, the jungle cruise, see India-rubber trees that are really trees—25 or more feet tall—as well as kangaroo ivy trailing 30 feet, and philodendrons with 3-foot leaves. A tourist still farther south, in the jungles of Guatemala, would be even more surprised. There, in its native habitat, the same Swiss cheese plant that modestly adorns living rooms all over North America lives up to its botanical name, *Monstera deliciosa;* it is indeed a delicious monster —an enormous vine that climbs 100 feet or more from the jungle floor, bearing fruit that tastes like a cross between a pineapple and a banana. And anyone who happened to stop at Norfolk Island, the out-of-the-way speck of land in the South Pacific that is the original home of my 3-foot Norfolk Island pine, would see even more spectacular progenitors: trees towering 200 feet in the air.

INDOOR TREES   The Norfolk Island pine grows so slowly—3 to 6 inches a year under living-room conditions—that no indoor gardener has to be concerned about cutting a hole through to the attic to accommodate its mature height. Nevertheless, a 15-year-old specimen makes a handsome indoor "tree" 4 to 6 feet tall, with rich, silky dark green needles and gracefully drooping branches that give it a distinctive Oriental look. Other plants also make good indoor trees. A friend of mine has his favorite chair under a spreading Australian umbrella tree; another, who lives in a modern house, has designed his whole living room around a sizable weeping fig tree that grows in a tub beneath a central skylight.

Trees are only one among several unusual forms in which house plants can be grown. Most people limit themselves to plants they can put on a window sill or table, but there are species that lend themselves to many other uses: in addition to upright types that grow into indoor trees in floor containers, there are trailing varieties that look well in hanging baskets or climbing on a trellis, and some plants that make arresting displays grow in plain water or even inside bottles. Species that are useful in these special ways are listed in the encyclopedia chapter starting on page 83 and in the quick-reference charts on pages 147-149. If you are looking for such a plant, first consult the chart under the column headed "special uses"; you can further narrow your choices by noting in other columns whether the candidates are palms or vines, whether they are green-leaved, have white or yellow markings, or are brightly colored, and whether their light and temperature needs suit the particular use you have in mind. You can then explore the ones that especially appeal to you by looking at the more detailed descriptions and illustrations of individual species and varieties given in the encyclopedia section. Plants that can be grown in these ways usually get along with the general care prescribed for their species, but a few special considerations should be kept in mind.

There is a wide choice of plants that lend themselves to hanging displays by growing outward in an arching manner—rabbit's-foot ferns, spider plants, and vines such as grape or Swedish ivy are

HANGING CONTAINERS

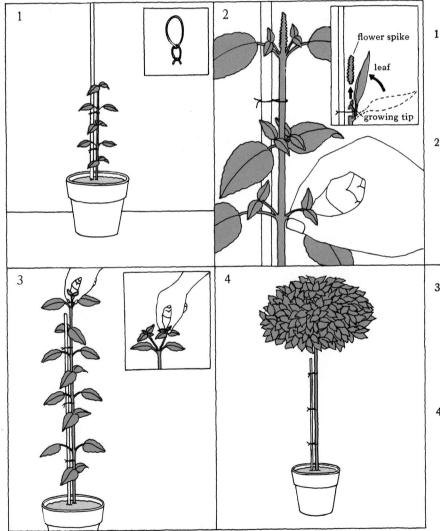

HOW TO TRAIN AN INDOOR "TREE"

1. *To make a treelike form out of a normally bushy plant such as a coleus, start with a single-stemmed, 4- to 6-inch plant in a 3-inch pot. Insert a 12-inch stake and tie soft cord first to the stake, then loosely to the stem (inset).*

2. *When the plant is about 10 inches tall, move it to a 5-inch pot, tie it to a 30-inch stake and begin to prune twin-leaved side shoots. With coleus, also remove the flower spike, and one side leaf and shoot (inset); tie the other leaf so its shoot forms the growing tip.*

3. *When the plant is about 2 feet tall, transfer it, stake and all, to an 8-inch pot, and for a "tree" that will be about 3 feet high, pinch off the central growing tip of the stem. As new shoots appear, pinch off their tips (inset) to encourage still more branching.*

4. *The result of the training over a period of a year or two is a compact crown of foliage atop a "trunk"; the leaves that grew along the sides of the stem fall off naturally with age and the stem itself may become stiff enough so that the stake can be removed.*

only a few of the most popular. Plants in hanging containers suspended from the top of a window frame, a protruding wall bracket or a ceiling hook can save space while allowing you to enjoy them at eye level (they also remain out of the reach of cats and other pets that might have a penchant for nibbling greenery). It is the container, rather than the choice of plant, that may pose a few problems. First, of course, you have to be sure to locate a hanging plant where it will not interfere with traffic, or people will bump their heads on your favorite fern. The best places to put hanging plants —provided they meet the plants' particular light requirements— are in windows or in corners where people are not apt to pass close by, high in stairway halls *(page 49),* or over large, permanently placed pieces of furniture such as a dining-room table or an island-type room divider *(page 53).*

The second problem with hanging plants is the design of the container. If you prefer the wire-basket type so popular outdoors, buy one with a waterproof liner to keep water from dripping on your living-room rug. Weight is also a consideration. A Mexican clay urn on rawhide ropes may be impressive, but when loaded with a plant and watered soil it can weigh as much as 50 pounds —too heavy to hang from most ceilings without creating a hazard.

The most practical container I have found is the lightweight

MAKING A CLIMBING LOG FOR VINES

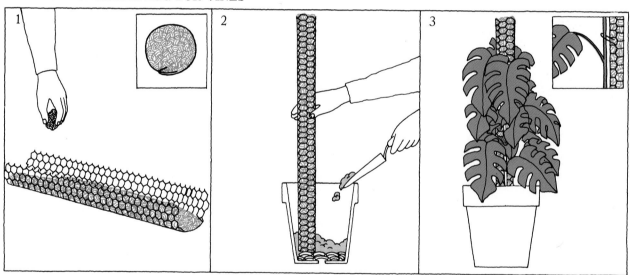

To create a support for climbing vines, heap moist, long-fibered sphagnum moss on an 8-by-24-inch piece of plastic-coated 1-inch wire mesh. Roll the mesh into a 2-inch log held by bending the wire (inset).

After lining an 8-inch pot with an inch of clay shards or gravel, hold the log near one edge and add potting mixture around the base to keep it upright. Pack more moss into the top of the log, if necessary, to fill it.

Pot the vine in front of the log and fasten the stems at 4- to 6-inch intervals to the mesh with pieces of bent wire or large hairpins (inset). Keep the sphagnum moss moist by pouring water into the top.

plastic type that has its own saucer built in to catch excess water as it drains through the soil. It also comes with its own chains and hanging hook, so that you can easily take the plant down for watering, fertilizing and other chores at the kitchen sink. Even plants in plastic pots, however, weigh more than you think; whenever I hang one from a ceiling or wall made of plaster or wallboard I anchor the hook solidly with expansion bolts made for such purposes.

Rather than suspend trailing vines in hanging containers, you can train many varieties to climb up from a pot with the help of a simple support such as a mesh "log" stuffed with moss *(page 12)*. This method leads to healthier, bigger plants, for it is a curious fact of nature that most vines grow slowly and produce relatively small leaves when allowed to trail, while if they are provided with vertical supports like those they find in the trunks and branches of a forest, their leaf size and vigor increase dramatically.

SUPPORTS FOR VINES

The rapid growth of some vines can create a minor problem; you probably have seen a vine in someone's house that has climbed up a wall, crossed the top of a window and looks prepared to keep on circling the room. Most vines, however, will stay within reasonable bounds if you nip off straggling ends occasionally.

Many plants grow not only in soil that is well watered, but in water alone. One of the best examples is that old favorite, the heart-leaved philodendron; I have kept it in book-end vases for years. Devil's ivy can be grown dramatically in a large shallow dish filled with water, over which it will quickly spread to form a handsome blanket of foliage. Other plants that take to water happily are the many varieties of English ivy, as well as arrowhead vine, wandering Jew, Sander's dracaena and Chinese evergreen.

PLANTS IN WATER

To prevent the tops of tall water-growing plants from falling over, anchor their roots in pin-point flower holders or in a ball of crumpled chicken wire. To keep the plants at their healthiest, change the water every month or so, adding a few drops of liquid fertilizer for nourishment and a handful of charcoal to neutralize wastes. One small caution is worth remembering: opaque containers or dark-colored glass ones are better than clear vases, which admit so much light that they encourage the growth of a green scum of algae in the nutrient-laden water.

There are many other ways to grow plants indoors, of course, and you will find ideas for quite a few of them scattered through the rest of this book, from the bottle terrarium shown on pages 29-32 to the dish gardens on pages 74-78. About the only limits are your own imagination—and the growing requirements of the plants themselves, a subject explored in detail in Chapter 2.

Surprises in form and color

If the mention of foliage house plants conjures up no more in your mind than the traditional images of philodendron and ivy, you are in for a delightful surprise. Foliage plants, gathered by collectors from every tropical and semitropical corner of the earth, present the indoor gardener with an almost endless assortment of sizes and shapes to choose from. Even if the choice must be determined by a factor as seemingly limiting as size, the selection is not severely restricted: for every size there is a greenhouse full of different-looking plants—broad-leaved and narrow-leaved, spindly and spreading, smooth and textured, green, red and many other hues.

This marvelous diversity did not, of course, come about merely to challenge the house-plant enthusiast. Plants form and change as a result of their environment and their ability to survive in that environment. Thus many of the most ornamental features of foliage house plants are the result of practical evolutionary adaptation. For example, the fuzzy hairs covering the leaves of the piggyback plant (*Tolmiea menziesii, page 20*) protect the fragile leaves from heavy rainfalls. The hairs shed some of the water, thus preventing the rain from rotting the leaf or weighing it down and breaking it. The shape of a plant's leaves can also serve a multitude of purposes: the leaves of many tropical trees like the *Ficus retusa nitida (page 16)* are slightly cupped to retain needed moisture in a light mist, but taper to a point called a drip tip that funnels excess amounts of water off the leaf during storms. The narrow swordlike leaves of plants like the *Dracaena draco (right)* and the deeply lobed foliage of plants like the *Philodendron selloum (page 19)* offer the least resistance to wind, so that they are less likely to be ripped to shreds by the hurricanes common in their native habitats.

In *Dracaena draco,* in fact, each of the visual elements that alone makes other plants attractive is a valued feature: its height and breadth are dramatic, its leaves are erect but slightly curved at the ends, and the leaves deepen in color from pale yellow when new to a rich green when mature.

A Dracaena draco, seen from above, has new pale yellow shoots growing in the center of dark green leaves.

NEPHROLEPIS EXALTATA 'WHITMANII'

FICUS RETUSA NITIDA

FICUS LYRATA

Plants that climb and cascade

Aside from the familiar tabletop house plants that sit sedately in their pots on window sills all over America, foliage plants are available as luxuriant arching types that cascade down from hanging baskets toward the floor and as sturdy trees that climb toward the ceiling.

One of the most graceful examples of the hanging variety is the feathery fern called *Nephrolepis exaltata* 'Whitmanii' *(above, left)*. At the other extreme is the stately and formal Indian laurel, *Ficus retusa nitida (far left)*, which has been trained as a standard, that is, a plant with a single treelike stem in which all growth has been concentrated in a sheared crown of foliage. Beside it is a smaller, bolder standing plant, a fiddle-leaved fig, *Ficus lyrata*. But probably the most popular large plant today is the erect, single-stemmed paradise palm, the *Howeia forsteriana*, several of which are generally combined, as at right, in one tub.

HOWEIA FORSTERIANA

17

BRASSAIA ACTINOPHYLLA

PTERIS TREMULA

DRACAENA MARGINATA

The shape that makes the leaf

Among the most distinctive leaf shapes are the fanlike tooth-edged foliage of the *Fatsia japonica (top right)* and the deeply lobed leaves of the ubiquitous *Philodendron selloum (right)*. But among the most popular of contemporary plants are the *Dracaena marginata (left)*, whose long sword-shaped leaves are edged with a reddish tinge, and the *Pteris tremula (top left)*, whose seemingly fragile but remarkably robust fronds are once again popular since their days of glory as a centerpiece at banquets.

Sometimes a plant is distinguished by the arrangement of its leaves on the stem rather than by their shape: the oval leaflets of the *Brassaia actinophylla (above)* radiate out from one point on the stem, whereas the leaves of the *Pleomele reflexa (far right)* break out from the center of the head in a rosettelike effect.

FATSIA JAPONICA

PHILODENDRON SELLOUM

PLEOMELE REFLEXA

19

The many different textures

Contrary to what many a novice believes, not all healthy plants necessarily have smooth and shiny leaves like those of the Japanese pittosporum, *Pittosporum tobira (below)*. An attractive contrast is the softer-looking hairy leaf of the *Tolmiea menziesii (right)*, commonly called the piggyback plant because of the curious way in which it produces tiny plantlets at the base of its mature leaves. An entirely different effect is created by the dainty, crinkly leaves of the recently introduced *Pilea crassifolia (top right)* and the bold, heavily quilted foliage of the Emerald Ripple peperomia, *Peperomia caperata* 'Emerald Ripple' *(far right)*.

TOLMIEA MENZIESII

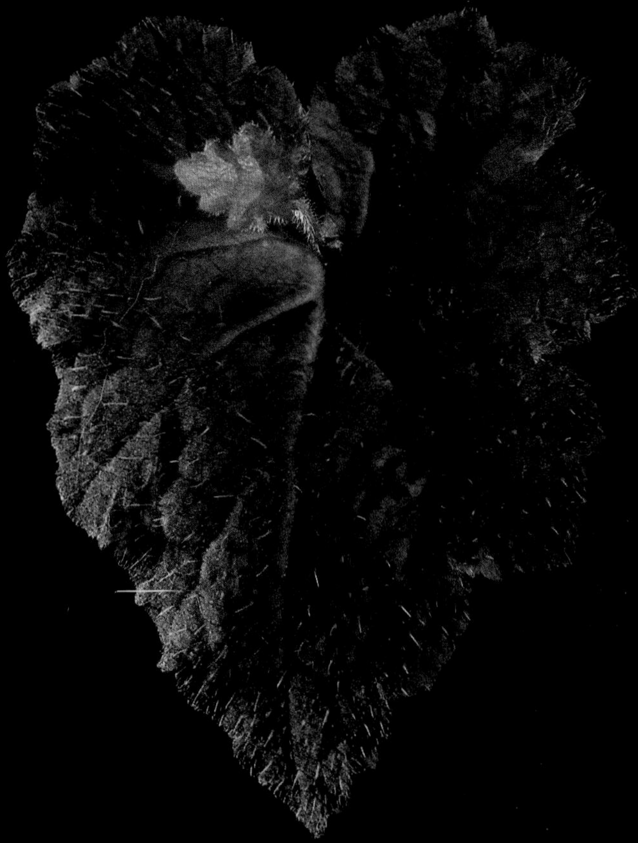

PITTOSPORUM TOBIRA

PILEA CRASSIFOLIA

PEPEROMIA CAPERATA 'EMERALD RIPPLE'

ACALYPHA 'CEYLON'

A spectrum of colorful foliage

Most foliage house plants with colorful leaves need bright sunlight to bring out the richness of their hues, which range from whites and yellows to purples and reds. Perhaps the greatest sun worshippers of them all are the crotons *(below, right)*, unique in that they may bear differently colored leaves on the same plant.

Among the most vivid of plants are the leaves of the *Gynura aurantiaca (below)*, covered with short purple hairs; the *Acalypha* 'Ceylon' *(left)*, daintily edged in red; and a rare shade seeker, the *Calathea makoyana (right)*, whose purple underside and green top are shown.

CALATHEA MAKOYANA

GYNURA AURANTIACA

CODIAEUM HYBRID

The advantages of tender loving care 2

While watering the tall dracaena in his office one day, a lie-detector expert named Cleve Backster attached his machine's electrodes to the plant; he wondered if the detector's recording of gradual changes in electrical resistance would indicate the length of time moisture took to get from the roots to the leaves. To his surprise, the machine indicated an almost instant response, one resembling that of a person under emotional stimulus. Intrigued, he decided to see what would happen if he lit a match underneath a leaf. Backster claims he never had time to reach for the match; the moment he thought of doing it the recording needle went right off the graph.

Backster's reports on what he calls plant sentience are only a few of many that attribute to plants an eerie responsiveness to all sorts of factors in their environment, including other living things. It has been said, for example, that plants are sensitive to sound vibrations, that they grow better than normally when soft music is played and that, conversely, they shrink under the constant noise of rock. A high-school science class proved, to the students' satisfaction at least, that plants can be made to grow extravagantly if they are praised every day and that they can be made to do poorly, and even die, if they are scolded.

While evidence like this may not make much of an impression on my botanist friends, it does support a contention I have held for a long time—that plants, like people, get along best with a little tender loving care. Of course plants, like people, cannot live on love alone; they need the right kind of care lovingly provided: the proper amounts and combinations of light, heat, moisture and nutrients as well as grooming, cleaning and protection against overcrowding and disease.

You can increase a house plant's chances of a long and healthy life if you choose a robust one to begin with. A wise buyer inspects plants closely before he chooses, for looks tell much about how the plant has been grown and readied for sale.

The majority of foliage house plants have been grown out-

Basic to the health of plants like the young English ivies at left is proper potting. A house plant needs a clean pot, a loose-textured soil mixture and drainage materials such as clay shards or large pebbles.

doors in places like Florida or Southern California, where they get ample sun and moisture and are fertilized frequently to stimulate maximum growth. When they are sent to less equable climates for sale the conditions change, often dramatically; the plants are shipped, displayed and sold for use in indoor environments where they get less light, lower humidity and less food. To minimize the shock of such changes, many growers and greenhousemen acclimatize, or "finish," their plants over a period of several days to several weeks, the time depending on the species. They gradually reduce light and moisture levels and withhold fertilizer so the plants become tough enough to withstand store and home conditions. Bargain plants, in contrast, may not have been allowed to remain in the greenhouse long enough to become acclimatized or to build up a root system capable of absorbing the considerable quantities of water they need when moved to the dry air of living rooms. They are not good buys, and their appearance gives them away.

WHAT TO LOOK FOR   When you are shopping for a plant, there are several ways you can tell whether a particular specimen is sound. First look at the leaves. They should be approximately the size and color specified for their species in the encyclopedia section *(Chapter 5)*. Moreover, they should exhibit no browning of the edges, a symptom of too much fertilizer or too much heat, and the lower leaves should show no indication of becoming pale or yellow, a sign of improper watering. Look critically at the intervals between leaves on the stems. On a plant that has been fed and watered heavily to promote abnormally fast growth, this spacing may be great enough to make the plant appear tall, sparse or leggy; new leaves will not grow to fill in the gaps. So unless the foliage is reasonably dense, reject the plant in favor of another, bushier one. While inspecting the leaves, you should also look closely for evidence of insects at the tips of new branches, at the places where the leaves join the stems and on the undersides of leaves (for specific insect symptoms and controls, see the chart on page 154).

In buying a plant it is also advisable to check the top of the soil in the pot and the drainage hole or holes in the bottom; if roots show above the surface or are growing out through the holes, the plant has outgrown its pot and may not be the best buy you can find. If in addition the leaves appear wilted and the new ones are smaller than the others, the plant may have already suffered from overcrowding and should be passed over.

INITIAL CARE   After you have selected a promising-looking plant and have brought it home, it is a good idea to put it in the kitchen sink and water it thoroughly from the top to dissolve any excess salts that may have accumulated as a result of heavy fertilizing by the grower; these salts can burn the roots, particularly if the soil is allowed to become dry. After watering, set the plant aside for half an hour or so and then water again to flush the dissolved salts away.

Younger plants, like younger people, seem to adjust to new conditions more easily than older ones, provided that their root systems are sufficiently developed. But even a young plant needs special attention to tide it over its adjustment period. After the initial soaking, set the plant in a relatively cool place to minimize water loss from the leaves and continue to keep the soil a little more moist than the average recommended for the species. To reduce the shock of moving from the greenhouse, where the humidity may have been 70 per cent or more, mist the foliage once or twice a day with tepid water from an atomizer bottle made for the purpose and sold in garden stores. Do not apply any fertilizer, even if the plant looks a little weak; fertilizer can injure a plant that is growing in relatively dim light, where it is not functioning very actively and cannot assimilate the extra food.

It is also good practice to quarantine a new plant, setting it away from your other plants for a couple of weeks to make sure it does not harbor any insects you may have missed on your first inspection. During this period do not be alarmed if a few lower leaves turn yellow and eventually die. This loss of foliage is essentially a survival mechanism: plants going through an adjustment to new conditions drop the older, lower leaves they cannot support, retaining the younger, more vigorous ones nearer the top. When a leaf yellows you can remove it for appearance' sake if you want to, snapping it off close to the main stem, but it is better to allow the leaf to drop off by itself; before falling it will seal the point where it was attached to the stem and thus leave no wound for infections to attack. If more than two or three leaves turn yellow and drop, you are probably giving the plant either too much water or too little water, or you may have placed it in too dark a location; check its needs in the encyclopedia section. If a plant drops most of its leaves you have a case of fatal shock on your hands; there is not much you can do but go back to the store and ask for a replacement.

After an adjustment period of two to three weeks, a new foliage house plant no longer needs special care and can go on the normal regimen. Of all its needs, none is more important to health and long life than the amount of light it receives. Light is the power source for the process of photosynthesis, by which the leaves produce sugars and starches to feed all parts of the plant.

The amount of natural daylight that enters a home through its windows is only a small fraction of the light outdoors under an

IVY FOR LUCK AND LOVE

For centuries one of the most beloved of domestic plants, ivy is the subject of countless legends that entwine in its history. According to Greek mythology, a dancer named Cissos performed at a feast of the gods with such abandon that she fell dead at the feet of Dionysus, the god of wine; Dionysus transformed her body into ivy, which the Greeks thereafter used to crown the victors in sports competitions. In folklore, ivy is often associated with love and luck. If it grows in profusion on a maiden's grave, an old American tale holds, the girl died of love; if it refuses to grow on a grave, the soul is unhappy in its new home. And in Wales the death of an ivy plant was thought to foreshadow the owner's loss of his house.

PROVIDING PROPER LIGHT

open sky. Outdoors, the summer sun at midday may produce as much as 10,000 or 12,000 foot-candles of light (a foot-candle being the amount of light cast by a candle on a surface 1 foot away). Inside a house, however, plants in a sunny window may receive only 4,000 or 5,000 foot-candles, and a few feet from the window the level may drop to 200 foot-candles or less. Still farther away the average light may range between 10 and 100 foot-candles (a book can be read comfortably in illumination of 50 foot-candles or less). Fortunately for gardeners, many tropical plants tolerate low light levels or they could not be grown indoors at all.

Within these low levels, however, the light needs of plants vary. The plants in this book are divided into three broad categories: those such as crotons, coleuses and tree ivies, which require full sun at a south-facing window or the bright reflected light bouncing off a light-colored wall; the intermediate plants, such as rex begonias, dracaenas and figs, which thrive in partial shade or the filtered light coming through a sheer curtain; and plants that get along on a minimum of illumination, such as Chinese evergreens, aspidistras and many ferns, which can survive in indirect, shadowless light coming through a north-facing window. Since most plant owners want their plants to be beautiful, yet not grow too quickly out of bounds, the light level recommended for each species in the encyclopedia is the least that will maintain health without encouraging fast growth. Window light is generally one-directional and causes the part of the plant away from the light to stretch toward it; if you want a plant near a window to grow symmetrically, give it a quarter turn every day—or at least every time you water —so that all parts of the foliage will get equal light.

It is a fairly simple matter to tell whether or not a plant is get-

(continued on page 33)

A garden in a climate of its own

Gardens planted inside decanters, apothecary jars or even 10-gallon demijohns like the one at right are as intriguing as ship models in bottles —but serve a practical purpose as well. Once such a container is sealed as a completely enclosed terrarium, the environment inside it becomes a moist microclimate ideal for humidity-loving plants that are often hard to grow in the dry atmosphere of most homes. As an added bonus, plants grown under glass tend themselves. When their leaves give off water vapor, it condenses inside the bottle and runs back down to moisten the roots; similarly, while the plants use carbon dioxide in making food, they simultaneously release oxygen, which they use to convert food into energy in a process that replenishes the carbon dioxide. Almost any bottle can be used as a terrarium provided that it is made of clear or lightly tinted glass in order to admit light and to permit a view of the garden inside.

The tools needed to plant a demijohn are household staples except for the spring-operated pickup tool, sold in hardware stores. The potting materials in the dishes are charcoal, packaged soil and pebbles.

Fitting it all into the bottle

The first step in creating a bottle terrarium is selecting plants that, like those listed below, will adapt to life under glass and are small enough for the container. The next steps, getting the plants settled inside a narrow-mouthed bottle, are not so tricky as they might seem. The pictures at right show the procedure used by Mrs. Jo Ubogy of Connecticut, who has planted dozens of bottle gardens for herself and friends. The foundation Mrs. Ubogy prefers for terrariums consists of about ½ inch of pebbles to provide drainage, plus a sprinkling of charcoal granules to neutralize fumes caused by decay in moist conditions. Enough packaged potting soil is then added to fill the bottom quarter of the bottle. The surface can be shaped like a landscape of hills and valleys.

Next, Mrs. Ubogy sets the plants in place one by one, starting with the tallest and finishing with the smallest ones. Then she moistens the garden, covers the bottle and puts it in shade for a few days. If the soil seems dry, she adds water; if it looks soggy, she removes the cover for a few hours each day to let water escape. When the moisture reaches the right balance, she sets the bottle on display in the light and temperature the plants require—avoiding direct sun, which can heat the bottle so much that the plants parboil. From this point on, the garden tends itself except for occasional watering with an atomizer; many bottle gardens have survived without attention for months, even years.

PLANTS FOR BOTTLE GARDENS

Low-growing plants:
devil's ivy, fittonia, small-leaved English ivy, Japanese sweet flag, prayer plant, striped inch plant.

Taller centerpiece plants:
calathea; Chinese evergreen; maidenhair fern; small-leaved philodendron; small specimens of dieffenbachia, dracaena, palm and umbrella plant.

1. *Using a funnel to keep the glass clean, pour pebbles over the bottom of the bottle, then coat them with charcoal and pour in the potting soil.*

2. *After shaking the bottle from side to side to spread the potting soil, use the end of a yardstick to tamp it down and shape the surface as desired.*

3. *Knock the largest plant out of its pot and gently brush the soil off the roots. If it is multistemmed like these parlor-palm seedlings, separate it.*

4. *If the crown of foliage is too large to fit comfortably through the neck of the bottle, prune it with scissors; also remove any yellowed leaves.*

5. *To prevent injury to trailing roots, wind them loosely into a ball that will slip safely through the neck and be easy to handle inside the bottle.*

6. *Bend the leaves up and grasp the roots in the claws of a pickup tool, keeping the stem and handle parallel. Lower the plant into the bottle.*

7. *Lay the plant on its side with its roots over the place they will be planted. Pressing the roots with the yardstick, remove the pickup tool.*

8. *Use the yardstick to push the roots into the potting soil and straighten the plant, making sure it grows at the same level that it did in the pot.*

9. *After all the plants are in place, add water a little at a time, letting it flow down the sides of the bottle; moisten the soil lightly but evenly.*

10. *To swab the inside surface of the bottle clean, use a wad of paper towel or lint-free cloth attached securely to the end of a bent wire coat hanger.*

ting the right amount of light in the location where you have placed it. If the distance between the new leaves on its stems is greater than the distance between the older ones, the plant is in effect stretching to get more light, and its stems indicate this by elongating, in some instances bending, toward the light source. In such a case, move the plant to a spot where it will get more light. If on the other hand the plant wilts during the hot part of the day and the leaves begin to develop yellow, then brown, patches, the plant is getting too much light and you should move it back from the window or draw the curtains during the middle of the day.

In situations where you cannot give a plant enough window light to meet its minimum needs, you can supplement the natural light with artificial light, or grow the plant under artificial lights alone.

Improvements in artificial lighting equipment and techniques have made it possible to grow virtually any foliage plant in places where natural light is dim or nonexistent: in dark halls and stairways, in the inside corner of a living room, in bookshelves and under kitchen counters, even in a windowless basement playroom. Any kind of artificial light as a supplement to daylight will help plants grow, even an ordinary 60-watt bulb in a table lamp. But where most of the light comes from an artificial source, particularly in the case of light-loving plants, special provisions must be made.

Since flowering is not important in most foliage plants, special plant-growing lamps are not essential; ordinary light, such as that provided by standard fluorescent or incandescent lamps, will keep foliage healthy. Among the most widely used standard light sources are fluorescent tubes of the cool-white type, which provide rays primarily in the yellow-green-blue portion of the spectrum. However, many people find the tone of cool-white lamps somewhat cold and harsh in a home setting, even if they do not object to it in offices and stores. Moreover, plants need a certain amount of light in the warm, or red, end of the spectrum for balanced growth. The simplest way to get these red rays is to combine one tube of the so-called warm-white type with each cool-white tube, or combine cool-white fluorescent tubes and ordinary incandescent bulbs in a ratio of 2 watts of fluorescent to 1 of incandescent.

Fluorescent tubes are rather ungainly looking and when they are used to keep plants growing they are usually concealed: mounted under a bookshelf, a ceiling valance or beneath the shelves on a plant-holding cart. Fluorescents are particularly useful for such concealed installations because they can be placed quite close to plants —up to 6 inches away—without generating enough heat to dry out or burn the foliage, as incandescent lights can. Moreover, they last longer—most fluorescent tubes have an average lifetime of

Having completed the terrarium, Mrs. Ubogy will stopper it and set it in a shaded place for a few days, checking the humidity level before putting the garden on display.

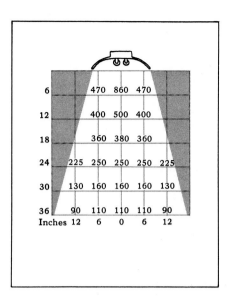

**LIGHT LEVELS PRODUCED
BY FLUORESCENT LAMPS**

*The number of foot-candles of light
that reach a plant from two 40-
watt fluorescent tubes in a shallow
reflector are shown above to
help guide lamp placement for
illumination levels suggested in the
encyclopedia. The vertical distance
from lamp to foliage is indicated at
left; the horizontal distance of the
plant from the center line is shown
at the bottom. A peperomia, which
requires 400 foot-candles, for
example, should be placed about a
foot below the lights if they are
the sole source of illumination.*

12,000 hours compared to 750 to 1,000 hours for most incandescent bulbs—and though fluorescents cost more, they use less electricity, being about three times as efficient per watt in converting power into light energy. For average use all that is needed is a pair of 40-watt fluorescent tubes placed at a distance from the plant that will provide the illumination the plant requires. The illumination requirement in foot-candles for each kind of plant is given in the encyclopedia, and the chart at left relates foot-candles to the distance between the tubes and the plant. To measure foot-candles directly, you can buy a foot-candle meter, sold in electrical supply stores, for about $20. If you have a camera with a built-in light meter you can convert its exposure readings to foot-candles by the simple method shown on page 36.

If plants must be placed much more than 3 feet from a pair of fluorescent tubes, the light is not sufficient to grow many species and you will either have to add more tubes or consider incandescent lamps. Incandescent reflector floodlights or spotlights of the so-called daylight type, mounted on a wall or ceiling, will maintain most foliage plants that have relatively low light requirements. A 150-watt floodlight, which is about the minimum size that will do any good, can provide some 50 foot-candles at a distance of 5 feet. A 150-watt spotlight, which gives a narrower, more concentrated beam than a floodlight, will deliver about 300 foot-candles at 5 feet. The relationships between foot-candles and distance for a 150-watt floodlight and a 150-watt spotlight are shown in the chart on page 35. The latest developments in artificial lighting are lamps that include a wide range of the colors of the natural light spectrum, making it possible for the first time to grow such notable sun lovers as cacti and succulents under artificial light alone. These lamps come in the same lengths as standard fluorescent tubes and fit into the same two-pronged sockets. When using any type of artificial light, keep it on for 12 to 16 hours a day if it is the sole source of illumination. Unless you can remember to turn the lights on when you get up and turn them off at a set time in the evening, an automatic-timer switch is a worthwhile investment.

THE ART OF WATERING

As important to plants as light is the amount of water they receive. Yet—and this may surprise you—many gardeners are too conscientious in this respect. In fact, the tendency to overwater is so common that I firmly believe more plants die from this cause than any other. One reason so many people make this mistake, I am sure, is that they are not aware that a plant's roots must have air as well as water; if the soil is kept constantly saturated, air is driven out, the roots rot and the rest of the plant dies for lack of nourishment from below. So after that first good flushing when you bring the plant home, be careful not to drown your plant. The harm caused by overwatering usually shows up first in yellowing leaves at the base; in severe cases the leaves drop off without changing color. Such an abrupt loss generally signifies that irreparable root damage has taken place—about all you can do is discard the plant, learn from the error and start over again.

Of course there is such a thing as underwatering, too, and its primary symptom is wilting leaves, beginning with the youngest ones at the tips of the stems. The older leaves, having larger, tougher cells, may not show any effect for a few days or more, but soon their edges begin to turn brown. If you catch the plant at the browning stage, there may be time to save it with watering; though the edges will not turn green again, they can be cut off with scissors.

Admittedly it is not easy to gauge the right amount of water. I am afraid I cannot provide any precise schedule for watering; the needs of different species vary, and the needs of a particular plant may also vary with the temperature of the room, the cloudiness of the sky outdoors and the size and material of the container it is growing in. But in general, plants fall into three broad categories of moisture needs, as the encyclopedia indicates. Water-loving plants such as dracaenas, Japanese sweet flags and the Hawaiian ti demand a soil that is constantly moist, but not so wet that it feels soggy to

LIGHT LEVELS PRODUCED BY INCANDESCENT LAMPS

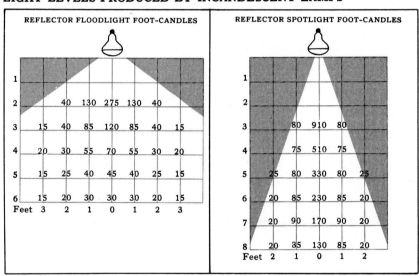

A 150-watt incandescent floodlight with built-in reflector casts a wide cone of light around a central point (rather than a central line as with fluorescents). Several overlapping lamps can build up light levels.

A 150-watt reflector spotlight gives high light levels up to about 8 feet away, but its light drops off sharply at each side so it is most suitable for single plants. It is hot and should be kept at least 3 feet from plants.

GAUGING FOOT-CANDLES

A camera equipped with a built-in light meter can be used to measure the foot-candles of light falling on a plant. Set the film-speed dial to ASA 25 and the shutter speed to ⅟₆₀ second. Place opaque white paper next to the leaves and point the camera at it from a distance no greater than the narrow dimension of the paper. Adjust the lens opening (f-stop) until the built-in meter indicates a correct exposure. If this lens opening is f/2, illumination is about 100 foot-candles; f/2.8 indicates 200 foot-candles; f/4, 370 foot-candles; f/5.6, 750 foot-candles; f/8, 1,500 foot-candles; f/11, 2,800 foot-candles; f/16, 5,000 foot-candles.

WATERING WITH TWO POTS

the touch. Other plants such as peperomias, dieffenbachias and pittosporums should be allowed to become moderately dry between thorough waterings. Still others such as monsteras, coleuses and many ferns should be kept barely moist at all times. To tell how moist or dry the soil is, simply poke your finger down into it about ½ inch and gauge by feel.

More problems connected with watering can be traced to improper drainage than to any other single cause. Foliage plants can be grown in almost anything from an old tomato can to a priceless Grecian urn—as long as excess water is not allowed to collect in it. Most plants are sold in simple flowerpots of clay or plastic with one or more drainage holes at the bottom, and these may be attractive enough until the plants become too large for them. Bear in mind, however, that clay pots, because their walls are porous, lose moisture by evaporation about three times as fast as plastic ones and should be checked more often for dry soil; put the other way around, plants in plastic pots should be watered less frequently.

In addition to standard clay and plastic pots, there are many kinds of decorative containers that do not have drainage holes. You can add holes by drilling carefully through the bottom with a special masonry bit. But the very lack of holes is appreciated by many people because it keeps water off the floor without need for a saucer. A holeless container, on the other hand, can pose serious overwatering problems. For one thing, you cannot readily tell whether excess water is accumulating at the bottom of the container, where it can rot the roots. To minimize this danger, line the bottom of the container with a generous drainage layer of broken clay flowerpots, pebbles or coarse gravel. This layer makes a reservoir deep enough to catch excess water beneath the soil ball. The depth of the drainage reservoir should vary with the pot size; a 10- to 12-inch container with a depth equal to its width should have about 2 inches of drainage material, a 15- to 18-inch container should have 3 to 4 inches. To keep the soil from filtering down into the broken clay or gravel and filling in the reservoir, cover the drainage material with a 1-inch layer of long-fibered sphagnum moss. If you want to use a decorative urn without the trouble of repotting the plant and the problems of overwatering, simply set the plant in its original pot inside the urn; prop the pot on a block or brick so that it will remain above any water that runs through the inner pot's drainage holes to accumulate in the urn *(drawing, page 38)*.

Plastic pots have gained in popularity not only because plants growing in them do not require watering as often as do plants growing in clay pots, but because they are lightweight, inexpensive and come in many colors. But clay pots are still a good bet, particularly for beginning gardeners: they are heavier and thus harder to tip over, and because of their porosity they are less likely to retain excess water if overwatered. Old-time gardeners learned years ago how to capitalize on this porosity, and virtually to eliminate the frequent watering demanded by clay-potted plants. The method they used, still a great timesaver, is called double potting (drawing, page 38). The clay pot is set within another, holeless pot or urn, the bottom of which is lined with broken clay pots or gravel, and the space between the pots is stuffed with long-fibered sphagnum moss. Water is then poured onto the moss rather than into the inner pot; it seeps through the clay walls to moisten the soil within. (To help a new plant adjust to this method, water the soil directly at first, gradually applying more and more of the total water to the moss.) One of the advantages of double potting is that the moisture transfer through the clay pot walls is not only constant but it is gradual as well. The soil can thus be readily maintained on the dry side; that is, with barely enough moisture to maintain the plant without encouraging fast growth. Because of this slow but even supply of moisture, double-potted plants live beautifully for years indoors.

Regardless of how a plant is potted, there are a few basic tips on watering I would suggest. First, use tepid water, at about 90°F., which is simply tap water that is pleasantly warm to the touch; plants take up tepid water more readily than cold water, and cold water can shock many plants and cause them to wilt. If the water is heavily chlorinated, let it stand in a pan overnight before using it on your plants so the chlorine can evaporate. Do not use water from a water softener unless it is equipped with a deionizing unit to remove the sodium used in the softening process; neither chlorine nor sodium is beneficial to plants.

TIPS ON WATERING

When you water a plant in a standard pot with drainage holes, add water until some comes out of the holes. Beware of water coming out too quickly, however; if the ball of soil around the roots has been allowed to become overly dry, the soil may have shrunk and pulled away from the pot's walls, and the water you have applied has just run down the gap on the inside of the pot, completely bypassing the roots. In such a case take the plant, pot and all, and immerse it in the sink or in a pail of water; leave the top of the soil covered with an inch or two of water until air bubbles stop rising, and then set the plant aside so the excess water can drain.

The health of foliage plants depends not only on the water in their soil but on the moisture in the air around them; they are also sensitive to air temperature. Cacti and other succulents, which are discussed in detail in Chapter 4, are by and large desert plants and

TEMPERATURE AND HUMIDITY

for this reason are generally the most adaptable to the dry, heated air of houses in winter, where the temperature averages around 70° and the relative humidity may be as low as 10 per cent. But many other species of foliage plants such as figs, crotons and scheffleras come from semitropical areas where daytime temperatures are about 70° to 80°, night temperatures are about 10° lower and the relative humidity ranges from 50 to 75 per cent; these too do well indoors without special treatment. Plants that originated in equatorial regions, however, particularly those that flourish at sea level where the temperatures are truly hot and the air is often very humid, cannot be grown successfully unless special provisions are made to create a miniclimate around them that is similar to their natural habitat. These plants, notably palms, staghorn ferns and fragrant dracaenas, do best in warm greenhouses and in former days were known as stove plants because of the amount of heat necessary to keep them growing satisfactorily. You may have seen some of these plants in a commercial greenhouse, where the temperature is kept up around 80° and the plants and the walkways around them are wetted down with a hose or sprinkler system several times a day to keep the humidity at a level of 70 or 80 per cent.

Long before I worked in greenhouses myself, I got an inkling of the importance of high temperature and humidity for certain

TWO WAYS TO CONTROL WATERING

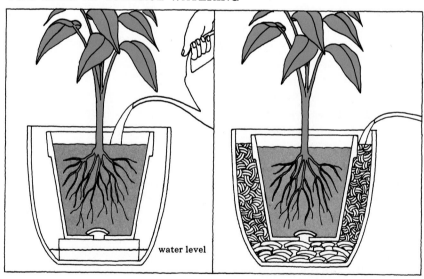

water level

A brick under a pot that is concealed in a watertight decorative container permits moisture to drain away from roots when the plant is watered. Excess water accumulates around the brick prop and evaporates.

To give a plant constant but limited moisture, set it in a clay pot on shards inside a watertight container and fill the side spaces with sphagnum moss. Water applied to the moss will seep into the pot.

plants in an unexpected place—the laundry in my hometown. The most interesting thing about the laundry to me at age 12 was not the handsomely starched shirts my father used to pick up there every Saturday, but the towering rubber tree that grew in a massive dragon-encircled urn in the front window. I can still see clearly those enormous leaves, dark green and glistening as though they had been varnished, so strange and exotic in an elm-shaded New England village. The reason the tree grew so well was that all the heat and steam from the laundry tubs and irons provided a climate almost identical to the jungle climate of the rubber tree's native Malaysia—as the brows of the poor laundry workers testified!

Of course few people will put up with the conditions of a laundry in their homes just to accommodate certain tropical plants, but there are ways an indoor gardener can raise the humidity level around the plants themselves without making a jungle out of the whole living room. The simplest method, and one that I use for my begonia treebine and velvet-leaved philodendron, is to place the potted plants on a shallow tray about 2 inches deep, filling the tray with an inch of pebbles or sand and ½ inch of water and making sure the water does not touch the bottom of the pots—if the roots stand in water they rot. The constant evaporation of the water raises the humidity in the air immediately around the plants to as much as three to five times that of the rest of the room, as I have measured by placing a small hygrometer just above the foliage.

Whether or not you use a tray, you can benefit almost any plant by placing it close to others; all plants constantly give off moisture through their leaves, and this moisture hangs in the air, raising the humidity near the foliage.

One of the best ways to assure a suitable miniclimate for plants —and a fine way to display small plants attractively—is to carry the pebble-tray idea a step further by unpotting the plants and planting them together in a dish garden. All that is required is that the plants have similar needs for light, moisture and temperature, and that they be small enough to fit together in a shallow container. You can make imaginative dish gardens using only cacti and other succulents, which like bright light and little water (pages 74-78), or you can group plants such as ferns, ivies and Chinese evergreens, which prefer moist conditions and less light. In either case, choose a container that is at least 3 inches deep; since it will have no drainage holes, line the bottom with ½ inch of coarse gravel or pebbles to act as a reservoir that will keep excess water away from the roots. Fill the container above this drainage layer with the potting mixture recommended for the plants. For most dish gardens, plants

RAISING THE HUMIDITY

MAKING A DISH GARDEN

growing in 2- to 3-inch pots are about the right size; unpot them and set them in holes scooped out of the potting mixture, making sure that they are planted at the same level as they were growing before, and firm the soil well around them with your fingers.

Except for dish gardens of cacti and other succulents, which must be watered sparingly, watering from above is generally inadequate. I take my dish gardens to the kitchen sink and give them the total immersion treatment, allowing the entire dish to remain under an inch of water until all bubbles stop rising to the surface. Then I lift the dish out and prop it at an angle for about half an hour so the excess water can drain away over the rim; if the plants were properly firmed down when planted they will not fall out.

MAKING A TERRARIUM Although many plants will do handsomely in a dish garden, some of the moisture lovers such as fittonias, marantas and most ferns do better if they are grown in an enclosed terrarium where the humidity can be kept at a very high level. This fact was first discovered back in 1827 by one of those happy accidents that dot the history of horticulture. Dr. Nathaniel Ward, a London physician, was experimenting with caterpillars, putting them in glass jars so he could observe them as they emerged from the pupa stage. One day he noticed that one of the jars he had used and left stoppered on a shelf had something growing in it that was not a caterpillar; he looked more closely and it was unmistakably a tiny fern. Somehow a fern spore had found its way into the jar and had germinated in a bit of mold that had formed on the jar's bottom. Dr. Ward was so excited about his discovery that he all but dropped his caterpillar research and set about building larger versions of the jar for further experiments—glass-sided boxes with removable covers in which he was able to grow ferns and other tropical plants in soil for as long as 15 years. Ward called his boxes terrariums, and they soon proved a boon to plant hunters who for the first time were able to bring back sensitive tropical plants in "Wardian cases" well protected from salt air and changing climatic conditions during their long sea voyages. Ward's terrariums also became popular for growing the plants; hardly a self-respecting Victorian household was without one, generally mounted on an ornate wrought-iron stand and containing as its center of attraction a billowing Lady fern, of which some 65 varieties existed even then.

Terrariums seem to be back in fashion today, and I have seen them made out of every kind of container imaginable: oversized brandy snifters, gallon pickle jars, even the 5-gallon water bottles used for drinking fountains. One of the most popular containers, and one that is actually quite similar to Dr. Ward's original, is a simple rectangular fish tank of the kind sold in pet stores.

Most of the plants I have recommended for terrariums in the encyclopedia are relatively small even when fully grown, and they will fit comfortably in a 10-gallon or even a 7½-gallon fish tank. Of course if you become really interested, you can make a bigger container for more or larger plants; a friend of mine has built an indoor greenhouse 4 feet wide, 8 feet long and 6 feet high, equipped with a battery of plant-growing lights, so that his wife, an invalid, can garden indoors. Most beginners prefer to start with something smaller; a wide-mouthed glass candy jar that comes with its own top makes a charming display if planted with a small fittonia, a couple of table ferns and a little moss picked up from the woods.

The container that I find most suitable for a terrarium is the 10-gallon fish tank, which is about 16 by 20 inches by 8 inches high. It is big enough to let you work inside it with both hands and to hold a fair-sized assortment of plants. It will need a removable cover. Have the hardware store or a glazier cut one out of sheet glass or clear plastic; such a cover will admit light but will keep the humidity in, and it can be lifted off or slid open an inch or two if the moisture level becomes too high.

PREPARING THE CONTAINER

Any container used for a terrarium must be scrupulously clean, for bacteria thrive just as well as the plants will in the high temperature and humidity of a closed environment. For this reason you should use packaged commercial potting soil that has been pasteurized to kill any organisms it may contain. And you should carefully inspect any plants for signs of insects or disease before putting them together in a terrarium, where infections and infestations will quickly spread among the closely grouped plants.

Plants for terrariums, like those for dish gardens, should be selected for the compatibility of their soil, light and moisture needs; even if you happened to like them together, cacti and ferns would not live long in each other's company. Whatever plants you choose, make sure first that there is an adequate drainage layer in the bottom of the container: 1 to 3 inches of coarse gravel or large pebbles is ideal, topped with a thin layer of sphagnum moss to keep the soil mix on top from sifting down.

PLANTING A TERRARIUM

The planting procedure for any terrarium is the same as the one shown for the bottle garden on pages 28-32, except that in wide-mouthed containers you will not have to use long-handled tools but can reach in with your hands. Do not add any fertilizer to the potting mix; it already has enough nutrients to last the plants for at least a year; after that you can add a small amount of half-strength house-plant fertilizer every six months, but use it sparingly or you will soon cause the plants to outgrow their surroundings.

A WINDOW GREENHOUSE

A decorative and practical device for displaying and maintaining plants is a miniature prefabricated greenhouse that fits to the outside of a house around a window. Its glass panels give maximum light for sun-loving plants such as coleuses, silk oaks and most cacti and succulents; the house windows can be removed for display and ease of access, or left on for close control of the environment inside. A hinged roof panel, its opening screened against insects, can be opened or shut as the need for ventilation is indicated by a temperature-humidity gauge (top shelf, left). The adjustable plant shelves are of wire mesh to allow air to circulate; the bottom is fitted with a tray that can be filled with water to increase humidity or supplied with a heating unit to raise temperatures in winter.

Once you have finished planting the terrarium, give it a light watering with an atomizer bottle or a bulb sprinkler, aiming the spray toward the sides of the container so as not to drench the leaves. Allow the foliage to become dry before putting the top in place. If the inside of the glass becomes heavily coated with moisture, take the top off for a few hours and replace it when only a fine mist of droplets can be seen on the glass. When you have thus stabilized the environment it will operate as a closed system: water will be drawn up by the roots and evaporated by the leaves into the air, from which it will condense on the glass and run down into the soil, where it can be used by the roots again. If the system is in balance it should not require watering again for months or even years, but if the foliage begins to crinkle at the edges or the moss at the bottom turns brown, it will need another light watering. After planting a terrarium, place it in the light conditions recommended for the group of plants you have chosen. However, never put a terrarium in full sunlight; the transparent container traps solar heat and the temperature would soon rise high enough to cook the plants.

The best way to control the environment for foliage plants is, of course, to grow them in a greenhouse. I have one outside my library; I open a door, step down a couple of steps and for a minute or an hour I am in another world. My greenhouse is a lean-to structure about 12 by 18 feet, divided into a warm section where I keep tropical foliage plants such as maidenhair ferns and saddle-leaved philodendrons as well as my orchids, and a cool section where row upon row of cacti get the low winter temperatures that ensure their flowering in spring. Simpler than even my lean-to is a miniature greenhouse mounted in a window, an ideal place for displaying not only cacti and succulents but such other sun-loving plants as coleuses and crotons. A ready-made model prefabricated of glass and aluminum, with built-in adjustable shelves and a top-opening vent protected by insect screening *(drawing, left)*, costs less than $200. The smallest types are designed to fit standard-sized windows and are attached to the outside of the frame so that nothing protrudes into the room. The regular windows can be removed and the greenhouse left open to the room, or sliding glass panels can be installed if the plants require a closed environment different from that of the house. The climate inside the greenhouse can be controlled by pebble trays filled with water to humidify the air, by heating cables or mats that work on a thermostat to maintain the desired temperature during cold weather, and by opening and closing the top vent when a temperature-humidity gauge indicates that this is in order. Strong summer sun that would burn many foliage plants can be softened by various shading devices: regular greenhouse whiting powder stirred in water and painted onto the outside of the glass, reed screening that can be rolled up and down from inside as needed, or green plastic shading.

A window greenhouse not only enables you to tailor a mini-climate quite precisely to the needs of particular plants, but it also provides more space than you may have inside a room for displaying them. One of the most stunning indoor gardens I have ever seen is a standard window greenhouse attached to the outside of a living-room window in a friend's house. In it she keeps an array of begonias, piggyback plants and kangaroo ivies, along with a few orchids and other flowering plants that provide a dash of color. At night, with the living-room lights dimmed and the plants dramatically lighted by fluorescent tubes concealed beneath the shelves, it becomes the focal point of the whole house.

While a greenhouse can provide optimum light and moisture conditions for plants, they also need proper feeding if they are to thrive for years. The first feeding rule is a simple one: when in doubt, don't do it. Frequent fertilizing simply makes house plants grow faster so that they become too big for their allotted space and have to be cut back severely or thrown away. And fertilizer, it should be remembered, is not a substitute for either moisture or light. In fact it is easy to damage or even kill a foliage plant that is growing in dim light by giving it too much food, for it is growing so slowly the roots cannot assimilate much fertilizer and the accumulating excess may burn the roots.

Most foliage plants should be fed no more frequently than once every three to six months, and this schedule should begin no sooner than six months after the plant is purchased; the soil and fertilizer given the plant by its commercial grower to bring it to salable size is generally more than enough to last that long. Any powdered, liquid or tablet fertilizer specifically designed for house plants can be used, but the best ones are those that have their nitrogen, phosphorus and potassium in a 1-2-1 ratio; a fertilizer marked 5-10-5 or 10-20-10 on the package, for example, is ideal. The reason for a 1-2-1 ratio is that it contains ample phosphorus, which promotes sturdy cell growth, but not so much nitrogen, which makes for fast leaf growth, or potassium, which also stimulates plant development. Follow the directions on the label and under no circumstances make the mixture stronger than the one suggested by the manufacturer; I generally use only half the minimum strength suggested.

Unlike fertilizing, which should be done at most every few months, the cleaning of foliage house plants should be frequent. They benefit from a good washing every two weeks or so. I am constantly amazed—and distressed—at the number of things people apply to

FEEDING FOLIAGE PLANTS

THE FORTNIGHTLY BATH

43

GROWING AN AVOCADO TREE

Avocado plants are not generally considered to be foliage house plants, but they sprout so readily and their large, dark green oval leaves are so decorative that many people grow them indoors in pots. To start one, wash the pit from a freshly eaten avocado, removing any pulp. Insert three or four toothpicks around the pit so that it will rest on the rim of a drinking glass with the broad end of the pit down. Add water until ½ inch covers the pit's base. Place the glass in a warm spot out of direct sunlight and replenish the water as needed. In a few weeks the pit should sprout. After a number of leaves and a mass of roots have formed, remove the toothpicks and bury the lower half of the pit in potting soil in an 8- to 10-inch pot. Water well and place in full sun. When the stem is a foot or so tall, tie it loosely to a stake. Your young avocado tree should grow handsomely for years—but it is unlikely to bear fruit indoors.

the leaves of plants in the belief that it will make them healthier or more beautiful; in addition to the commercial leaf shines, which make foliage a bit glossier but otherwise seem to do no particular good or harm, I have heard of plant owners applying olive oil, vegetable shortening, milk and even furniture polish. Any one of these concoctions not only collects dust but can easily block the pores in the leaves, through which the plant breathes, and kill it. Fortunately most people coat only the topsides of the leaves, allowing the majority of the breathing pores, or stomata, which are located on the undersides, to keep working.

In any case, the leaves of foliage plants are so lovely and endlessly varied in color and texture that any attempt to give them all a uniform gloss seems inappropriate. The only treatment I give my plants is a regular fortnightly bath to wash away accumulated dirt and dust and any insects that may have gathered, and to freshen the leaves so they can function normally. I take the smaller plants to the kitchen sink and medium-sized ones to the bathroom shower and give them a gentle spray of tepid water. Plants too large to move easily I wipe clean, leaf by leaf, using a soft damp cloth and supporting the leaf from underneath with one hand. If the weather is mild, I sometimes take plants outside and wash them down with a fine spray from a garden hose, then let them dry before bringing them back indoors.

Some plants, such as the piggyback plant and the purple passion vine, have hairy leaves that trap dirt yet are too delicate to be cleaned by a direct spray; in these cases invert the plant while holding one hand across the top of the pot; then swish the upside-down pot back and forth in a sinkful of tepid water containing a little soap (not detergent); then rinse it in clear tepid water.

Probably the one thing that worries people most about indoor plants is not when to fertilize or bathe them, but what to do with them when the family is off on a vacation and there is no one to watch after their watering needs. The ideal solution is to have a mutual-aid pact with a neighbor who will take care of your plants while you are away, in return for the same service on your part. If you cannot get a plant sitter, however, there are several ways you can help your plants to tend themselves. With a small plant, simply water it, cover it with a clear plastic food bag, tuck the bag under the bottom of the pot and set the bagged plant out of direct sun; if properly done, the water will recycle as in a terrarium, condensing on the inside of the plastic and running down where it can be taken up through the drainage hole. Larger plants, or a group of several plants, can be covered in similar fashion with a large clear plastic garment bag from the dry cleaner's; if a single large plant is potted in a container without drainage holes, tie the open end of the bag loosely around the stem of the plant instead of folding it under the bottom; that way moisture running down the inside of the plastic will drip into the soil of the pot.

Plants as well as people seem to like vacations, and after a long winter indoors they often benefit from a summer on the porch or terrace. If you move your plants outside, however, you would be wise to follow a few basic rules. First, do not move them out until all danger of a late spring frost has passed. Second, when safe weather does arrive, put them in deep shade for a week or more. The reason for this precaution is that their foliage, tender because it developed under weak indoor light, can be easily burned by the much higher light levels outdoors. After a couple of weeks, when the plants have had a chance to adjust to the outdoor environment, you can move them to more permanent summer locations, but even the light-loving types should still be kept only in partial sunlight or dappled shade. Third, keep the plants out of windy spots where they will quickly dry out and where their tender foliage can be whipped and damaged. To prevent clay pots from drying too quickly, they can be double potted in decorative urns lined with damp sphagnum moss. Fourth, bring your plants indoors again in early fall, well before the first expected frost and at a time when temperatures outside are virtually the same as temperatures within; waiting any longer may force them to adjust too quickly from a cool environment to a heated one and you may lose a few plants.

Even with good care and an eye to maintaining health rather than promoting growth, foliage plants can eventually become either too big for their pots or their setting. The best way to delay this moment is to train a plant to stay compact, starting when it is young. Prune back long, straggly stems to within ⅛ inch of a leaf joint; this will force the plant to retrench and send out new growth from the base of the leaf, a process that may require months. During this period the plant makes no upward growth but remains within bounds and perfectly healthy.

When a plant does become large, you may have to repot it. Unfortunately there is no easy rule to follow. I have a 6-foot-high rubber tree that has been growing happily in the same 8-inch pot I bought it in when it was less than 3 feet high. This species, as well as certain other plants such as palms and scheffleras, seems to do best when its roots are crowded in a pot that seems too small; the pot restricts any tendency to exuberant growth without seeming to hurt the plant in any way. But when a plant begins to produce new leaves that are smaller than average, if it wilts between normal waterings, if the lower leaves yellow, and particularly if roots

A SUMMER OUTSIDE

REPOTTING PLANTS

HOW TO REPOT
A LARGE HOUSE PLANT

1. *When a plant has outgrown its pot, roots may emerge through the drainage hole or crop out on the soil surface, or the plant may wilt between normal waterings. Before removing it for transfer to a larger pot, moisten the soil so the plant will slip out easily.*

2. *Set the pot on its side, place a cloth pad over the top of the rim, and holding the plant firmly, rap the edge of the pot with a mallet or the side of a hammer. Turn the pot a few inches and repeat until the soil ball slides out.*

3. *Untwist matted roots by combing the soil with a fork. Keep the ball as intact as possible, but trim long, twisted or dangling roots.*

4. *Prepare a new pot 2 inches wider and deeper than the old one by adding about an inch of moist potting mixture over drainage layers: at the bottom should be clay shards in a layer about 2 inches deep for pots 10 to 12 inches across, about 3 inches for larger ones, covered by an inch of long-fibered sphagnum moss. (The moss will be compressed when the plant rests on it.)*

5. *When the plant is set in the pot, the top of the soil ball should be 1 inch below the rim of an 8-inch pot (⅛ inch lower for each additional inch of pot diameter). Adjust to this level by adding potting mixture to the bottom of the pot, then add more mix around the sides, tamping with a stick to eliminate air pockets.*

6. *Smooth and firm the top surface with your fingers, adding potting mixture if necessary to cover exposed roots. Finally, soak the plant until water seeps out the drainage hole at the bottom.*

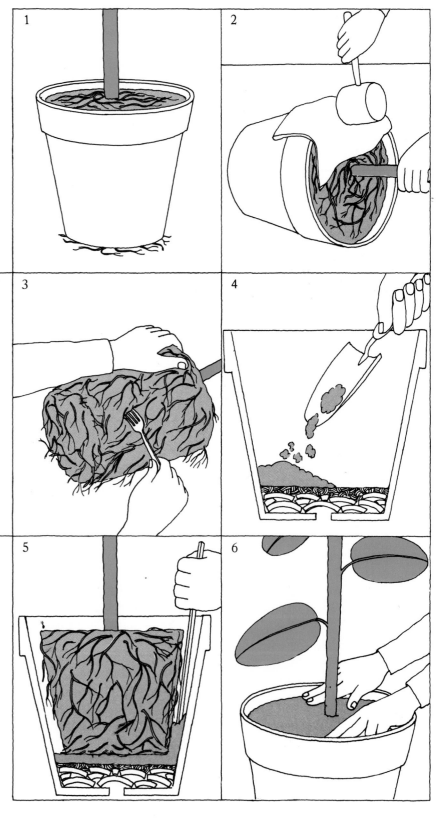

appear on the soil surface or emerge from the drainage holes, it is time to unpot the plant and have a look. If the roots are massed and tangled around the soil ball, the plant needs a larger pot.

The best time to repot most plants is in early spring as new growth is beginning; then the new roots that form will have fresh soil to grow into. But some plants such as Swedish ivy or coleus never really stop their growing and can be repotted at any time. The potting mixture you use will depend on the type of plant, but the basic requirement is a high percentage of organic matter so that the soil stays soft and spongy for years, allowing air to get to the roots and the roots to grow easily to gather moisture and nutrients. The mixture best suited for most house plants consists of 1 part loam (garden soil that has a good balance of clay, silt and sand and retains moisture and nutrients), 1 part organic matter such as peat moss or leaf mold, and 1 part coarse, or sharp, sand for good drainage. To each gallon pailful of this mix add 1 tablespoon of ground limestone to counteract the acidity of the peat moss, leaf mold and most soils; the limestone will also provide calcium, which strengthens cell walls. Also add 2 teaspoons of a chemical fertilizer such as 5-10-5, and to get a still higher concentration of phosphorus so vital to plant growth, add 1½ teaspoons of 20 per cent superphosphate. Because loam from the garden may contain fungus diseases, insects and weed seeds, it should be pasteurized in a covered baking dish in a 180° oven for 30 minutes before use.

If you are only repotting one or two plants and do not want to go to the trouble of preparing your own mix, simply use in place of the formula outlined above a packaged general-purpose potting soil of the kind sold at garden stores. All contain sterile ingredients; the best ones for house plants have a rather coarse texture and a high percentage of organic material.

For plants such as philodendrons, which need a highly organic growing medium, omit the garden soil and use 1 part peat moss or leaf mold and 1 part perlite or vermiculite as described in the encyclopedia. Other variations on the basic mix are desirable for ferns, and for cacti and succulents; these too are described in the encyclopedia. Unless specified otherwise in the encyclopedia, plants repotted in these mixtures do not need fertilizing for six months. The procedure for repotting is shown at left.

Whether or not a plant is repotted, one day it may simply outgrow its location in the house. If the plant has reached old age and displays long tired-looking stems with few leaves, the easiest thing to do is replace it with a new specimen of more manageable size. You do not necessarily have to buy the replacement, however; if the old plant is still healthy you can use it to produce new, smaller plants—a fascinating business that is the subject of Chapter 3.

Plants that solve problems

Most people simply collect a few house plants that appeal to them and enjoy their greenery on a convenient table or window sill. But foliage plants in particular offer an opportunity for much more: imaginatively used, they not only create stunning displays, but they can also provide a simple and economical way to solve interior-decorating problems. In the severe look-alike interiors of many modern houses and apartments, the varied foliage of house plants adds pattern and color, modifies straight lines and softens harsh contours. And in homes of any vintage where the proportions of rooms no longer suit their owners' needs, plants, properly placed, can shape old spaces into new ones.

The many ways in which plants are employed as elements of interior design are made feasible largely by modern lighting techniques, which can keep the plants healthy anywhere in the house. Today it is possible to move plants from their traditional inflexible positions near windows into any corner—even a dark stairway or hall *(right)*. This very freedom, however, can overwhelm the indoor gardener unless he follows a few basic guidelines:

Scale. First of all, plants should be chosen with an eye to the size and character of the space. A large-leaved fiddle-leaved fig tree would look badly out of place in a small dressing room; conversely, a tiny, lone peperomia might appear lost in a large, boldly furnished living room.

Repetition. In groupings of plants, the use of many different plants of different species can lead to a spotty and incoherent effect. Massed plants of the same kind, on the other hand, make a strong impact.

Emphasis. The focus should be on the plant, not the pot. The container design should suit the plant, not fight it; the safest choice is an unadorned pot of a neutral color.

None of these axioms, of course, need be taken as a hard and fast rule, but each can be put to work in a variety of ways, as the photographs and sketches on the following pages show. And each can add greatly to the enjoyment of plants indoors.

Gracefully adorning a bare stair hall, a piggyback plant and a Boston fern hang above a spider plant and English ivy.

Foliage to brighten inside walls

Since the majority of foliage plants thrive in something less than full sunlight, they can be grown even near windowless interior walls. Some will need supplementary artificial light, which can be supplied by either fluorescent tubes or incandescent bulbs incorporated into the room design. Whether these fixtures are installed on ceiling, wall or shelf, or set on the floor, they can be wired to timers that turn the light on and off on schedule to give the plants their daily rations of illumination. Incandescent bulbs can also be fitted with dimmer switches, which soften the light when the bulbs are used as the room's ordinary lighting source.

To a fireplace wall of stark white brick, form and color are added by a dieffenbachia (far left), two saddle-leaved philodendrons and a butterfly palm; in the open glass shelves are Swedish and English ivies and an Emerald Ripple peperomia.

Potted plants composed in close array against a wall create a living picture. Here, a base of trailing English ivy gains height from pileas and peperomias. Lights can be hidden on the floor behind the couch.

Massed foliage, like that of bird's-nest ferns, gives an empty fireplace an elegant look in summer, especially when framed by a pair of stately paradise palms. Floodlights on the ceiling can illuminate the display.

Small plants like cascading silver pothos and upright peperomias and prayer plants thrive on shelves under fluorescent tubes concealed by valance strips; they will also grow successfully in dim natural light supplemented by a lamp (right).

Organizing space with plants

Tall plants and planter boxes filled with greenery provide a handsome alternative to remodeling. Strategically placed, the plants can camouflage such architectural problems as the leftover space in the living room below. As shown at right, they can also serve to separate a large room into inviting areas for different activities, to provide additional wall space for furniture placement, or to shorten the apparent length of a long, narrow room. The planters can be simple plywood boxes, lined with sheet metal or plastic trays and finished to blend with the style of the room.

Plant boxes set on casters can be arranged in a variety of ways to divide a long room or create an entrance hall where none exists. For an airy effect, upright bird's-nest ferns are used in the planters and delicate, arching brake ferns in the hanging containers above.

In a room short of wall space, a central island garden provides a background for furnishings. Directly above it is a ceiling-mounted lighting box, fitted with a bank of fluorescent tubes to light the dieffenbachias and philodendrons below it.

A long, narrow room can be made to look shorter by a low floor planter built across one end. The one shown here is filled with a bold display of tall monsteras and medium-sized dieffenbachias flanked by shorter caladiums.

In an oddly shaped room, a wedge of space behind the couch is filled by (from left) a butterfly palm, Swedish ivy, coleus, a saddle-leaved philodendron, a Dracaena hookeriana, a red-margined dracaena and a dieffenbachia. On the floor is another saddle-leaved philodendron.

Rounding out awkward corners

Corners have always posed difficult decorating problems. Except for the wedge-shaped china cupboards popular in Colonial times and the fanciful whatnot shelves of the Victorian period, little furniture has been designed to fit in these troublesome angles. Properly chosen and placed, however, foliage plants bring a deserted corner to life—and are far less expensive than furniture.

Plants can be used singly, in groupings or in a small "garden" arranged on different levels. And unlike pieces of furniture, which should be accessible, they benefit rather than suffer from being tucked away in hard-to-reach corners out of the way of traffic.

Softening the sharp angles of a living-room corner is a miniature jungle of several bamboo palms surrounded by (left to right) a red-margined dracaena, a dieffenbachia, a fancy-leaved caladium, pots of English ivies and a young Dracaena hookeriana.

A striking focal point in a modern
room is made by hanging a single
plant large enough in size to dominate
a corner. Shown here is a staghorn
fern; other attractive choices would be
basket begonias and Boston ferns.

A hanging plant positioned above a
standing plant carries the line of
greenery from floor to ceiling. Here
Canary Island ivy trails down toward
a voluminous Japanese fatsia
surrounded by more ivy at its base.

A simple three-tiered structure of
wood supports a multilevel garden of
large and small plants. The shelves
are painted the same color as the walls
and are further concealed by dense
English ivy and Japanese fatsia.

A glass-topped table makes a living piece of furniture if a bed of glossy foliage is set on the bottom shelf. The plants shown are heart-leaved philodendrons, which grow successfully in either soil or a shallow dish of water and do not require much light.

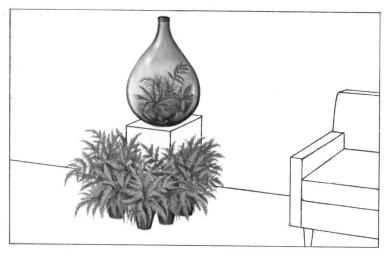

A bottle garden, such as the one pictured on pages 29-32, can be displayed as a piece of sculpture on a plant stand or a simple pedestal made of wood. The base of the pedestal is set off by a feathery semicircle of ferns.

Uplighting, from floodlights set on the floor, emphasizes bold patterns of foliage and creates dramatic shadows on a ceiling or wall. The effect is most striking with large-leaved plants such as palm trees, dieffenbachias and saddle-leaved philodendrons.

Swedish ivy cascading from a hanging pot looks twice as lavish when hung before a mirror. Other ivies and plants, like wandering Jews and spider plants, that require little light can be used to decorate bathrooms, where they thrive in the high humidity.

Plants can be used with a theatrical flourish to give a decorating scheme fresh life. Putting a single striking plant or a carefully composed bottle garden on a pedestal, for example, creates an unusual focal point. A glass-topped table can be turned into a showcase for a collection of smaller trailing plants. Mirrors, whether wall-hung or built-in like the one below, amplify the visual impact of any plant by reflecting the greenery, and lighting from beneath or beside a grouping can cast attention-getting shadows on flat white surfaces behind, above or below the plants.

Creating an effect of drama

Helping your plants multiply 3

Many years ago, during a trip to the 1939 New York World's Fair, I remember buying a novel little souvenir at one of the exhibit stands: a chunk of wood about 2 or 3 inches long wrapped in a small plastic bag. Inside the bag was a slip of paper proclaiming that here was a "Hawaiian Ti Log" and promising that if you set the log in a pot of soil and added water it would grow into an exotic Polynesian plant with leaves a foot long. The logs were going like hot cakes at $1 apiece, and they were no fraud. When buyers like myself got home and followed the instructions, lo and behold, they got fine foliage plants that would grow for years in their own living rooms, serving as living reminders of their trips to the fair.

Ti logs are still sold as novelties at fairs, flower shows and florists' shops, and they still delight people with their amazing ability to summon forth life from the most unlikely, dead-looking pieces of wood. Indeed, if you have a ti plant, or another plant such as a dieffenbachia or dracaena that grows on long main stems, or canes, you can reproduce it in much the same way (drawings, page 60) to provide new plants for your own collection or to give to friends. In fact, the plant you already own may well have been propagated from a cane: the popular Massange's dracaena is often grown commercially from cane cuttings that are 3 to 4 feet long; the bare canes form roots and leafy crowns so rapidly that within about six months they are ready for the florist's window.

Of course, not all foliage house plants have canes, nor can all that do be multiplied in this fashion. But there are few house plants that cannot be propagated by one or more of a number of other methods, and to many people experimenting with propagation is the most interesting part of gardening indoors. Almost all plants can be multiplied from seeds and, in fact, some cannot be multiplied successfully in any other way. But the seeds of the less well-known house plants are not always readily obtainable, and some require controlled greenhouse conditions to germinate into seedlings, not to mention patience on your part before the seedlings be-

The stem of an India-rubber tree, being propagated by air layering, is partially cut and bundled in damp sphagnum moss and plastic wrap. Within a few months new roots will grow out through the moss.

come plants large enough to enjoy. For these reasons the most common method, the one that produces the quickest results, is vegetative propagation, which means simply that part of the plant's vegetation instead of its seed is used to make a new plant.

PROPAGATION BY DIVISION

Vegetative propagation takes several different forms, the simplest of which is division. Almost any plant that has more than one stem rising from the soil in its pot can be divided into two or more plants, each retaining part of the original root system and top growth; among the most common foliage house plants that are propagated this way are the aspidistra or cast-iron plant, the umbrella plant, the spider plant, the Japanese sweet flag and many ferns.

The best time to divide a plant is in spring when new growth is starting. Simply knock the plant out of its pot and pull the sections apart with your hands. If they resist being pried apart, as they will in the case of caladiums and other plants that have thick fleshy roots, cut them apart with a large sharp kitchen knife. First shake the soil off the roots so they are exposed, then cut down through the crown of the plant, the area where the roots and top growth join. Repot the divisions immediately so the roots do not dry out, using the potting mixture specified for the plant in the encyclopedia (Chapter 5). Water each new plant thoroughly and set

STARTING PLANTS FROM CANE CUTTINGS

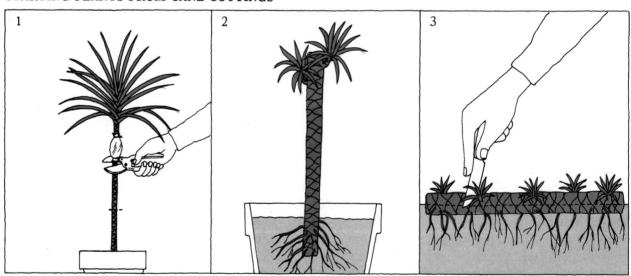

After a dracaena or dieffenbachia is air layered (page 58), the stem, or cane, remaining can be cut into 12-inch lengths (dashed lines) that will propagate plants. The stub in the pot will also sprout new branches.

To transform a cane cutting into a plant with one or more branches, stand it in moist sand or vermiculite, setting it 2 to 3 inches deep. When new leaf clumps grow 3 to 4 inches across, pot the plant in soil.

To get a number of small plants, lay a cane cutting horizontally, half buried in rooting medium. When shoots are 2 inches tall, cut them off and set them in rooting medium to let roots develop; then pot them.

it out of direct sunlight; water it again whenever the soil surface becomes dry. When the leaves appear firm and healthy, give it the light, temperature and moisture conditions recommended.

RUNNERS AND SUCKERS

A variation on division works well for certain plants that naturally multiply themselves by sending out small new plants. These sprouts generally appear in spring or summer, either on long slender trailing stems called stolons or runners, or in the form of small shoots, or suckers, that grow near the base of the plant. One of the most familiar examples of runner propagation is furnished by the spider plant, which produces miniature replicas of itself at the ends of long arching stems. In their natural habitat in South Africa the little plants send down roots and become independent while still anchored to the mother plant. It is easy to duplicate this process indoors by leading a runner to the top of a soil-filled pot placed next to the larger plant. Hold the tiny plant in place in its pot with a hairpin or bent paper clip until it is well rooted—generally two to three weeks—and then cut off the umbilical cord. Spider plants root so easily, in fact, that many indoor gardeners simply cut off the baby plants when their aerial roots, little white nubs on the undersides of the plants, are about ¼ inch long, and then plant them directly in moist potting mix to grow on their own.

Other foliage plants such as screw pines and many succulents such as echeverias, agaves and aloes send out from their bases a number of suckers. Given an opportunity to develop, suckers crowd against the original plant and in time form clusters of plants. All that is needed to make new plants is to cut away the suckers, using a sharp knife and cutting as close to the main stem as possible. Although suckers seldom have roots, they usually grow their own if they are simply potted in the proper soil for the species.

STEM AND LEAF CUTTINGS

For plants that do not form natural divisions or new baby plants, the commonest form of propagation is from cuttings. It is so common, in fact, that almost everyone who has house plants tries it sooner or later. One of our neighbors is a typical cuttings enthusiast; she always has at least a dozen old jelly jars, plastic tumblers and other assorted containers filled with water lined up on her kitchen counter and window sill, each with a sprig of greenery of some sort sticking out of it. Some of these turn into plants that she happily pots and puts in the living room; others gradually turn pale and limp and she throws them in the garbage with minor regrets. Sometimes she adds a pinch of sugar or even a dash of Angostura bitters to the water to help things along, but so far these experiments have failed to guarantee results.

You can propagate plants the way my neighbor does, and

you may well have, but it is pretty much a hit-or-miss affair with many plants and I suggest that you go about multiplying your plants a little more knowledgeably, according to their particular needs. If the proper procedures are followed, many kinds of plants can be grown from cuttings, either stem cuttings from the ends of branches or, in the case of some plants, a single leaf; these cuttings are best detached from the plant during its period of active growth, generally spring or summer, and induced to form roots on their own.

Cuttings form roots most readily if the stem is cut about ¼ inch below a leaf joint, or node. Plants such as coleus, devil's ivy and heart-leaved philodendron will grow roots easily from cuttings that are simply placed in a glass of water, but experienced gardeners have found that roots form more sturdily and adapt more easily to permanent potting if the cuttings are inserted in a moistened rooting medium. Satisfactory materials are sharp (i.e., coarse) sand, peat moss, sphagnum moss, vermiculite, perlite or an equal-part mixture of two or more of these materials, all of which combine a high water-holding capacity with an open structure that allows air to enter. The stem ends of the cuttings can be dipped before potting into a rooting-hormone powder, available at garden stores; the hormone will shorten the rooting time.

Before setting a cutting into the rooting medium, remove any leaves that would be below the medium; they will decay if they are covered. Certain plants such as philodendrons have such long petioles, or leaf stems, that the lowest leaves do not need to be removed even though the petioles are buried. So long as the leaf blades themselves protrude above the rooting medium, burying the petioles does no harm and in fact often results in bushier, more compact plants because extra stems are apt to rise from the point between the petiole and the main stem. The procedure for rooting stem cuttings is shown in detail on the opposite page.

Peperomias, some begonias, piggyback plants and many succulents can be grown from cuttings consisting of a single leaf; rex begonias and sansevierias can even be grown from sections of a leaf (drawings pages 66, 67). The stem of an ordinary leaf cutting is inserted in the rooting medium and the leaf itself is left exposed; if the leaf is stemless or has a short stem, as is the case with many succulents and some peperomias, or if sections of leaves are used, the base of the leaf or section is partially buried. In either case, a new plant develops from beneath the rooting medium and the mother leaf that has given birth to the young plant eventually dies.

Cuttings wilt quickly unless they are provided with high humidity since their leaf surfaces evaporate moisture readily and, without roots to supply normal amounts of moisture, they lose moisture faster than they can take it up. To ensure humid conditions,

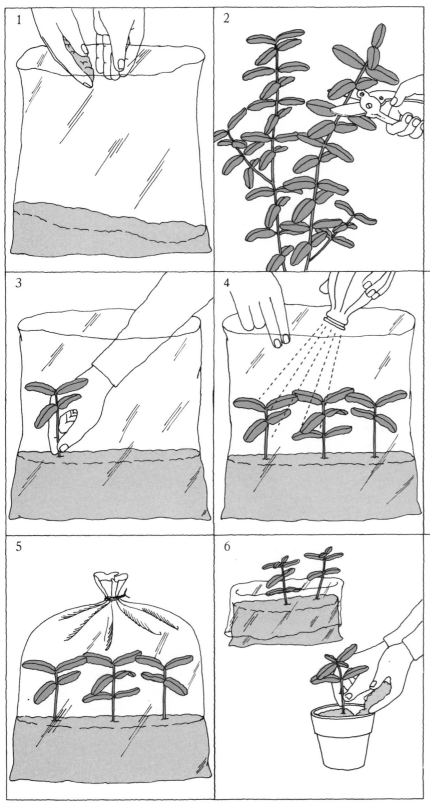

STARTING PLANTS FROM STEM CUTTINGS

1. *A simple way to start new plants such as Pearl Edge euonymus is to plant pieces of stem in a self-contained improvised environment from a clear plastic 1-gallon food storage bag. Use a rooting medium of 2 parts peat moss and 1 part sharp sand; moisten this mix and put it into the bag to make a base 4 inches deep.*

2. *Take 3- to 6-inch-long cuttings from the ends of young, light green stems, slicing just below a leaf joint with pruning shears or a knife. Strip off the lower leaves.*

3. *Insert the ends of the cuttings 1 to 3 inches deep in the rooting mixture. The ends may be dipped in hormone powder beforehand to stimulate root formation. To prevent rot, space the cuttings so the leaves do not touch. Firm the rooting mix around the stems to keep them upright.*

4. *Using a spray bulb or atomizer, mist just enough water over the leaves to wet them. Then pull the edges of the plastic together at the top and blow into the opening to inflate the bag before sealing it with a plastic wire twist.*

5. *Keep the cuttings in bright light, out of full sun. Inside the bag, water vapor from the leaves will collect on the plastic and run down to keep the rooting mix moist. If many large drops form, open the bag for a few hours to let the excess water evaporate.*

6. *When the roots are an inch long, open the bag and gradually roll down the sides (top) over a period of about a week to let the cuttings adjust to room conditions before potting them (bottom). To see when roots are big enough, lift a cutting with a spoon.*

set your cuttings in a clear plastic food bag filled with the moistened rooting medium as shown in the drawings, or in a flowerpot filled to within ½ inch of the rim. Firm the medium well around the bases of the stems or leaves, then sprinkle the cuttings with tepid water. If you use a plastic bag, simply tie the top closed; if you use a pot, slip the pot into a plastic bag and fold the open end under the pot. In either case, set this small greenhouse in bright light, but not full sun, in a place where the temperature is at least 60°F.; 75° to 80° is even better to speed the rooting process.

The length of time required for rooting varies with the kind of plant: species with tender moisture-filled stems—like the wandering Jew, velvet plant or coleus—will usually root within a week; plants having tougher stems, such as English ivy and evergreen euonymus, require about 10 days; types with very tough, woodlike stems, such as dracaena, podocarpus and aralia, may take a month or longer. New gardeners often ask how to tell when new roots have formed. The way professionals do it is simply to pull up a cutting or two once a week and look at them. When my wife sees me inspecting cuttings this way she accuses me of being an impatient gardener, and she may be right, but in any case it does not hurt the cuttings because the rooting medium is so soft that they pull out easily if you pry them up gently with a spoon, nail file or wooden plant label. If the cuttings have not yet grown roots, stick them back into the rooting bed and water them lightly. When the roots have formed and are about an inch long, the cuttings are ready for individual pots. Use the potting material specified in the encyclopedia entry for the species and set each new plant in its pot at the depth at which it stood in the rooting medium; this level can easily be determined by color—the stem of the rooted cutting will be slightly darker aboveground than below.

AIR LAYERING PLANTS   Although many plants are easy to grow from cuttings, large-leaved types such as rubber trees, scheffleras, crotons and the monstera, or Swiss cheese plant, lose so much moisture from their leaf surfaces that they would wilt before roots could form. Yet even these plants can be multiplied by inducing roots to grow on stems. The trick is to start the rooting process on stems that remain attached to the mother plant. The method is an ancient form of plant propagation known as air layering or Chinese layering. To use it, choose a healthy, sizable stem near the top of the plant, make an upward-slanting cut one third to one half way through the stem and insert a match stick in the cut to hold it open. The open cut is then dusted with rooting-hormone powder and wrapped in a tightly bound bundle of moist sphagnum moss about as big as a baseball. The moss ball in turn is bound in ordinary plastic wrap to retain the moisture within the moss, as seen in the photograph on page 58. After a few months roots can be seen under the clear plastic, working their way through the moss, and the plastic can be removed. The whole stem tip is then cut just below the new roots and is planted, moss and all, in the type of potting mixture recommended for the species.

If you want only one or a few replicas of plants you already have in the house, air layering, division and cuttings are the easiest and quickest methods. But if you want a number of new plants—to create a display across a bare window sill or to give away as presents—you should consider growing them from seeds. Seeds, of course, are much less expensive to buy than grown plants, and although you may have to wait as long as a year for full-foliaged specimens, you will have the satisfaction of growing something yourself from the ground up. Coleuses, begonias, rubber trees, pittosporums and silk oaks, as well as a number of other foliage plants and many cacti and other succulents, are especially easy to grow from seeds without special equipment or care.

Almost every gardener who raises seedlings has his own favorite soil mixture and containers. I use a mixture of equal parts of leaf mold or peat moss, garden soil or packaged potting soil and coarse sand. This medium retains enough but not too much moisture, and it also provides adequate nutrients without the need for added fertilizers. If you use ordinary garden soil, pasteurize it first in a 180° oven as described in Chapter 2.

An ordinary flowerpot makes a good container in which to start seedlings, but the type of flowerpot known as a pan is preferable; it is twice as wide as it is deep and is thus easier to handle without tipping; it holds more than enough potting mix to accommodate all the seedlings most people want. If the pot is not new, it should be thoroughly cleaned with soap and hot water to get rid of any bacteria that may have been left over from its previous use; if it is a clay pot, it can be put in the oven with soil that is being pasteurized to kill germs. Any clay pot should be soaked for several hours before it is used so that it becomes thoroughly wet and will not absorb moisture from the soil after the seeds are planted.

When you have your pot ready, fill it to the rim with potting mix and firm the mix with the heel of your hand or with the bottom of another clean flowerpot, compressing the soil to a level about ½ to ¾ inch below the rim of the pot. Sprinkle the seeds sparsely over the surface so that they will not crowd one another when they begin to grow. Unless the seeds are very small they should be covered lightly, to a depth of once or twice their diameter, to help keep them moist during the process of germination. As a covering material I use either a fine grade of vermiculite or finely ground (milled) sphagnum moss, both available at garden stores. The sphagnum moss is difficult to moisten with cold water; sprinkle it with hot tap water, which it absorbs quickly, then let it drain before spreading it evenly over the seeds. If the seeds are tiny, that is, the size of grains of sand or smaller, they should be sprinkled on top of the moss or vermiculite. The material should be moistened and spread in a ¼-inch layer on top of the potting mixture and then the seeds should be dusted lightly over it; they will sift down into the covering to the right level.

Whether the seeds are large or small, do not water them from the top of the pot or you will wash them too deep; instead, set the pot in a dish of tepid water and leave it there until the potting mix has become moist all the way to the surface. Then take the pot out of the water and let it drain for about an hour. To keep the soil moist and to maintain a high humidity in the air above the seedbed —both conditions essential to germination—slip the flowerpot into a clear plastic bag and fold the top of the bag under the pot. Set the pot where the temperature will be about 70° to 80° and where there is ample light without direct sun.

Moistened and enclosed in its own miniature plastic greenhouse, your seed pot should not require additional watering until after the seedlings have sprouted. At that time the plastic covering

PROPAGATING SANSEVIERIAS FROM LEAF SECTIONS

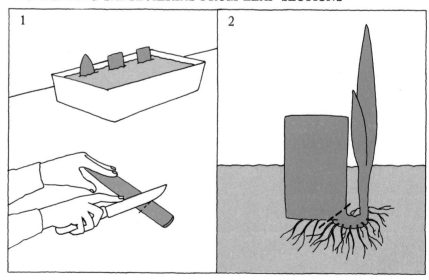

To produce many plants from a single sansevieria leaf, cut the leaf into 3- to 4-inch lengths and press the base end of each section halfway down into a flat filled with moist sand, perlite or vermiculite.

Keep the cuttings moist and out of direct sun for several weeks until the new shoot beside each leaf section is 3 to 4 inches high. Then pull it up, cut off the shoot (dashed line) and transplant it to potting mixture.

should be removed and the pot should be set in the light and temperature conditions recommended for the species. Keep the soil mix under the seedlings moist but not wet. Water in the morning so that the top of the soil is dry at nightfall; this procedure helps prevent the disease called damping off, a fungus that destroys the cells of seedlings at soil level and can topple the young plants overnight.

As the seedlings of most species grow, they will develop what are called seed leaves, generally a pair of small, rounded leaves that are not shaped like the typical mature leaves of the plant. Exceptions are conifers such as the Norfolk Island pine, which bear needle-shaped leaves like their mature relatives even as they sprout, and asparaguses and palms, which usually have grasslike leaves from the beginning. In plants that produce seed leaves, the true leaves develop from a bud between the seed leaves; when the true leaves take on the recognizable shape of the species, pry up the seedlings gently with a spoon or wooden plant label, taking the soil around the roots with them, and transplant each to its own pot in the potting mix recommended for the plant.

As you become more interested in indoor gardening, you may want to try a variation on growing plants from seed: reproducing ferns from the spores that grow on the undersides of their fronds. One of

GROWING FERNS FROM SPORES

PROPAGATING THICK-LEAVED PLANTS FROM LEAF CUTTINGS

Fleshy-leaved house plants such as peperomias and crassulas can be multiplied by snapping off single leaves. Choose healthy, medium-sized leaves, removing them at the points where they meet the stem.

Insert the stem of each leaf at an angle into equal parts of moistened peat moss and sharp sand; bury one edge of the leaf to support it. Angled planting keeps the leaf from shading new growth when it appears.

Set the pot in bright indirect light until the new leaves are about one third the size of the parent. Then gently lift and separate the old growth from the new and transplant the shoots to potting mixture.

The time and effort required to create a new type of hybrid foliage plant is demonstrated by the history of the Burgundy philodendron (page 131), a plant that bears striking arrow-shaped leaves with wine-red ribs and stems. To develop it, Robert McColley of Florida's Bamboo Nurseries, Inc. first combined two species with arrow-shaped leaves, one a vigorous type with red stems, and got a fast-growing, shapely plant with reddish leaves. But the leaves were too widely spaced so he crossbred the new hybrid with a third, more densely foliaged kind of philodendron to make it more compact. Then he crossed the result of this merger with two disease-resistant species to produce a plant tough enough to survive any ailment. In the process McColley discarded more than 200,000 seedlings before he found the single plant he wanted. To make sure it was ready for the market, he subjected specimens to overfertilizing and underwatering, extremes of light and temperature, and even simulated shipping conditions to see how long it took the plant to recuperate from mistreatment. Satisfied with its performance, he launched into volume production of the plant for marketing. Eight years from the initial hybridizing experiment, his first Burgundy philodendron was ready to be sold.

the fascinating things about ferns is that they are living fossils, closely resembling the species that were the most abundant plants in the world some 200 million years ago and whose fossilized remains account for the majority of coal deposits on every continent today. The unusual reproductive process that has enabled them to survive down to this day does not involve what we normally think of as seeds; ferns do not bear flowers and thus have no seeds, but they do produce immense numbers of spores, dustlike particles enclosed in spore cases that appear as rows of symmetrical dots beneath the leaves at any time from April to September, depending on the species. A single fern may produce millions of spores a year, each capable of becoming a new fern; in the case of plants growing in the wild, these spores fall to the ground where, if conditions are right, they develop into new plants. Obviously, few of these millions of spores do find just the right conditions.

The gardener who wants to observe the process, however, can easily supply close to ideal conditions indoors, using a procedure very similar to that for sowing very tiny seeds. The most important condition for ferns is ample moisture, so the potting mixture should have a high proportion of organic material to help it retain water. I use 2 parts of garden soil, pasteurized in the oven and sifted fine through a piece of window screening; to this I add 2 parts of peat moss or leaf mold, screened in the same manner, and 1 part sharp sand. If you do not have access to good garden soil, substitute packaged potting soil in the formula. I use a clay flowerpot of the pan type, soaked for several hours so it will not absorb moisture from the potting mix, or a plastic pot, which needs no soaking and is helpful in retaining the moisture ferns must have. As an added precaution against bacteria—and against the algae that are present in ordinary tap water—I boil a large pot of water and after it has cooled use some of it to soak the flowerpot. I save the rest for moistening the spores in the potting mix. When I am ready to sow the spores I fill the pot completely with the mix and firm it so the surface is ½ to ¾ inch below the rim. Make sure the surface is perfectly level; otherwise only the low spots will stay moist while the high spots will dry out.

When the spore cases on the fern become ripe, remove a leaf, drop it into a small brown paper bag and leave it there until the cases dry out and disintegrate, usually in about a week. Then empty the contents of the bag onto a sheet of paper and remove the pieces of dried leaf so that only the brown dustlike spores remain. Crease one end of the paper so you can use it as an open funnel to tap the spores onto the top of the potting soil, or simply pick up a tiny pinch of the spores between your thumb and forefinger and sprinkle them across the surface. Hold your hand or the paper close to the surface and make sure there is no draft in the room; the slightest breeze will blow the spores away. Set the pot in a dish of water until the surface darkens to indicate the mix is thoroughly moistened. Then, to provide a steady supply of moisture, place the pot in a shallow saucer of water, slip a clear plastic bag over it and fold the top under the saucer. Keep the covered pot and saucer in a well-lighted spot out of direct sun in a place where the temperature remains constant at about 65° to 70°.

Within a few days to a few weeks in the case of table ferns (*Pteris*) and maidenhair ferns (*Adiantum*), or as long as a year in the case of the staghorn fern (*Platycerium*), the surface of the mix will be carpeted with what appears to be a green slime. At this point many a beginner has thought to himself, "I must have done something wrong—I planted ferns and got seaweed!" But this is just the intermediate stage in the fern's life cycle; ferns evolved during the period when life on earth was changing from a water to a land environment, and the "seaweed" reflects their amphibious past. Actually it consists of flat green heart-shaped bits of growth called prothallia; when the prothallia become about ¼ inch across they produce on their undersides the male and female organs of the fern. As each prothallium matures, the male organ, called the antheridium, bursts open, releasing sperms that swim through the film of water on the underside of the prothallium until one fertilizes the egg cells contained within the female organ, or archegonium. With the union of sperm and egg a new fern begins its life. The tiny new plant sends up leaves and its roots descend into the soil; the prothallium, its work done, dries up and vanishes.

About six months after the spores were sown, the young ferns send up their own tiny fronds. When the fronds become 1 to 1½ inches tall, remove the plastic bag, lift the plants gently in little clumps, several to a clump, and reset them 1 to 2 inches apart in separate pots or a gardener's flat or planting tray. The container should be filled with a potting mixture of equal parts of pasteurized or packaged potting soil and peat moss or leaf mold. Be careful not to set the plants too deep; the prothallia, which will still be in evidence, should just rest on the surface of the mix. About a year from the time the spores were sown the clumps can be pulled gently apart and each fern repotted separately, using the potting mix and light and temperature conditions recommended for the species. Since most ferns continue to do best under humid conditions, I often place the little plants, pots and all, in a tank-type terrarium to brighten a north window sill. Later on, as they grow into mature plants, I transfer some of them to a decorative wall or floor container or a hanging basket, to take their place as handsome conversation pieces in the study or living room.

The fascinating family of cacti and succulents

Anyone interested in foliage house plants should consider the special group of cacti and other succulents that are the evolutionary oddities of the plant world. Every bit as beautiful as they are bizarre, they are among the easiest of plants to grow indoors. Many a gardener has found that even if he cannot seem to raise anything else in cramped quarters and dry, heated air, he can at least grow a couple of dwarf opuntias or echeverias on a sunny window sill.

Like many people, I once thought of cacti as funny-looking prickly plants, a kind of living barbed wire that people used to fall into in old western movies. It was a revelation to discover the almost infinite variety of these strange plants and the fascination they afford. There are some 2,000 known species of cacti, ranging from the tiny 1-inch-high plaid cactus, to giant saguaros that send candelabralike trunks to heights of 50 feet or more. The word cactus comes from *kaktos* (spiny plant), used by the ancient Greeks to describe a species that turned out to be not a cactus at all but a type of artichoke; 2,000 years later the name was adopted by the great plant classifier Linnaeus to embrace a large group of plants whose peculiar traits included succulent, or fleshy, stems that served to store water, prickly or hairy coverings and few if any leaves.

Long ago in their evolutionary history, apparently, cacti had leaves. All cacti still do in their seedling stage; some species sprout small leaves on new growth for a short time each spring and one or two species bear leaves throughout the year. But in adapting to slowly changing climatic conditions that turned their native habitats into deserts, most cacti gradually lost their leaves, which evaporated too much scarce water into the dry air. Instead they began to store what water was available in their stems, which became fat and rounded to hold a maximum of moisture while exposing a minimum of surface to the drying sun and air; many species of cacti can even change their shape to adjust the area of their evaporating surfaces to varying conditions, being equipped with accordionlike ribs that expand when moisture is plentiful and contract

Trays of young cacti, including ball-shaped notocactus and columnar myrtillocactus, await buyers in a greenhouse. Their striking shapes and easy maintenance make them highly popular among indoor gardeners.

during times of drought. Some species have also developed sharp spines or woolly hairs that not only help to shade their fleshy tissues from the fiercest rays of the sun but also make these juicy reservoirs less appetizing to hungry, thirsty desert animals.

HOW SUCCULENTS EVOLVED

While true cacti are the most spectacular of the plants called succulents, there are some 6,500 other species of water-storing plants that fall into that class. Unlike the cacti, which are all of the *Cactaceae* family and are natives of the Americas, these others belong to 44 different botanical families that are spread around the world and include close relatives of the poinsettia and the geranium, the lily and the grape. Most succulents such as aloes, haworthias, crassulas and echeverias evolved under less severe conditions than cacti, in areas where rainy seasons are followed by long dry periods. And in contrast to the generally leafless cacti, most other succulents have leaves. To tide the plants over the dry spells, their leaves gradually became fattened by water-storing tissues and covered with a waxy or horny material that reduces evaporation from the surface.

GROWING SUCCULENTS

The surprising variety of sizes, shapes and colors among the cacti and other succulents makes them decorative as house plants in a wide range of situations. Miniature varieties of *Mammillaria, Gymnocalycium* and *Notocactus,* and succulents such as *Gasteria* and *Haworthia* will fit on the narrowest window sill. Trailing types such as rattail cactus and burro's tail sedum provide striking displays in hanging baskets, and tall upward-growing species such as the elephant-foot tree and some euphorbias can be set in a container on the floor in a sunny corner.

If cacti and other succulents are given the proper conditions and a minimum of basic care, most will provide pleasure for years. Being largely desert plants, they tolerate and even thrive in the 10 to 30 per cent relative humidity of heated houses and apartments. Many have tough skins that make them unappetizing to destructive insects, all require only occasional watering and practically no feeding, and most grow so slowly they will not soon become too large for the location you have put them in.

As easy to grow as they are, however, these plants do have a few definite needs, all deriving from their natural life outdoors where sun is generally plentiful, water is scarce and the growing season is short. The first rule is: give them plenty of light. Because the amount of light that penetrates into a house is so much less than cacti normally get in the open desert, you should set them in the sunniest location available; some other succulents, however, are used to less light. If you do not have a window that gets the requisite amount of sun, you can supplement whatever daylight you have with artificial light *(Chapter 2)*. Like other house plants, cacti and succulents can be moved outdoors in summer, but there they should be set in a spot that provides them with light shade or filtered sunlight during the hot part of the day; if you set them in full sun they will almost surely suffer sunburn because their tissues have developed under relatively weak indoor light.

The second rule in growing succulents, especially cacti, is to avoid the temptation to water them as much as you would other house plants. They have adapted to life in arid climates; when they are given too much water, their roots simply cannot take up the moisture and they rot away. I know of one lady who has a novel method of determining when to water her cacti: she looks at the weather

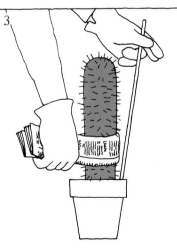

MOVING A CACTUS TO A LARGER POT

1. *Before transplanting a cactus that has outgrown its pot, select a new pot one third to one half as wide as the plant is tall—or 1 inch wider than a globe-shaped plant —and line the bottom third with shards, gravel and charcoal. Add an inch of potting mix.*

2. *Wearing gloves, unpot the cactus and hold it in the new pot with a loop of folded newspaper so that its soil line is ½ inch below the rim of a pot up to 6 inches wide (1 inch below in larger pots). Fill around the sides with potting mix.*

3. *Still gripping the cactus with the newspaper, tamp down the potting mix around the root ball with a small stick, adding more mix if necessary; this step eliminates air pockets that cause water to drain down the sides of the pot, away from the roots.*

4. *Smooth the top surface of the soil with the back of a kitchen spoon. To help the broken roots heal after transplanting, leave the cactus dry for three or four days, then soak the soil until excess water seeps through the drainage hole at the bottom of the pot.*

potting mixture

crushed charcoal

coarse gravel

clay shards

listings in the newspaper every day to see if it has rained in the desert city of Tucson during the previous 24 hours; if it has, she waters her plants, if not, she waits. Her "natural" method is not a bad one, but it does not allow for the extremes of rainfall and drought that come even to Tucson; by and large you are better off watering according to the needs of each plant.

Proper watering depends not only on the type of plant, but on the type of container, the size of the plant and the time of year. During the active growing season from spring to fall, the soil around most cacti should be allowed to dry out thoroughly between waterings; the drying process may take from a few days to two weeks. In winter, from about November through February, most species of cacti go into a semidormant state when growth processes almost stop. During this period they should be watered only enough to keep the plants from shriveling; under average conditions one watering about every two or three weeks is enough. Large cacti and cacti in plastic or glazed containers, which do not lose moisture as rapidly as clay pots, need less frequent watering.

Other types of succulents generally need slightly more frequent watering than cacti. The soil should be allowed to become only moderately dry between waterings from spring through fall; during the winter resting period they need watering only often enough to keep the leaves from shriveling—about once every two weeks is sufficient if the plant is in a clay pot, less often if it is in a nonporous one.

Whatever species you are dealing with among cacti and other succulents, always water on a dry, sunny day rather than a humid or cloudy one. Morning is the best time, for then the roots can absorb as much moisture as possible while the plant, using the

(continued on page 79)

A miniature landscape for a dish

One of the best ways of showing off the sculptural qualities of cacti and other succulents is to create a landscape in miniature by planting one or several compatible plants—those with similar light, soil and water requirements—in a shallow container such as a casserole. In such a dish the individual features of each plant become secondary to the total design of the tiny garden; the effect depends on the balance of elements —the plants, the color and shape of the container, and the texture of the pebbly materials used to top the potting mixture. Although dish gardens can be created with many types of plants, succulents and cacti are especially popular—they grow almost untended, are widely available in diminutive sizes and come in bold, often bizarre shapes. Perhaps most important, succulents grow very slowly, so that the passage of time does not disrupt the carefully planned composition of the miniature landscape.

A handsome composition in a casserole includes an opuntia cactus (center) and rebutias grafted onto a hylocereus (right).

A pair of tall thrixanthocereuses and small round mammillarias are balanced against a backdrop of gravel and small stones.

Two cuttings from a jade plant rise like miniature trees above a mound of gravel-topped soil in an au gratin dish.

Contrast in height, shape and texture is provided by three of the many succulents that belong to the Crassula genus.

The yellow rim of a soup bowl and pale gravel emphasize the delicacy of an echeveria.

An echeveria, dramatically set off-center against a background of charcoal chips, grows in a shiny black ceramic dish.

A milk-striped euphorbia, resembling the giant saguaro cactus, is set against echeverias in a miniature desert scene.

Tumblers stacked to different levels make a rearrangeable cactus garden.

Colorful pebbles surround an aloe (top), a crassula, haworthias and a sedum.

Builders' sand and a clay pot provide a rugged setting for such succulents as gasterias (upper right) and a tall myrtillocactus.

Set off-center in a red ceramic dish is a panda plant flanked by a hairy white old-man cactus and a spiny mammillaria.

An abstract pattern uses 11 kinds of succulents in the compartments of a plastic silverware tray.

sunlight, works to pull the water up through its tissues and to evaporate the excess into the air; if you water on a humid or cloudy day or in the evening, the plant cannot take up the moisture as rapidly and it will remain around the roots, inviting rot. When watering, always use tepid water; cold water can shock the plants and can even cause some succulents to drop their foliage.

The third rule for growing these desert plants applies to temperatures. Since all the succulents come from regions that are warm during their growing season, ordinary house temperatures are satisfactory much of the year. But if you want your cacti to bear flowers, they will need cool temperatures during the winter rest period (most other succulents do not). Ideally cacti should be given night temperatures of 40° to 45° F. and day temperatures no higher than 65° from fall to spring; under these conditions they will bear flowers when they resume growing, as they do in nature. If temperatures remain much above these levels the plants will not blossom, and because they cannot really rest they will weaken and may become spindly. The ideal temperatures are admittedly not easy to achieve in most homes, but they can be approximated if you place the plants on an unheated porch where the temperature does not drop below freezing, in a window in a cool part of the basement or in a window greenhouse where the temperature can be regulated.

Since most cacti and other succulents grow slowly, they seldom need repotting more frequently than once every two years. The best time to repot is in early spring just as new growth is beginning. Choose a container that allows for neither too little nor too much soil mix around the plant. Since overwatering is common, it is better to have the plant in a pot that seems a little too small for it than one that is too large; water drains quickly if there is little soil to hold it, while if the pot is too large, the soil will remain wet longer than it should. If the plant is an upright-growing type, use a pot whose width equals from one third to one half the height of the plant. If the plant is globular, use a pot 1 inch greater in diameter than the body of the plant. The smallest miniatures look best if you group several together in a 3- or 4-inch pot, leaving about an inch of space between the plants and the sides of the pot.

Because these dry-climate plants are so sensitive to excess moisture, they should have a generous drainage layer of coarse gravel at the bottom of the pot *(drawings, page 73)* and they should be planted in a mixture that allows for even better drainage than the mixture recommended for other house plants. I use a standard mix composed of equal parts of loam, leaf mold and sharp sand, and ½ part crushed charcoal (or 1 part packaged potting soil and 1 part sharp sand), with 1 tablespoon of ground limestone and 1 table-

REPOTTING SUCCULENTS

spoon of bone meal added to each gallon pailful of mixture. The sand should be very gritty, without fine particles; the best kinds are so-called water-washed sand, available at building supply stores, and aquarium sand, sold in pet shops. Also available at pet shops, as well as at many garden and hardware stores, is the crushed charcoal that helps to draw harmful substances from the soil, keeping it fresh and open in structure. The ground limestone is the same material used to overcome the acidity of garden and lawn soils; it not only assures neutral to slightly alkaline conditions, which most succulents prefer, but its calcium content serves a special function in helping cacti build the sturdy, brightly colored spines that add so much to their beauty. The bone meal supplies the plants with the nutrients, primarily phosphorus, that promote steady, healthy

GRAFTING ONE CACTUS ONTO ANOTHER

1. *To graft a globe-shaped cactus on top of a columnar one, remove the top of the columnar plant, the stock, with a sharp knife; a flat board held behind the plant will steady it so you can cut with a single clean stroke.*

2. *Bevel the top edge of the stock downward to trim spines out of the way and to keep the stock from lifting the upper plant as the cut dries. Sterilize the knife with alcohol and make a thin, flat slice below the top (inset); leave the slice in place to keep the cut moist.*

3. *After the cactus that will be used as the upper plant, or scion, has been unpotted, slice off its roots and bevel the rim upward. Then make a thin slice with a sterilized knife just above the cut surface.*

4. *Just before scion and stock are joined, the slices are discarded and the two plants pressed together with their central growth rings matched; strings weighted with hardware nuts are draped over the top to hold the graft. Keep dry and out of direct sun for a few days until the graft takes, then remove the strings.*

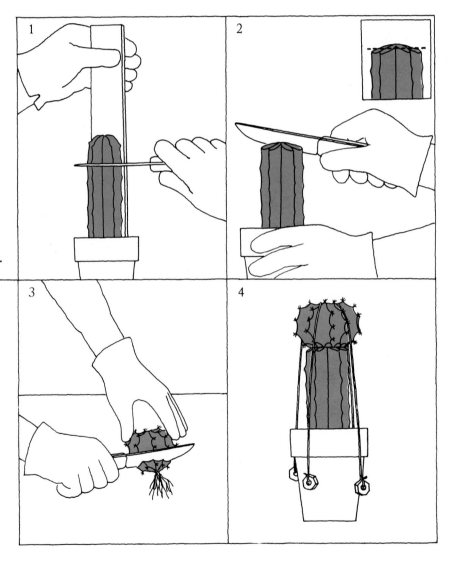

growth: it will provide enough nourishment to see a plant through the first year. Unless the plant is repotted the following year, with fresh bone meal in the mix, it is a good idea to give it one feeding annually early in spring with any house-plant fertilizer. Use half the strength recommended on the manufacturer's label.

Both cacti and other succulents can be propagated by a number of the methods described in Chapter 3—from divisions, stem and leaf cuttings, and seeds. Stem cuttings should lie in a dry place out of the sun for three or four days so the juicy cut ends can dry out and heal before they are placed in the rooting medium. Seeds should be started in a mixture of 2 parts packaged potting soil, 2 parts sharp sand and 1 part crushed charcoal.

The most intriguing method of producing your own new plants, however, involves the unique ability of most cacti and a few other succulents to attach themselves and grow on others by the grafting process *(drawing, page 80)*, providing truly new plants not found anywhere in nature. By grafting, which joins a stem section from one plant to a cut in the rooted stem of another, a tiny globe-shaped crown cactus can be grown on the padlike stem of a bunny ears cactus, or a trailing type such as a rattail cactus can be placed atop the stem of a columnar cereus cactus. Only true cacti and the euphorbia succulents lend themselves to grafting, for in them the inner ring of growth tissue that carries nutrients through the plants is clearly defined. When the stems are cut, these supply channels are easy to recognize so that the channels of one cut stem can be lined up precisely with the channels of the other as the joint is made between the two, thus guaranteeing a free flow of food and water from the rooted parent plant to the grafted section. The two cut surfaces should be joined together with slight pressure to force out any air bubbles that might allow the cut surfaces to dry or bacteria to cause rot. They should then be secured in place under light pressure with rubber bands or string stretched over the top of the grafted plants. The rubber bands or string can be removed within a few days. Grafting can be done at any time, but the best time of year is early spring when new growth is just beginning.

A friend of mine who has a cactus farm in California grafts beautiful trailing orchid cacti to the giant pads of opuntias, or prickly pears, whose strong root systems nourish the orchid cacti into spectacular growth. It is even possible to graft a number of different kinds of cacti onto a single supporting plant, so that the composite displays a different shape on every "branch." I myself have not gone quite that far. I get my main pleasure out of my house plants, be they cacti, succulents or whatever, pretty much as they are; the way nature made them is more than lovely enough for me.

GETTING NEW PLANTS

THE USEFUL CACTUS
Cacti have so many uses in Mexico that the government has forbidden their export and promotes their cultivation. The nopal cactus is harvested by desert cattle ranchers to provide their stock with both water and nourishment. The fruit of the tuna cactus is made into a tasty jam; it is also fermented and distilled into wine, and the residue is used for chicken feed. The delicious fruit of the prickly-pear cactus is eaten whole, served in salads and made into candy; the organ-pipe cactus is planted to form impenetrable living fences along property lines. The peyote cactus, which induces hallucinogenic visions when eaten, has played a part in Indian rituals since the days of the Aztecs.

An encyclopedia of foliage house plants 5

Most foliage house plants flourish with little care if their specific needs are tended. Some, like acalyphas, require as much light as you can give them, while others, such as the cast-iron plant, thrive even in a dimly lighted corner. A few—dracaenas, for example—need constantly moist soil, but devil's ivy does best if the soil is allowed to become moderately dry between waterings.

Such growing requirements, as well as the characteristics, uses and methods of propagating the plants, are given for 103 genera in the following section. The entries specify light and moisture needs, together with temperature ranges that allow the plant to grow by day and rest at night. Fertilizing instructions are based on the assumption that plants were potted in a nourishing mixture before purchase. Since some plants can become too big for the space allotted to them, all directions are aimed at maintaining the plants' health rather than stimulating their growth.

To keep the plant healthy for its full normal life span where natural light is inadequate, provide as much artificial light as possible, but at least the foot-candles specified, for 12 to 16 hours a day; however, plants will usually live for at least a year with less light. Avoid overheating the foliage. Spotlights should be at least 3 feet away from the plant, floodlights 2 feet away. Even ordinary incandescent bulbs should be distant enough so that you cannot feel the warmth of the bulb when you place your hand next to the leaves. Fluorescent tubes can be located as close as 6 inches to the foliage without danger of overheating the plants.

The plants are listed alphabetically by their internationally recognized Latin botanical names. For example, the dwarf Veitch screw pine, *Pandanus veitchii compacta*, is listed under the genus name *Pandanus;* its species name, *veitchii*, is followed by the varietal name, *compacta* (dwarf). Common names are cross-referenced to their Latin equivalents. For quick reference, a chart of the characteristics, requirements and special uses of the recommended species and varieties appears on pages 147-151.

House plants provide foliage of every color and pattern—from the red-and-green caladium (lower left) to the spikes of dracaena (upper right)—as shown in this painting of 23 of the plants in the encyclopedia.

A

ACALYPHA

A. godseffiana (acalypha), *A. wilkesiana* (copperleaf, beefsteak plant, acalypha)

Acalyphas are bushy plants that either can be maintained at a height of 2 to 3 feet by being pruned or can be allowed to grow to as much as twice that height. The species *A. godseffiana* has oval leaves, 2 to 3 inches long, that are distinguished by a broad white stripe along their edges. The copperleaf, or beefsteak plant, derives both of its common names from the red, copper and pink mottling on its 3- to 4-inch pointed leaves.

HOW TO GROW. Acalyphas do best where they get four or more hours a day of direct sunlight, or where they get artificial and natural light that average 800 foot-candles over 12 hours a day, but they will grow fairly well in bright indirect light, such as that reflected from light walls. Acalyphas prefer night temperatures of 60° to 65°, day temperatures of 75° to 85° and a high relative humidity, above 40 per cent. Keep the soil barely moist at all times. Fertilize established plants at three- to four-month intervals, but wait four to six months before fertilizing newly purchased or newly potted plants. When the plants become overcrowded, repot them in spring. For best results use a mixture of 1 part loam, 1 part peat moss or leaf mold and 1 part sharp sand; to each gallon pailful of this mixture add 1½ teaspoons of 20 per cent superphosphate, 1 tablespoon of ground limestone and 2 teaspoons of 5-10-5 fertilizer. Otherwise, use a packaged general-purpose potting soil. To rejuvenate old and straggly plants, cut them back in early spring to a height of 8 to 12 inches. New plants may be started from stem cuttings at any season, but they root most easily from new growth in summer.

ACORUS

A. gramineus, also called *A. japonicus* (Japanese sweet flag)

Although the basic species of the Japanese sweet flag is seldom grown as a house plant, two easy-to-grow varieties have been cherished for a long time. Both are grasslike plants that hold their leaves stiffly in fan-shaped tufts. The white-striped or variegated Japanese sweet flag, *A. gramineus variegatus,* reaches a height of 8 to 12 inches and bears leaves that are attractively marked with lengthwise stripes of white and green; it will grow quite well in plain water. The dwarf Japanese sweet flag, *A. gramineus pusillus,* is a perky miniature that becomes only 3 to 4 inches tall and has green leaves. Japanese sweet flags tolerate a wide range of temperatures and are particularly valuable in drafty locations where more delicate plants would be likely to fail.

HOW TO GROW. Japanese sweet flags do best in bright indirect or curtain-filtered sunlight; if only artificial light is available, provide at least 400 foot-candles. The plants prefer night temperatures of 40° to 55° and day temperatures of 65° or lower, but will tolerate a temperature range of 40° to 80°. Keep the soil wet at all times. Newly purchased or newly potted plants should not be fertilized for six months; once established, the plants should be fed at six-month intervals. Repot overcrowded plants at any season. For best results use a mixture of 1 part loam, 1 part peat moss or leaf mold and 1 part sharp sand; to each gallon pailful of this mixture add 1½ teaspoons of 20 per cent superphosphate, 1 tablespoon of ground limestone and 2 teaspoons of 5-10-5 fertilizer. Otherwise, use a packaged general-purpose potting soil. Propagate new plants at any season by dividing the rhizomes, the thickened roots from which the leaves sprout.

COPPERLEAF
Acalypha wilkesiana macafeana

ADIANTUM

A. capillus-veneris (southern maidenhair fern, Venus's maidenhair fern), *A. raddianum,* also called *A. cuneatum* (delta maidenhair fern), *A. tenerum* (delicate maidenhair fern)

Maidenhair ferns are unexcelled in daintiness, holding aloft clouds of wedge-shaped leaflets about ¼ to ½ inch across on glossy black wirelike stems. They are slightly more difficult to grow than many other house plants and prefer the humid environment of a terrarium. They also do well in the shade of a summer patio if the air is moist. The leaves of most species unfold pink, then turn pea green.

The southern maidenhair fern grows 6 to 20 inches tall and has exceedingly delicate fronds. The delta maidenhair fern reaches a height of 6 to 15 inches and is one of the easiest species to grow; a favorite among its many varieties is Goldelse, which has extremely feathery fronds. The basic species of the delicate maidenhair fern is seldom grown, but its variety Farleyense, which grows 15 to 24 inches tall, is popular because of the arching habit of its dense plumelike fronds. Another variety, the fan maidenhair fern, *A. tenerum wrightii,* is similar in size and is notable for its fan-shaped leaflets, which sometimes overlap.

HOW TO GROW. All types of maidenhair ferns do best in the shadowless light of a north window; if only artificial light is available, provide at least 150 foot-candles. Night temperatures of 50° to 55° are preferred by the southern maidenhair fern, 55° to 60° by the other species. Day temperatures of 60° to 70° and a high humidity of about 50 per cent are ideal for all. Keep the soil wet at all times from spring through fall, but during the winter, water the plants only enough to keep the fronds from wilting. Newly purchased or newly potted ferns should not be fed for six months, but once the plants are established, feed them every six months with any standard house-plant fertilizer diluted to one half the minimum strength recommended on the label. When the plants become overcrowded, repot them in late winter just before new growth begins. For best results use a mixture of 1 part loam, 1 part peat moss or leaf mold, 1 part finely ground fir bark and 1 part sharp sand; to each gallon pailful of this mixture add 2 tablespoons of bone meal. Otherwise, use a mixture composed of equal parts of a packaged general-purpose potting soil and peat moss or leaf mold. Propagate in late winter by cutting the fronds to soil level and dividing the wiry roots.

ADROMISCHUS

A. clavifolius (pretty pebbles), *A. cooperii* (Cooper's adromischus), *A. cristatus* (sea shells), *A. festivus* (plover eggs), *A. maculatus* (calico hearts, leopard's spots). (This genus was formerly called *Cotyledon.*)

These succulent plants have thick 1- to 2-inch leaves that are practically stemless and often seem to lie on the surface of the soil, forming neat clumps best displayed in shallow 3- to 4-inch flowerpots. The plants sometimes send up insignificant flowers, bell-shaped and white or pink, on thin wiry stalks in summer.

Pretty pebbles have club-shaped gray-green leaves with tiny reddish flecks. Cooper's adromischus has egg-shaped blue-green leaves with dark green blotches. Sea shells have wedge-shaped, wavy-edged light green leaves on tiny red stems that are covered with fine hairs. Plover eggs have egg-shaped blue-green leaves with reddish brown spots. Calico hearts have somewhat heart-shaped gray-green leaves spotted with reddish brown.

HOW TO GROW. *Adromischus* species do best where they get four or more hours a day of direct sunlight, or where artificial and natural light average 1,000 foot-candles, but they will grow fairly well in bright indirect light, such as

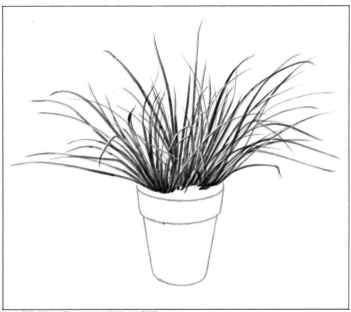
WHITE-STRIPED JAPANESE SWEET FLAG
Acorus gramineus variegatus

FAN MAIDENHAIR FERN
Adiantum tenerum wrightii

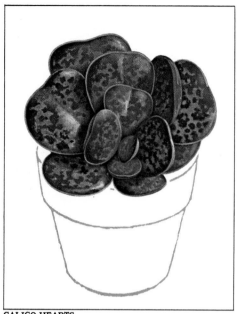

CALICO HEARTS
Adromischus maculatus

QUEEN VICTORIA CENTURY PLANT
Agave victoriae-reginae

that reflected from light walls. Night temperatures of 50° to 55° and day temperatures of 68° to 72° are ideal. Allow the soil to become moderately dry between thorough waterings from spring through fall; in winter, water only enough to keep the leaves from shriveling. Do not feed newly potted plants for a year; established plants should be fed once each spring with a standard house-plant fertilizer diluted to half the minimum strength recommended on the label. Repot overcrowded plants in spring. For best results use a mixture of 1 part loam, 1 part leaf mold, 1 part sharp sand and ½ part crushed charcoal, or else use a mixture of equal parts of a packaged general-purpose potting soil and sharp sand; to each gallon pailful of whichever of these mixtures you use, add 1 tablespoon of ground limestone and 1 tablespoon of bone meal. Propagate from leaf cuttings at any season.

AGAVE
A. filifera (thread-bearing century plant), *A. picta* (painted century plant), *A. victoriae-reginae* (Queen Victoria century plant)

These succulent plants are called century plants because they take so long to bloom—not really a century but 10 to 50 years. When the moment does arrive, the plant sends up from the center of its rosette of leaves a tall flower spike, which then dies, usually leaving behind a number of smaller rosettes at its base. Most species are too massive for use as house plants, but the ones listed here have been selected for their slow growth; if they are purchased when the rosettes are only 2 to 4 inches across, they may take 10 years or more to outgrow a wide window sill. All produce stiff sword-shaped leaves, often edged with sharp teeth and tipped with needlelike points.

The thread-bearing century plant has bright green leaves that after many years become 10 inches or more long. The leaves have white edges that dry and split to display curled threadlike fibers. The painted century plant has blue-green leaves that eventually grow 12 inches or more long; their white edges are occasionally tinged with pink and are studded with small blackish brown teeth. The Queen Victoria century plant is the most decorative small species for indoor use. Its stiff, tightly compressed leaves, 4 to 6 inches long, have white markings and edges.

HOW TO GROW. Century plants do best where they get four or more hours a day of direct sunlight, or where artificial and natural light average 1,000 foot-candles over 12 hours a day, but they will grow fairly well in bright indirect light, such as that reflected from light walls. Night temperatures of 50° to 55° and day temperatures of 68° to 72° are ideal. Let the soil become moderately to nearly dry between thorough waterings from spring through fall; in winter, water only enough to keep the leaves from shriveling. Do not fertilize newly potted plants for a year; established plants should be fed once each spring with any standard house-plant fertilizer diluted to half the minimum strength recommended on the label. Repot overcrowded plants at any season, using heavy gloves and thickly rolled newspaper to handle the prickly plants. For best results use a mixture of 1 part loam, 1 part leaf mold, 1 part sharp sand and ½ part crushed charcoal, or else use a mixture of equal parts of a packaged general-purpose potting soil and sharp sand; to each gallon pailful of whichever of these mixtures you use, add 1 tablespoon of ground limestone and 1 tablespoon of bone meal. The Queen Victoria century plant must be propagated from seeds; the other species can be grown from seeds or from the young shoots, or suckers, that spring up near the base of the plants. New plants can be started at any season.

AGLAONEMA

A. commutatum, also called *A. marantifolium* and *Schismatoglottis commutatum* (Chinese evergreen); *A. costatum* (spotted Chinese evergreen); *A. crispum,* also called *A. roebelinii* and *Schismatoglottis roebelinii; A. modestum,* also called *A. sinensis* (Chinese evergreen). (All also called aglaonema)

Aglaonemas are tough plants that grow in the dark corners of a room where most other, more delicate plants would perish. All the species listed here will also grow remarkably well in plain water. Several varieties of *A. commutatum* are particularly useful. Three of these varieties grow 1 to 2 feet tall and have gleaming, dark green lance-shaped leaves 6 to 9 inches long and 2 to 3 inches wide: they are the variegated Chinese evergreen, *A. commutatum maculatum,* which has silvery bars on its leaves; White Rajah—until recently considered a separate species and often sold as *A. pseudo-bracteatum*—whose leaves are heavily marked with white; and Pewter, whose leaves are marked with silver. Two smaller varieties, also with silver markings, grow up to 12 inches tall: they are Silver Queen, a strikingly beautiful plant, and *A. commutatum treubii,* whose leaves are a bluish green. The spotted Chinese evergreen, *A. costatum,* grows slowly, seldom exceeding 10 inches in height. It has heart-shaped leaves, 6 inches long and 3 inches wide, which form a dense clump 12 to 18 inches across. The shiny green leaves have white spots and white central ribs.

A. crispum is the most robust of the aglaonema species listed here. It grows up to 3 feet tall, with a spread equal to its height, and bears stems that are crowded with thick leathery leaves 10 to 12 inches long and 4 to 5 inches wide; the leaves look as if they are brushed with gray, except for their edges and ribs, which are a soft green. *A. modestum,* the first of the aglaonemas to be introduced to Western gardeners, grows to a height of 2 or 3 feet. It bears slender wedge-shaped leathery leaves, usually 6 to 8 inches long and about 3 inches wide, with tapering points that sometimes dip at the ends.

HOW TO GROW. Aglaonemas do best in the shadowless light of a north window; if only artificial light is available, provide at least 150 foot-candles. The spotted Chinese evergreen can get along with somewhat less light than the other species. Night temperatures of 65° to 70° and day temperatures of 75° to 85° are ideal. Keep the soil barely moist at all times. Wait four to six months before feeding newly purchased or newly potted plants; once established, plants should be fed at four-month intervals. Repot overcrowded plants at any season, using a mixture of 1 part loam, 1 part peat moss or leaf mold and 1 part sharp sand; to each gallon pailful of this mixture add 1½ teaspoons of 20 per cent superphosphate, 1 tablespoon of ground limestone and 2 teaspoons of 5-10-5 fertilizer. Otherwise, use a packaged general-purpose potting soil. Propagate at any season from stem cuttings, from sections of main stems or by the method known as air layering.

ALOE

A. aristata (lace aloe), *A. brevifolia* (short-leaved aloe), *A. nobilis* (gold-toothed aloe), *A. variegata* (tiger, partridge breast, pheasant wing or Kanniedood aloe), *A. vera* (true aloe)

Aloes were grown as pot plants at least as long ago as the days of the Roman Empire. The chief species in ancient times was the true aloe, cultivated then as now for the soothing ointment that can be made from the juice of its leaves. All of the aloes described here produce rosettes of succulent leaves that resemble those of the century plant

WHITE RAJAH CHINESE EVERGREEN
Aglaonema commutatum 'White Rajah'

TIGER ALOE
Aloe variegata

(*Agave, page 86*). The plants often bear clusters of small tubular red, orange or yellow flowers in winter.

The lace aloe forms a rosette, 4 to 6 inches across, containing as many as a hundred 4-inch slender dark green leaves that are studded on the back with white dots called tubercles. The short-leaved aloe grows 3 to 4 inches across and has 3- to 4-inch pale green leaves that are edged with small teeth. The 6- to 10-inch gold-toothed aloe has pale green leaves with prickly teeth along their edges. The tiger aloe is the most attractive species for use as a house plant. The leaves, which eventually form a mound nearly 12 inches tall and 6 inches across, are accented by bands of white and may eventually become tinted with bronze if they grow in bright light. The true aloe has pale green leaves 18 to 20 inches long. Old plants of this species become too large for most indoor locations and should be discarded, but new plants are easy to propagate.

HOW TO GROW. Aloes do best where they get four or more hours a day of direct sunlight, or where artificial and natural light average 1,000 foot-candles over 12 hours a day, but they will grow fairly well in bright indirect light, such as that reflected from light walls. Night temperatures of 50° to 55° and day temperatures of 68° to 72° are ideal. Allow the soil to become moderately dry between thorough waterings. Do not fertilize newly potted plants for the first year; established plants should be fed once each fall with standard house-plant fertilizer diluted to half the minimum strength recommended on the label. Repot overcrowded plants at any season, but be especially careful not to set aloes any deeper than they grew previously. For best results use a mixture of 1 part loam, 1 part leaf mold, 1 part sharp sand and ½ part crushed charcoal, or else use a mixture of equal parts of any packaged general-purpose potting soil and sharp sand; to each gallon pailful of whichever of these mixtures you use, add 1 tablespoon of ground limestone and 1 tablespoon of bone meal. Propagate at any season from the young shoots, or suckers, that spring up from the base of larger plants.

ALUMINUM PLANT See *Pilea*
ANTHERICUM See *Chlorophytum*

APOROCACTUS
A. flagelliformis, also called *Cereus flagelliformis* (rattail cactus)

The rattail cactus has trailing stems, only about ½ inch across but as much as 3 feet long. They bear short, densely set spines of yellow or reddish brown and, in late spring, pink flowers 2 to 3 inches long. The rattail cactus is usually grown either in a hanging container or grafted to the top of a tall-growing cactus so that its trailing stems create a fountainlike effect. Both methods display the plant well and also keep the stems clean by preventing them from touching the soil—an important consideration with cacti, since the plants cannot be washed or wiped.

HOW TO GROW. The rattail cactus does best where it gets four or more hours a day of direct sunlight, or where artificial and natural light average 1,000 foot-candles over 12 hours a day, but it grows fairly well in bright indirect light, such as that reflected from light walls. In winter, night temperatures of 40° to 45° and day temperatures under 65° are ideal, but from spring through fall, night temperatures of 65° to 70° and day temperatures of 75° to 85° are preferable. Allow the soil to become moderately dry between thorough waterings from spring through fall; in winter, water only enough to keep the plants from shriveling. Do not fertilize newly potted plants for the first year; established plants should be fed once each spring. For fast growth repot annually in early spring; otherwise, repot in spring only when the plants become overcrowded. For best results use a mixture of 1 part loam, 1 part leaf mold, 1 part sharp sand and ½ part crushed charcoal, or else use a mixture of equal parts of a packaged general-purpose potting soil and sharp sand; to each gallon pailful of whichever of these mixtures you use, add 1 tablespoon of ground limestone and 1 tablespoon of bone meal. Propagate at any season from seeds or stem cuttings or by grafting a piece of stem to the top of a less attractive tall-growing cactus.

ARALIA, BALFOUR See *Polyscias*
ARALIA, FALSE See *Dizygotheca*
ARALIA, JAPANESE See *Fatsia*
ARALIA, PENNOCK'S See *Polyscias*
ARALIA, VICTORIA See *Polyscias*
ARALIA BALFOURIANA See *Polyscias*
ARALIA ELEGANTISSIMA See *Dizygotheca*
ARALIA IVY See *Fatshedera*
ARALIA JAPONICA See *Fatsia*
ARALIA PAPYRIFERA See *Tetrapanax*
ARALIA SIEBOLDII See *Fatsia*

ARAUCARIA
A. heterophylla, also called *A. excelsa* (Norfolk Island pine)

The Norfolk Island pine is often used as a Christmas tree, but it also makes a handsome long-lived house plant the year round. It grows 3 to 6 inches a year and bears branches thickly covered with ½-inch needles. The plant grows wild on the 3-by-5-mile speck of land in the South Pacific for which it was named, becoming a 200-foot-tall tree with a trunk 9 to 10 feet across.

HOW TO GROW. Norfolk Island pines do best in bright indirect or curtain-filtered sunlight; if only artificial light is available, provide at least 400 foot-candles. In winter the plants can stand full sun. They prefer night temperatures of 50° to 55° and day temperatures of 68° to 72°, but can tolerate a range from 45° to 85°. Keep the soil barely moist. Feed established plants every three or four months, but wait four to six months before feeding newly purchased or potted plants. Repot when plants become overcrowded (usually at three- to four-year intervals). For best results use a mixture of equal parts of peat moss or leaf mold and perlite or vermiculite; to each gallon pailful of this mixture add 1½ teaspoons of 20 per cent superphosphate, 1 tablespoon of ground limestone and 2 teaspoons of 5-10-5 fertilizer. Otherwise, use a highly organic packaged potting mixture formulated for African violets. Home propagation of Norfolk Island pines is difficult. Most commercial growers start plants from seeds, but potted plants are not mature enough to bear seeds and they are seldom available at retail nurseries. Cuttings of branches will take root, but the new plants grow sideways like branches rather than upright like stems. If a cutting is taken only from the tip of a tree, the new plant will grow erect but, of course, the original plant's shape will have been ruined.

ARECA PALM See *Chrysalidocarpus*
ARROWHEAD VINE See *Syngonium*
ARROWROOT See *Maranta*

ASPARAGUS
A. densiflorus sprengerii, also called *A. sprengerii* (Sprenger asparagus fern); *A. myersii*, also called *A. densiflorus myersii* (foxtail asparagus fern); *A. myriocladus* (many-branched asparagus fern); *A. plumosus* (asparagus fern); *A. retrofractus* (twisted asparagus fern)

RATTAIL CACTUS
Aporocactus flagelliformis

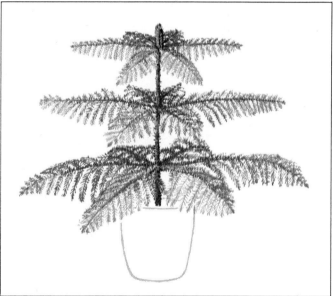

NORFOLK ISLAND PINE
Araucaria heterophylla

FOXTAIL ASPARAGUS FERN
Asparagus myersii

CAST-IRON PLANT
Aspidistra elatior

The asparagus species listed here make excellent easy-to-grow house plants. All have filmy "needles," which are actually flattened stems, technically called phylloclades, that serve the purpose of leaves.

The Sprenger asparagus fern has been a favorite for generations. It has deeply arching 18- to 24-inch stems that are covered with loose billows of bright green inch-long flat needles. The foxtail asparagus fern has stiffly upright or arching 1- to 2-foot stems so covered with needles they look like furry plumes—hence the species' common name. The many-branched asparagus fern usually grows 4 to 6 feet tall with spiny arching stems that branch out into many zigzag branchlets, each densely covered with ¾-inch dark green needles. The asparagus fern is a twining vine that sends out several 12- to 18-inch arching stems before one emerges that is strong enough to climb a 2- to 3-foot trellis. The spiny stems are thickly set with ⅛-inch dark green needles. Flat, roughly triangular branchlets extend horizontally from the main stems. If a bushy plant is desired, the ends of long stems can be pinched off. Florists often include cut stems of the asparagus fern in bunches of roses. The twisted asparagus fern is similar in appearance to the many-branched asparagus fern, except that its needles are 1 inch long and bright green.

HOW TO GROW. These ornamental asparagus species do best in bright indirect or curtain-filtered sunlight; if only artificial light is available, provide at least 400 foot-candles. Night temperatures of 50° to 55° and day temperatures of 68° to 72° are ideal. Keep the soil barely moist at all times. Feed established plants at three- to four-month intervals with a standard house-plant fertilizer, but wait four to six months before feeding newly purchased or newly potted plants. Repot overcrowded plants at any season, using a mixture of 1 part loam, 1 part peat moss or leaf mold and 1 part sharp sand; to each gallon pailful of this mixture add 1½ teaspoons of 20 per cent superphosphate, 1 tablespoon of ground limestone and 2 teaspoons of 5-10-5 fertilizer. Otherwise, use a packaged general-purpose potting soil. Propagate at any season by dividing the thick fleshy roots of old plants; several good-sized plants can be started from one old plant. When dividing old clumps, cut the stems to soil level and discard them to make room for the fresh ones that will rise from the roots.

ASPIDISTRA
A. elatior, also called *A. lurida* (cast-iron plant)

The cast-iron plant lives up to its name—it withstands not only heat, cold, wet soil and drought, but also dust, neglect and dimly lighted places. But with such maltreatment it only survives; with good care it grows about 3 feet tall and bears handsome arching leaves 15 to 30 inches long and 3 to 4 inches wide. The variegated cast-iron plant, *A. elatior variegata,* has leaves with white and green stripes that revert to solid green if the plant is given more than the prescribed amount of fertilizer or less than the prescribed amount of light.

HOW TO GROW. Both cast-iron plants and variegated cast-iron plants do best in the shadowless light of a north window; if only artificial light is available, provide at least 150 foot-candles. The plants prefer night temperatures of 50° to 55° and day temperatures of 68° to 72°, but will tolerate extremes from 45° to 85°. Keep the soil barely moist at all times. Fertilize established plants monthly from early spring through early fall; do not fertilize during the rest of the year and wait until the following spring before feeding newly potted plants. Repot overcrowded plants in early spring before new growth starts. For best results use a mixture of 1 part loam, 1 part peat moss or leaf mold and 1 part sharp sand; to each gallon pailful of this mixture add 1½ teaspoons of 20 per cent superphosphate, 1 tablespoon of ground limestone and 2 teaspoons of 5-10-5 fertilizer. Otherwise, use a packaged general-purpose potting soil. Propagate plants by dividing the roots in early spring. Several pieces of root, each with one or more leaves, can be planted together to make a large plant.

ASPIDIUM FALCATUM See *Cyrtomium*
ASPIDIUM TSUS-SIMENSE See *Polystichum*

ASPLENIUM
A. bulbiferum (mother fern, mother spleenwort), *A. nidus* (bird's-nest fern), *A. viviparum* (Mauritius mother fern). (All also called spleenwort)

The three spleenworts listed here have graceful arching fronds 10 to 15 inches long. Those of the mother fern are featherlike with shallowly scalloped leaflets, while the fronds of the Mauritius mother fern are divided into slender, almost threadlike, leaflets. Both species produce tiny bulbs on the upper surfaces of their leaves that develop into miniature replicas of the plants themselves. The bird's-nest fern has smooth undivided fronds that rise from a black hairlike center resembling a bird's nest. Of the three species, the bird's-nest fern is the easiest to grow because it tolerates drier air than the others.

HOW TO GROW. Spleenworts do best in the shadowless light of a north window; if only artificial light is available, provide at least 150 foot-candles. Night temperatures of 50° to 55° and day temperatures of 68° to 72° are recommended. Spleenworts are at their best in the humid atmosphere of a terrarium, but they will do reasonably well on a tray that is filled with pebbles and water to increase the humidity around the plants to 40 per cent or more. Keep the soil moist at all times except from midautumn through early spring, during which time it should be kept barely moist. Do not fertilize newly potted plants for six months. Once established, the plants should be fed at six-month intervals with any standard house-plant fertilizer diluted to one half the minimum strength recommended on the label. When the plants become overcrowded, repot them in late winter just before new growth starts. For best results use a mixture of 1 part loam, 1 part peat moss or leaf mold, 1 part finely ground fir bark and 1 part sharp sand; to each gallon pailful of this mixture add 2 tablespoons of bone meal. Otherwise, use a mixture composed of equal parts of a packaged general-purpose potting soil and peat moss or leaf mold. Before potting, put a ½- to 1-inch layer of crushed charcoal at the bottom of each pot. The bird's-nest fern can be propagated at any season from spores, the dustlike reproductive particles of ferns. Propagate mother ferns and Mauritius mother ferns at any season either from spores or by plucking off and potting the plantlets that develop on the fronds.

AUCUBA
A. japonica (Japanese aucuba)

The Japanese aucuba reaches a height of 3 feet or more and has 4- to 6-inch glistening green oval leaves. Among its varieties, *A. japonica variegata*, the gold-dust tree, has leaves speckled with yellow; *A. japonica picturata* has leaves with bright yellow centers and deep green edges, while Sulphur has green centers and yellow edges. The plants withstand cold and draft.

HOW TO GROW. The Japanese aucuba does best in bright indirect or curtain-filtered sunlight; if only artificial light is available, provide at least 400 foot-candles. It prefers night temperatures of 40° to 55°, day temperatures of 65° or

BIRD'S-NEST FERN
Asplenium nidus

GOLD-DUST TREE
Aucuba japonica variegata

ELEPHANT-FOOT TREE
Beaucarnea recurvata

lower and a high relative humidity of at least 40 per cent. The soil should be kept barely moist at all times. Fertilize established plants at three- to four-month intervals, but wait four to six months before feeding newly purchased or newly potted plants. When the plants become overcrowded, repot them in early spring before new growth starts. For best results use a mixture of 1 part loam, 1 part peat moss or leaf mold and 1 part sharp sand; to each gallon pailful of this mixture add 1½ teaspoons of 20 per cent superphosphate, 1 tablespoon of ground limestone and 2 teaspoons of 5-10-5 fertilizer. Otherwise, use a packaged general-purpose potting soil. Plants that become too tall should be cut to the desired height in winter or early spring just as new growth begins to develop. Propagate from root cuttings at any season.

AUSTRALIAN UMBRELLA TREE See *Brassaia*

B
BALFOUR ARALIA See *Polyscias*
BALL CACTUS See *Notocactus*
BALL FERN See *Davallia*

BEAUCARNEA
B. recurvata, also called *Nolina recurvata* and *N. tuberculata* (elephant-foot tree, beaucarnea, pony tail)

The elephant-foot tree is a carefree plant that can live indefinitely indoors, limited only by the height of your ceiling; it is capable of becoming 30 feet tall, and when it outgrows its space, the best thing to do is to put it in a tub for your patio—or give it to your local botanical garden. It grows with one or several trunks, each crowned with a plume of ¾-inch-wide leaves up to 4 feet long. The plant is distinguished by a bulbous swelling of the trunk at soil level; this strange characteristic, coupled with the grayish brown color and wrinkled texture of the bark, accounts for the common name elephant-foot tree. The swollen trunk serves as a water tank, enabling the tree to survive drought.

HOW TO GROW. Elephant-foot trees do best where they get four or more hours a day of direct sunlight, or where artificial and natural light average 800 foot-candles over 12 hours a day, but they will grow fairly well in bright indirect light, such as that reflected from light walls. They prefer night temperatures of 50° to 55° and day temperatures of 68° to 72°, but can withstand temperatures ranging from 40° to 90°. The soil should be allowed to become moderately dry between thorough waterings. Feed established plants once a year, in spring, with a standard house-plant fertilizer, but wait a full year before feeding newly purchased or newly potted plants. Plants will live for years in small containers. Repot overcrowded elephant-foot trees in very early spring before new growth starts, using a mixture of 1 part loam, 1 part peat moss or leaf mold and 1 part sharp sand; to each gallon pailful of this mixture add 1½ teaspoons of 20 per cent superphosphate, 1 tablespoon of ground limestone and 2 teaspoons of 5-10-5 fertilizer. Otherwise, pot in a packaged general-purpose potting soil. Propagate from seeds at any season.

BEAVERTAIL CACTUS See *Opuntia*
BEEFSTEAK PLANT See *Acalypha*

BEGONIA
Species and hybrids of three classes: rex begonias, rhizomatous begonias and basket begonias

Begonias have been so crossbred that neat classification is impossible. For convenience' sake, the begonias listed here are divided into three classes based on their dominant characteristic: rex begonias, noted for their brilliantly colored foliage; rhizomatous begonias, identified by thick succulent stems, or rhizomes, which creep along the top of the soil, sending out long-stemmed leaves at their ends; and basket begonias, whose lax stems trail gracefully over the edges of hanging containers to show the undersides of their leaves, which in some varieties are brightly colored. Yet none of these characteristics are unique to a class; rex begonias grow from rhizomes, many rhizomatous types have colorful leaves and trailing stems, and many basket begonias grow from rhizomes and also have colorful leaves. In the following descriptions, the predominant characteristic determines the plant's class.

Rex begonias are the most spectacular of the three types. Blended into or overlaid on the green leaves can be found a kaleidoscope of colors—red, pink, silver, gray, lavender and a maroon sometimes so deep it appears nearly black. Thousands of named varieties have been developed since the original rex begonia was found growing with a potted orchid imported into England in 1856. Three excellent ones are Merry Christmas, also called Rhurthal, 10 to 12 inches tall with smooth leaves shaped like lopsided hearts; Silver Sweet, an especially easy-to-grow 12- to 18-inch variety whose leaves are like those of Merry Christmas but are silver-colored with green veins; and Helen Teupel, about 12 inches tall with pointed, sharply lobed leaves that are purplish red brushed with pink and silver. The leaves are all 6 to 8 inches long and 3 to 4 inches wide.

Rhizomatous begonias come in many leaf shapes and colors. *B. erythrophylla,* a pond-lily, or beefsteak, begonia —so called because of the rounded lily-pad shape of its leaves and the blood red of their undersides—becomes 10 to 12 inches tall but spreads as much as 2 feet across; its 5-inch leaves have glossy green top surfaces. Bessie Buxton, named for a begonia enthusiast who stimulated an interest in the genus through her writings in the 1930s, is a 2-foot-tall upright version of *B. erythrophylla* with 4-inch leaves and only a 10- to 12-inch spread. Maphil, sometimes called Cleopatra, is extremely easy to grow; it forms a dense compact mound about 8 inches tall and has 3- to 4-inch star-shaped green leaves irregularly blotched with brown. Joe Hayden, 12 inches tall but with an 18- to 24-inch spread, is sometimes called the black begonia because its 4- to 6-inch star-shaped leaves have a deep bronze-black hue on their top surfaces; the undersides are dark red. The Iron Cross begonia, *B. masoniana,* 8 to 10 inches tall, has bumpy green leaves up to 7 inches long and 5 inches wide that are prominently marked with a dark pattern reminiscent of the German military medal. The Stitchleaf begonia, *B. mazae viridis* 'Stitchleaf,' 18 inches tall, has 1½-inch heart-shaped green leaves with purplish black marks around the edges that look as though they were stitched by a seamstress. Though this variety is relatively short-stemmed, it is effective in hanging containers because its leaves tumble down attractively over the edges.

Basket begonias include such fine types as D'Artagnon, whose 4- to 6-inch cup-shaped hairy leaves have rich green tops and plum-colored undersides; Abel Carriere, with green-veined silver leaves, heart-shaped and about 6 inches long and 4 inches wide, that turn pink in sunlight but need protection from hot sun and dry air; and Foliosa, the smallest-leaved begonia, whose ½-inch green leaves are canoe-shaped. All grow 10 to 12 inches high and 18 to 20 inches wide, except Foliosa, which spreads only about a foot, and all have stems 12 to 14 inches long.

HOW TO GROW. The begonias listed here do best in bright indirect or curtain-filtered sunlight all year round in areas south of the 38th parallel, which runs through or near Sac-

IRON CROSS BEGONIA
Begonia masoniana

MERRY CHRISTMAS BEGONIA
Begonia 'Merry Christmas'

ramento, Denver, St. Louis and Washington, D.C., but they will benefit greatly if they are given four or more hours a day of direct sunlight from midautumn through midwinter in areas north of the 38th parallel; if only artificial light is available, provide at least 400 foot-candles. Night temperatures of 60° to 65° and day temperatures of 70° to 75° are ideal. Begonias cannot tolerate wetness, so keep the soil barely moist, and err on the side of underwatering rather than overwatering: wilted plants recover when watered but overwatered plants die. Fertilize established plants at two-month intervals from midwinter until late fall with standard house-plant fertilizer diluted to half the minimum strength recommended on the label; do not feed them the rest of the year, and wait at least four to six months before feeding newly potted plants. Overcrowded begonias can be repotted at any season, but spring is preferred. For best results use a mixture of 1 part loam, 1 part peat moss or leaf mold, 1 part perlite or vermiculite and 1 part sharp sand; to each gallon pailful of this mixture add 1 tablespoon of ground limestone and 2 tablespoons of bone meal. Otherwise, use a packaged general-purpose potting soil. Because begonias have shallow roots and spread as they grow, they do best and are most attractive in squat pots one half to three fourths as tall as they are wide. All types discussed here can be propagated from stem cuttings at any season. Rex begonias can also be started at any time from leaf cuttings, and rhizomatous begonias, as well as rex begonias and basket begonias that grow from rhizomes, can be propagated by division of the rhizomes in spring or fall.

BEGONIA, WATERMELON See *Peperomia*
BEGONIA TREEBINE See *Cissus*
BIRD'S-NEST CACTUS See *Mammillaria*
BIRD'S-NEST FERN See *Asplenium*
BOAT-LILY See *Rhoeo*
BOSTON FERN See *Nephrolepis*
BOTANICAL WONDER See *Fatshedera*
BOWSTRING HEMP See *Sansevieria*
BOX See *Buxus*
BOXWOOD See *Buxus*
BRACKET PLANT See *Chlorophytum*
BRAKE FERN See *Pteris*

BRASSAIA
B. actinophylla, also called *Schefflera actinophylla* and *S. macrostachya* (schefflera, Australian umbrella tree, Queensland umbrella tree, octopus tree)

Scheffleras are superb long-lived house plants. Young seedlings bear leaves only 2 to 3 inches wide with three to five tiny leaflets; as the plants mature, the leaves change dramatically, eventually developing up to 16 leaflets, each 1½ inches wide and up to 12 inches long. The plants, usually 2 to 3 feet tall when sold, can reach 6 feet or more.

HOW TO GROW. Scheffleras do best where they get four or more hours a day of direct sunlight, or where artificial and natural light average 800 foot-candles over 12 hours a day, but they will grow fairly well in bright indirect light, such as that reflected from light walls. Night temperatures of 65° to 70° and day temperatures of 75° to 85° are ideal. Keep the soil moderately dry between thorough waterings. Newly purchased or potted plants should not be fed for six months; established plants should be fed at six-month intervals. Repot overcrowded plants at any season, using a mixture of 1 part loam, 1 part peat moss or leaf mold and 1 part sharp sand; to each gallon pailful of this mixture add 1½ teaspoons of 20 per cent superphosphate, 1 tablespoon of ground limestone and 2 teaspoons of 5-10-5 fertilizer. Otherwise, use a packaged general-purpose potting

SCHEFFLERA
Brassaia actinophylla

soil. To keep plants small, snip off the tips of the stems just above a leaf. Propagate from seeds at any season.

BRYOPHYLLUM See *Kalanchoe*
BUNNY EARS See *Opuntia*
BURRO'S TAIL See *Sedum*
BUTTERFLY PALM See *Chrysalidocarpus*

BUXUS
B. microphylla (little-leaf boxwood or box), *B. sempervirens* (common boxwood or box)

Boxwoods have long enjoyed a well-deserved reputation as excellent outdoor evergreens, but in recent years they have moved indoors. They are famous for the shiny deep green of their 1-inch oval leaves and for their dense branches, which respond well to pruning or shearing. Boxwoods grow slowly—perhaps 2 to 4 inches a year—and although they may grow as much as 4 feet tall if left unpruned, they are easily trained to become miniature trees, or standards, perhaps only a foot tall. Their roots tolerate cramped conditions, making young boxwoods suitable for terrariums or dish gardens. They also withstand cool temperatures and are therefore excellent for drafty places.

HOW TO GROW. Boxwoods do best where they get four or more hours a day of direct sunlight, or where artificial and natural light average 800 foot-candles over 12 hours a day, but they will grow fairly well in bright indirect light, such as that reflected from light walls. Night temperatures of 40° to 55° and day temperatures of 65° or lower are ideal. Keep the soil barely moist at all times. Newly potted plants should not be fed the first year; established plants should be fed annually in early spring before new growth starts, using a mixture of 1 part loam, 1 part peat moss or leaf mold and 1 part sharp sand; to each gallon pailful of this mixture add 1½ teaspoons of 20 per cent superphosphate, 1 tablespoon of ground limestone and 2 teaspoons of 5-10-5 fertilizer. Otherwise, use a packaged general-purpose potting soil. Propagate from stem cuttings in late summer or early fall.

C
CACTUS, BALL See *Notocactus*
CACTUS, BEAVERTAIL See *Opuntia*
CACTUS, BIRD'S-NEST See *Mammillaria*
CACTUS, CHIN See *Gymnocalycium*
CACTUS, COB See *Lobivia*
CACTUS, GOLDEN EASTER LILY See *Lobivia*
CACTUS, GOLDEN LACE See *Mammillaria*
CACTUS, GOLDEN STAR See *Mammillaria*
CACTUS, MAMMILLARIA See *Mammillaria*
CACTUS, OLD LADY See *Mammillaria*
CACTUS, OLD-MAN See *Cephalocereus*
CACTUS, OPUNTIA See *Opuntia*
CACTUS, PAPERSPINE See *Opuntia*
CACTUS, PINK EASTER LILY See *Echinopsis*
CACTUS, PLAID See *Gymnocalycium*
CACTUS, POWDER PUFF See *Mammillaria*
CACTUS, RATTAIL See *Aporocactus*
CACTUS, REDBIRD See *Pedilanthus*

CALADIUM
C. hortulanum (fancy-leaved caladium)

Caladiums offer unusually colorful foliage, combining red, pink, silver, white and green. The leaves, up to 24 inches long, are shaped like gigantic spearheads. The plants, 12 to 15 inches tall, grow from bulblike masses of storage tissue called tubers and go through a four- to five-month annual rest period during which the leaves wither away.

EDGING BOXWOOD
Buxus sempervirens suffruticosa

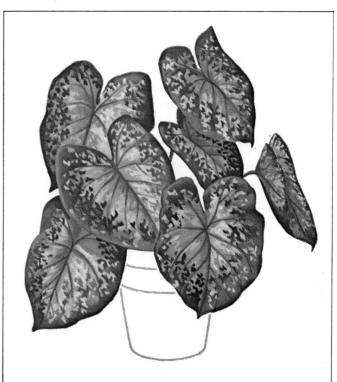

ACE OF HEARTS FANCY-LEAVED CALADIUM
Caladium hortulanum 'Ace of Hearts'

PEACOCK PLANT
Calathea makoyana

STRIPED INCH PLANT
Callisia elegans

HOW TO GROW. Caladiums do best in bright indirect or curtain-filtered sunlight; if only artificial light is available, provide at least 400 foot-candles. Night temperatures of 65° to 70° and day temperatures of 75° to 85° are ideal. During the growing period, keep the soil moist and feed every two or three weeks. For year-round display despite the semiannual dormancy, start a second plant approximately six months after the first. To start tubers into growth, press them 1 inch deep, bud side down, into damp peat moss or vermiculite. When leaves appear, pot the plants in a mixture of 2 parts loam, 2 parts peat moss, 1 part well-rotted or dried cow manure and 1 part sharp sand. Otherwise, use a mixture composed of equal parts of a packaged general-purpose potting soil and peat moss or leaf mold. When the foliage begins to wither (seven or eight months after growth began), gradually withhold water until the foliage shrivels completely. Allow the soil to become dry, then knock the plant out of its pot and shake the soil off the roots; pull away any dead tops. Dust the tubers with a combination fungicide-insecticide; store them in dry peat moss, perlite or vermiculite at 55° to 60° for four or five months, then start them into growth again. Propagate by dividing the tubers just before replanting.

CALATHEA
C. makoyana (peacock plant, calathea)

The peacock plant has almost as many bright colors as its name suggests: red stalks and shaded green leaves with purple-and-red undersides. It grows 1 to 2 feet tall and needs high humidity.

HOW TO GROW. Peacock plants do best in bright indirect or curtain-filtered sunlight; if only artificial light is available, provide at least 400 foot-candles. Night temperatures of 65° to 70° and day temperatures of 75° to 85° are ideal. The plants are at their best in a terrarium, but do quite well on a tray filled with pebbles and water to raise the humidity to about 50 per cent. Keep the soil moist but not soggy. Feed established plants every two weeks with standard house-plant fertilizer diluted to half the minimum strength recommended on the label; wait two or three months before feeding newly purchased or potted plants. Divide the strong roots and repot early each spring before new growth starts. For best results use a mixture of 1 part peat moss or leaf mold, 1 part perlite or vermiculite, 1 part sharp sand and ½ part well-rotted or dried cow manure. Otherwise, use a packaged highly organic potting mixture formulated for African violets.

CALICO HEARTS See *Adromischus*

CALLISIA
C. elegans, also called *Setcreasea striata* (striped inch plant)

Gardeners familiar with the wandering Jew *(Tradescantia, page 145, and Zebrina, page 146)* will recognize the striped inch plant as a relative. Its 1- to 1½-inch green-and-white leaves have purple undersides. The plant is especially suited for hanging containers where the tops and bottoms of the leaves can be seen simultaneously.

HOW TO GROW. The striped inch plant does best in bright indirect or curtain-filtered sunlight; if only artificial light is available, provide at least 400 foot-candles. Night temperatures of 50° to 55° and day temperatures of 68° to 72° are ideal. Keep the soil barely moist at all times. Feed established plants at three- to four-month intervals, but wait four to six months before feeding newly purchased or potted plants. Repot overcrowded plants at any season, using a mixture of 1 part loam, 1 part peat moss or leaf mold and 1 part sharp sand; to each gallon pailful of this mixture add 1½ teaspoons of 20 per cent superphosphate, 1 tablespoon of ground limestone and 2 teaspoons of 5-10-5 fertilizer. Otherwise, use a packaged general-purpose potting soil. Propagate from stem cuttings at any season.

CANDLE PLANT See *Plectranthus*
CANE PALM See *Chrysalidocarpus*

CARYOTA
C. mitis, also called *C. furfuracea* (tufted, clustered or Burmese fishtail palm)

The tufted fishtail palm, so called because of the shape of its leaflets, sends up a number of stems, and the taller they become the longer are their fronds; a fishtail palm 5 feet tall, for instance, usually has deeply arching fronds 3 to 4 feet long. The plant grows 6 to 8 inches a year, but eventually may outgrow its space, for it cannot be pruned.

HOW TO GROW. Fishtail palms do best in bright indirect or curtain-filtered sunlight; if only artificial light is available, provide at least 400 foot-candles. Night temperatures of 65° to 70° and day temperatures of 75° to 85° are ideal. Keep the soil wet at all times, but do not let the pots stand in water. Feed fishtail palms monthly from spring until fall; do not fertilize during the rest of the year, and wait until the following spring before feeding newly potted plants. These palms do best in pots that seem too small for them. When they become extremely crowded or the soil ball is completely filled with roots, repot in early spring. For best results use a mixture of 1 part loam, 1 part peat moss or leaf mold, 1 part sharp sand and ½ part well-rotted or dried cow manure; to each gallon pailful of this mixture add 2 tablespoons of bone meal. Otherwise, use a packaged general-purpose potting soil. Firm the fresh soil around the soil ball especially well. Propagate at any season from seeds or from the young shoots, or suckers, that spring up from the base of the plant.

CAST-IRON PLANT See *Aspidistra*
CENTURY PLANT See *Agave*

CEPHALOCEREUS
C. chrysacanthus, also called *Cereus chrysacanthus* (golden old-man cactus); *C. senilis,* also called *Cereus senilis* (old-man cactus)

The old-man cacti have single upright columnar stems, sometimes branched and usually not over 12 inches tall, with numerous vertical ridges, or ribs, running the length of the stems. The stems are covered with long hairlike bristles and needle-sharp spines. All species are exceptionally easy to grow. The golden old-man cactus has glossy deep green stems with 10 to 12 ribs. Short golden hairs surround its ½- to 1-inch golden spines. The old-man cactus, a favorite of many gardeners, may have 12 to 30 closely set ribs covered with 2- to 4-inch white hairs that hide slender 1- to 2-inch yellow spines.

HOW TO GROW. Old-man cacti do best where they get four or more hours a day of direct sunlight, or where artificial and natural light average 1,000 foot-candles over 12 hours a day, but they will grow fairly well in bright indirect light, such as that reflected from light walls. In winter, night temperatures of 40° to 45° and day temperatures under 65° are ideal; from spring through fall, night temperatures of 65° to 70° and day temperatures of 75° to 85° are preferable. Let the soil become moderately dry between thorough waterings from spring through fall; in winter, water only enough to keep the plants from shriveling. Do not feed newly potted plants the first year;

TUFTED FISHTAIL PALM
Caryota mitis

OLD-MAN CACTUS
Cephalocereus senilis

ROSARY VINE
Ceropegia woodii

established plants should be fertilized once each spring. For fast growth repot annually in early spring; otherwise, repot in spring only when the plants become overcrowded. For best results use a mixture of 1 part loam, 1 part leaf mold, 1 part sharp sand and ½ part crushed charcoal, or else use a mixture of equal parts of a packaged general-purpose potting soil and sharp sand; to each gallon pailful of whichever of these mixtures you use, add 1 tablespoon of ground limestone and 1 tablespoon of bone meal. Propagate at any season from seeds or stem cuttings.

CEREUS CHRYSACANTHUS See *Cephalocereus*
CEREUS FLAGELLIFORMIS See *Aporocactus*
CEREUS MULTIPLEX See *Echinopsis*
CEREUS SENILIS See *Cephalocereus*
CERIMAN See *Monstera*

CEROPEGIA
C. woodii (rosary vine, hearts entangled)

The rosary vine has 3-foot trailing purplish stems that bear ¼-inch heart-shaped succulent leaves with silver-mottled tops and purplish undersides. The plant grows from bulblike storage tissue called a tuber. Tiny tubers and occasional tiny purplish flowers form at the leaf joints. It is attractive in hanging containers or on a small trellis.

HOW TO GROW. The rosary vine does best in bright indirect or curtain-filtered sunlight; if only artificial light is available, provide at least 400 foot-candles. Night temperatures of 50° to 55° and day temperatures of 68° to 72° are ideal. Let the soil become moderately dry between thorough waterings from spring through fall; in winter, water only enough to keep the leaves from shriveling. Feed twice a month from spring until midsummer with standard houseplant fertilizer diluted to one half the minimum strength recommended on the label; do not feed the rest of the year. Do not feed newly potted plants until the following spring. Repot overcrowded plants at any season. For best results use a mixture of 1 part loam, 1 part leaf mold, 1 part sharp sand and ½ part crushed charcoal, or else use a mixture of equal parts of a packaged general-purpose potting soil and sharp sand; to each gallon pailful of whichever of these mixtures you use, add 1 tablespoon of ground limestone and 1 tablespoon of bone meal. Propagate at any season from stem cuttings or by planting the tiny tubers.

CHAMAEDOREA
C. elegans, also called *C. pulchella* and *Neanthe bella* (parlor palm, Neanthe palm)

The parlor palm is a dwarf species that, when young, is commonly used in dish gardens and terrariums because of its ability to live in cramped conditions at that stage. Grown by itself in a pot, it becomes 12 to 18 inches tall and has 9- to 12-inch-long arching featherlike fronds.

HOW TO GROW. Parlor palms do best in the shadowless light of a north window; if only artificial light is available, provide at least 150 foot-candles. Night temperatures of 65° to 70° and day temperatures of 75° to 85° are ideal. Keep the soil moist but not wet. Fertilize parlor palms monthly from early spring until fall; do not fertilize the rest of the year. Wait until the following spring before fertilizing newly potted plants. Repot in early spring, but only when the plants are thoroughly root-bound. For best results use a mixture of 1 part loam, 1 part peat moss or leaf mold, 1 part sharp sand and ½ part well-rotted or dried cow manure; to each gallon pailful of this mixture add 2 tablespoons of bone meal. Or use a packaged general-purpose potting soil. Firm the fresh soil around the soil ball especially well. Propagate from seeds at any season.

PARLOR PALM
Chamaedorea elegans

CHAMAEROPS

C. humilis (European fan palm)

The European fan palm, a dependable palm for indoor use, rarely exceeds 6 feet in height and has stiff fan-shaped deeply cut leaves about 1½ feet long and equally wide. The leaves, pale gray when they unfold, become gray green as they mature. The leaf stalks rise from rough trunks notable for their black hairlike covering, eventually forming a clump of several stems of varying ages so that foliage often appears at different levels at the same time.

HOW TO GROW. The European fan palm does best where it gets four or more hours a day of direct sunlight, or where artificial and natural light average 800 foot-candles over 12 hours a day, but it will grow fairly well in bright indirect light, such as that reflected from light walls. Night temperatures of 50° to 55° and day temperatures of 68° to 72° are ideal. Keep the soil wet at all times, but do not let the pots stand in water. Feed the plants monthly from early spring until fall; do not feed them the rest of the year, and wait until the following spring before feeding newly potted plants. Repot overcrowded plants in early spring, using a mixture of 1 part loam, 1 part peat moss or leaf mold, 1 part sharp sand and ½ part well-rotted or dried cow manure; to each gallon pailful of this mixture add 2 tablespoons of bone meal. Otherwise, use a packaged general-purpose potting soil. Propagate at any season from seeds or from the young shoots, or suckers, that spring up from the base of the plant.

CHIN CACTUS See *Gymnocalycium*
CHINESE EVERGREEN See *Aglaonema*
CHINESE FAN PALM See *Livistona*
CHINESE RUBBER PLANT See *Crassula*

CHLOROPHYTUM

C. comosum, also called *Anthericum comosum* and *A. sternbergianum* (spider, ribbon or bracket plant)

Spider plants are grasslike members of the lily family whose arching green leaves spread out like the legs of a daddy longlegs; varying from 4 to 16 inches in length and from ½ to 1 inch in width, they are prominently striped with yellow or white. Spider plants grow from fleshy roots that send out, along with the leaves, wiry stems up to 2 feet long lined with small protuberances that produce either tiny white flowers or small versions of the plants themselves. If these new plantlets touch the soil, they will quickly send out roots, but if the plantlets cascade over the edge of a hanging container, they will cling to the stems for many years, increasing in size and adding to the plant's fountain of foliage. Manda's spider plant, *C. comosum mandaianum,* has dark green leaves, 4 to 6 inches long and ½ inch wide, each marked with a bright yellow central stripe. The variegated spider plant, *C. comosum variegatum,* has white-edged pale green leaves 10 to 16 inches long and up to 1 inch wide. The common spider plant, *C. comosum vittatum,* has pale green leaves 4 to 8 inches long with white central stripes.

HOW TO GROW. Spider plants do best in bright indirect or curtain-filtered sunlight; if only artificial light is available, provide at least 400 foot-candles. Night temperatures of 50° to 55° and day temperatures of 68° to 72° are ideal. Keep the soil moist at all times. Feed established plants at three- to four-month intervals, but wait four to six months before feeding newly purchased or potted plants. Spider plants generally do not need repotting for several years, but when they do become overcrowded, repot at any season. For best results use a mixture of 1 part loam, 1 part peat moss or leaf mold and 1 part sharp sand;

EUROPEAN FAN PALM
Chamaerops humilis

COMMON SPIDER PLANT
Chlorophytum comosum vittatum

BUTTERFLY PALM
Chrysalidocarpus lutescens

MEXICAN TREE FERN
Cibotium schiedei

to each gallon pailful of this mixture add 1½ teaspoons of 20 per cent superphosphate, 1 tablespoon of ground limestone and 2 teaspoons of 5-10-5 fertilizer. Otherwise, use a packaged general-purpose potting soil. Propagate at any season from the plantlets along the stems or by dividing the fleshy roots.

CHRYSALIDOCARPUS

C. lutescens, also called *Areca lutescens, Hyophorbe commersoniana* and *H. indica* (butterfly, golden butterfly, golden feather, cane, areca or Madagascar palm)

The many common names for this long-lasting plant point to its popularity. It grows in clumps and bears featherlike arching fronds composed of many slender leaflets. The fronds are relatively long, reaching 3 feet or more on a 5-foot plant. Stems of old plants are ringed with bamboo-like scars where leaves once appeared. The plants grow 6 to 10 inches a year, but may eventually outgrow their space, for they cannot be pruned; an overgrown plant should be discarded or, in frost-free climates, moved outdoors.

HOW TO GROW. The butterfly palm does best in bright indirect or curtain-filtered sunlight; if only artificial light is available, provide at least 400 foot-candles. Night temperatures of 65° to 70° and day temperatures of 75° to 85° are ideal. Keep the soil wet at all times, but do not let the pots stand in water. Feed butterfly palms monthly from spring until fall; do not feed them the rest of the year. Do not feed newly potted plants until the next spring. Repot overcrowded plants in spring, using a mixture of 1 part loam, 1 part peat moss or leaf mold, 1 part sharp sand and ½ part well-rotted or dried cow manure; to each gallon pailful of this mixture add 2 tablespoons of bone meal. Or use a packaged general-purpose potting soil. Firm the fresh soil around the soil ball especially well. Propagate from seeds at any season.

CIBOTIUM

C. chamissoi, C. menziesii (both called Hawaiian tree fern), *C. schiedei* (Mexican tree fern)

Tree ferns spread as much as 6 feet, but in spacious homes they are superb, imparting a tropical aura hard to achieve any other way. Hawaiian tree ferns are often sold as 4- to 8-foot trunks without leaves or roots. They send out shoots *(center in drawing)* so tightly curled they are called crosiers, after the bishop's staff they resemble. The fronds eventually become 4 to 6 feet long. These plants are among the few that live for years if set in water with pebbles or rocks to hold them erect. The Mexican tree fern is usually sold without any discernible trunk, its light green airy 2- to 3-foot-long fronds rising directly from the soil and spreading up to 5 feet across.

HOW TO GROW. Tree ferns do best in bright indirect or curtain-filtered sunlight; if only artificial light is available, provide at least 400 foot-candles. Night temperatures of 50° to 55° and day temperatures of 68° to 72° are ideal. Keep the soil barely moist at all times. Do not fertilize newly purchased or newly potted plants for six months; once established, plants should be fed at six-month intervals with any standard house-plant fertilizer diluted to one half the minimum strength recommended on the label. Repot root-bound plants in early spring. For best results use a mixture of 1 part loam, 1 part peat moss or leaf mold, 1 part finely ground fir bark and 1 part sharp sand; to each gallon pailful of this mixture add 2 tablespoons of bone meal. Otherwise, use a mixture composed of equal parts of a packaged general-purpose potting soil and peat moss or leaf mold. Propagate at any season from spores, the dust-like reproductive particles of ferns.

CISSUS

C. antarctica, also called *C. glandulosa* and *Vitis antarctica* (kangaroo ivy); *C. discolor,* also called *C. velutina* (begonia treebine); *C. rhombifolia,* also called *Vitis rhombifolia* (grape ivy)

Plants now called *Cissus* used to be classified in the genus *Vitis,* for grapes, because of the grapelike tendrils by which the plants cling to any support. And the begonia treebine does indeed grow best on a light trellis. But the other species do not have to climb to be attractive; in fact, the kangaroo ivy and the grape ivy are usually grown in hanging containers so that their weak stems will cascade over the edges. The kangaroo ivy is especially tolerant of dry indoor air. Its 4- to 6-inch-long oval sawtooth-edged leaves are a shiny leathery dark green. The more compact dwarf kangaroo ivy, *C. antarctica minima,* has 3-inch-long leaves. The begonia treebine, one of the most colorful foliage plants, has slender heart-shaped 3- to 4-inch leaves that resemble those of rex begonias *(page 92).* They have top surfaces marked with purple, violet and silver, and undersides of reddish purple. Even the stems are deep red. The grape ivy has shiny three-lobed leaves, 4 inches long and 3 to 4 inches wide, that unfold bronzy, then turn deep green. New buds and the undersides of mature leaves are covered with soft brown fuzz.

HOW TO GROW. *Cissus* species prefer bright indirect or curtain-filtered sunlight; if only artificial light is available, provide at least 400 foot-candles. Kangaroo and grape ivies do best with night temperatures of 50° to 55° and day temperatures of 68° to 72°. The begonia treebine prefers 65° to 70° at night, 75° to 85° during the day, and a high humidity, about 50 per cent. Let the soil for all species become moderately dry between thorough waterings. Newly purchased or potted plants should not be fed for four to six months; feed established plants every four months. Repot overcrowded plants at any season, using a mixture of 1 part loam, 1 part peat moss or leaf mold and 1 part sharp sand; to each gallon pailful of this mixture add 1½ teaspoons of 20 per cent superphosphate, 1 tablespoon of ground limestone and 2 teaspoons of 5-10-5 fertilizer. Otherwise, use a packaged general-purpose potting soil. Pinch off stem tips to encourage compact, bushy growth. Propagate from stem cuttings at any season.

CISSUS PORPHYROPHYLLUS See *Piper*
COB CACTUS See *Lobivia*

CODIAEUM

C. variegatum pictum (croton)

Crotons come in more than 100 varieties. Leaf colors include yellow, green, copper, red, pink, orange, brown and ivory, and may spread over the whole leaf or appear as veining, spots, blotches or other patterns. Leaf shapes also vary: they may be slender and up to 18 inches long, flat and up to 6 inches wide, lobed, ribbed, crinkled or twisted into corkscrew shapes. Crotons grow fast: plants less than 12 inches tall may become bushy 3- to 5-foot shrubs within two or three years if not pruned.

HOW TO GROW. Crotons do best where they get four or more hours a day of direct sunlight, or where artificial and natural light average 800 foot-candles over 12 hours a day, but they grow fairly well in bright indirect light, such as that reflected from light walls. Night temperatures of 65° to 70° and day temperatures of 75° to 85° are ideal; leaves drop off in drafts. Keep the soil barely moist at all times. Feed crotons every two months from early spring through midsummer; do not fertilize them the rest of the year. Do not fertilize newly potted plants until the following spring.

BEGONIA TREEBINE
Cissus discolor

CROTON
Codiaeum variegatum pictum

101

Repot overcrowded plants in early spring, using a mixture of 1 part loam, 1 part peat moss or leaf mold and 1 part sharp sand; to each gallon pailful of this mixture add 1½ teaspoons of 20 per cent superphosphate, 1 tablespoon of ground limestone and 2 teaspoons of 5-10-5 fertilizer. Otherwise, use a packaged general-purpose potting soil. To encourage dense growth, prune overgrown plants in early spring. Propagate in spring or summer from stem cuttings or by the method known as air layering.

COLEUS

C. blumei (common coleus) and *C. rehneltianus* (Rehnelt coleus)

Coleuses are prized both indoors and outdoors for their colorful foliage. The common coleus and its variety *C. blumei verschaffeltii* have been so cultivated that now their leaves usually combine many shades of green, yellow, pink, red and maroon. The leaves grow 1 to 4 inches long, and the plants themselves grow about 2½ feet high in a bushy fashion. The Rehnelt coleus is a trailing plant with 1- to 1½-inch leaves. Three Rehnelt varieties are especially fine: Lord Falmouth, pink and red; Red Trailing Queen, purple, red and green; and Trailing Queen, red, yellow and purple. All grow in plain water.

HOW TO GROW. Coleuses do best where they get four or more hours of direct sunlight a day, or where artificial and natural light average 800 foot-candles over 12 hours a day, but they will grow fairly well in bright indirect light, such as that reflected from light walls. Night temperatures of 65° to 70° and day temperatures of 75° to 85° are ideal. Keep the soil barely moist at all times. Feed established plants every three months with standard house-plant fertilizer diluted to half the minimum strength recommended on the label, but wait four to six months before feeding newly purchased or potted plants. Repot overcrowded plants at any season, using 1 part loam, 1 part peat moss or leaf mold and 1 part sharp sand; to each gallon pailful of this mixture add 1½ teaspoons of 20 per cent superphosphate, 1 tablespoon of ground limestone and 2 teaspoons of 5-10-5 fertilizer. Otherwise, use a packaged general-purpose potting soil. Coleuses grow rapidly; to encourage dense but not tall growth, pinch off stem tips at any time. Propagate from stem cuttings at any season. Common coleuses can also be grown from seeds.

COPPERLEAF See *Acalypha*

CORDYLINE

C. terminalis (Hawaiian ti)

In their native Polynesia, Hawaiian ti plants provide long tough leaves for roof thatching and hula skirts. Several varieties are widely grown as house plants but require very humid growing conditions. Most have leaves 12 to 18 inches long and grow 1 to 3 feet tall, though some plants may reach 6 feet or more. Typical are *C. terminalis bicolor,* pink and green, and *C. terminalis tricolor,* pink, red and creamy white. Both grow well in plain water.

HOW TO GROW. Hawaiian ti plants are most colorful where they get four or more hours a day of direct sunlight, or where they get artificial and natural light averaging 800 foot-candles over 12 hours a day, but they grow fairly well and have attractive though less colorful foliage in curtain-filtered or bright indirect light, such as that reflected from light walls. Night temperatures of 65° to 70° and day temperatures of 75° to 85° are ideal. High humidity—about 60 per cent—is essential; keep the plants on a tray filled with pebbles and water, but do not let the water touch the pots. Keep the soil wet at all times. Feed established plants

COMMON COLEUS
Coleus blumei

HAWAIIAN TI
Cordyline terminalis bicolor

every three or four months, but wait four to six months before feeding newly purchased or potted plants. Repot overcrowded plants at any season, using a mixture of 1 part loam, 1 part peat moss or leaf mold and 1 part sharp sand; to each gallon pailful of this mixture add 1½ teaspoons of 20 per cent superphosphate, 1 tablespoon of ground limestone and 2 teaspoons of 5-10-5 fertilizer. Otherwise, use a packaged general-purpose potting soil. Prune overgrown plants to desired size at any season. Propagate at any season from sections of the main stem.

COSTUS
C. malortieanus, also called *C. elegans* and *C. zebrinus* (stepladder plant); *C. sanguineus* (spiral flag)

On these two species of *Costus* the leaves spiral around the stems instead of growing opposite one another or alternating. Both grow 1½ to 3 feet tall and occasionally bear spikes of small red or yellow flowers. The stepladder plant has hairy bright green oval leaves up to 12 inches long with dark green lengthwise bands; the undersides are pale green. The spiral flag has 3- to 4-inch pointed oval bluish green leaves accented with silvery central ribs; the undersides are reddish, as are the leaf stems.

HOW TO GROW. *Costus* plants do best in bright indirect or curtain-filtered sunlight; if only artificial light is available, provide at least 400 foot-candles. Night temperatures of 65° to 70° and day temperatures of 75° to 85° are ideal. Keep the soil moist at all times. Feed established plants at three- or four-month intervals, but wait four to six months before feeding newly purchased or potted plants. Repot overcrowded plants in early spring, using a mixture of 1 part loam, 1 part peat moss or leaf mold and 1 part sharp sand; to each gallon pailful of this mixture add 1½ teaspoons of 20 per cent superphosphate, 1 tablespoon of ground limestone and 2 teaspoons of 5-10-5 fertilizer. Otherwise, use a packaged general-purpose potting soil. Propagate by dividing the roots in spring or by cutting sections of the main stem at any season.

COTYLEDON See *Adromischus*
COTYLEDON ELEGANS See *Echeveria*

CRASSULA
C. arborescens, also called *C. cotyledon* (silver dollar plant); *C. argentea,* also called *C. portulacea* (jade plant, Chinese rubber plant)

These two easy-to-grow succulent species grow 18 to 30 inches tall and have 1- to 2-inch smooth rounded or oval leaves often edged with red. The silver dollar plant has gray-green leaves with tiny red dots. Varieties of the jade plant have leaves marked with combinations of white, yellow, orange, pink, red and purple. Jade and silver dollar plants live indefinitely indoors; many are used in dish gardens and often take the form of miniature trees. They sometimes bear tiny pinkish white flowers.

HOW TO GROW. Jade and silver dollar plants do best where they get four or more hours a day of direct sunlight, or where they get artificial and natural light averaging 1,000 foot-candles over 12 hours a day, but they will also grow well in curtain-filtered sunlight and in bright indirect light, such as that reflected from light walls. The plants prefer night temperatures of 50° to 55° and day temperatures of 68° to 72° but tolerate a range from 40° to 100°. Let the soil become nearly dry between thorough waterings. Feed established plants every three or four months, but wait four to six months before feeding newly purchased or potted plants. When necessary, repot at any season, but the plants generally live for years while root-bound. For

SPIRAL FLAG
Costus sanguineus

JADE PLANT
Crassula argentea

103

best results when repotting, use a mixture of 1 part loam, 1 part peat moss or leaf mold and 1 part sharp sand; to each gallon pailful of this mixture add 1½ teaspoons of 20 per cent superphosphate, 1 tablespoon of ground limestone and 2 teaspoons of 5-10-5 fertilizer. Otherwise, use a packaged general-purpose potting soil. Propagate at any season from stem or leaf cuttings.

CROTON See *Codiaeum*
CROWN OF THORNS See *Euphorbia*
CURLY PALM See *Howeia*
CUT-LEAVED PHILODENDRON See *Monstera*
CYANOTIS See *Zebrina*

CYATHEA

C. arborea (West Indian tree fern)

Travelers to Puerto Rico and Jamaica have been awed to find, high in the mountains, 50-foot tree ferns with feathery fronds up to 6 feet long. Indoors the same species grows far more slowly, in five or six years producing fronds only 1½ to 2 feet long.

HOW TO GROW. West Indian tree ferns do best in bright indirect or curtain-filtered sunlight; if only artificial light is available, provide at least 400 foot-candles. Night temperatures of 60° to 65° and day temperatures of 68° to 72° are ideal. Keep the soil wet at all times, but do not let the pots stand in water. Newly purchased or potted plants should not be fertilized for six months; established plants should be fed at six-month intervals with a standard house-plant fertilizer diluted to half the minimum strength recommended on the label. Repot root-bound plants in early spring. For best results use a mixture of 1 part loam, 1 part peat moss or leaf mold, 1 part finely ground fir bark and 1 part sharp sand; to each gallon pailful of this mixture add 2 tablespoons bone meal. Otherwise, use a mixture composed of equal parts of a packaged general-purpose potting soil and peat moss or leaf mold. Propagate at any season from spores, the dustlike reproductive particles of ferns.

CYCAS

C. circinnalis (fern palm); *C. revoluta,* also called *C. inermis* (sago palm)

Fern and sago palms are ancient plants with shiny leatherlike dark green leaves shaped like fern fronds. The leaves, seldom more than 2 feet long, grow upward and outward from stubby trunks a few inches tall.

HOW TO GROW. Fern and sago palms do best in bright indirect or curtain-filtered sunlight; if only artificial light is available, provide at least 400 foot-candles. Night temperatures of 50° to 55° and day temperatures of 68° to 72° are ideal. Let the soil become moderately dry between thorough waterings. Feed established plants every two months from early spring until midsummer; do not feed during the remainder of the year. Do not fertilize newly potted plants until the following spring. Repot overcrowded plants in early spring, using a mixture of 1 part loam, 1 part peat moss or leaf mold and 1 part sharp sand; to each gallon pailful of this mixture add 1½ teaspoons of 20 per cent superphosphate, 1 tablespoon of ground limestone and 2 teaspoons of 5-10-5 fertilizer. Otherwise, use a packaged general-purpose potting soil. Propagate at any season from seeds or from the young shoots, or suckers, that spring up from the base of the plant.

CYPERUS

C. alternifolius (umbrella plant); *C. diffusus,* also called *C. laxus* (dwarf umbrella plant); *C. haspan viviparus* (pygmy papyrus)

WEST INDIAN TREE FERN
Cyathea arborea

SAGO PALM
Cycas revoluta

Umbrella plants and papyri are water-loving plants with leaves that radiate from the tops of bare slender stalks, arching downward like the ribs of an umbrella. The umbrella plant grows 2½ to 4 feet tall, each stalk bearing 20 or so 4- to 8-inch shiny green leaves. The variegated umbrella plant, *C. alternifolius variegatus,* has stalks and leaves striped green and white. The slender umbrella plant, *C. alternifolius gracilis,* grows only 12 to 18 inches tall and has thinner green stalks and leaves than the basic species. The dwarf umbrella plant grows about 12 inches tall and has coarse grasslike green leaves at its base, as well as 8 to 10 leaves at the top of each stalk; the top leaves are 4 to 15 inches long and about ⅜ inch wide. The pygmy papyrus grows about 18 inches tall and bears great numbers of stiff upright-growing grasslike green leaves 2 to 3 inches long at the top of its stalks. All grow well in plain water.

HOW TO GROW. *Cyperus* species do best where they get four or more hours a day of direct sunlight, or where they get artificial and natural light averaging 800 foot-candles over 12 hours a day, but they will grow fairly well in bright indirect or curtain-filtered sunlight. Night temperatures of 50° to 55° and day temperatures of 68° to 72° are ideal. Keep the soil wet at all times by placing the pots in saucers filled with water. Fertilize the plants weekly from early spring until late summer with any standard house-plant fertilizer diluted to one half the minimum strength recommended on the label, but do not fertilize them during the balance of the year. Repot overcrowded plants in early spring, using a mixture of 1 part loam, 1 part peat moss or leaf mold and 1 part sharp sand; do not add fertilizer. Otherwise, use a packaged general-purpose potting soil. Measure the soil pH with a testing kit and adjust the pH to 7.0 (neutral): add limestone if the soil is acid, sulfur if it is alkaline. Propagate at any season from seeds or by dividing the roots.

CYRTOMIUM
C. falcatum, also called *Aspidium falcatum* (holly fern)

Holly ferns are splendid ferns for growing indoors, not only because of the gleaming green of their fronds, but because they withstand dry air, drafts and low light levels. They usually grow 1 to 2 feet tall, and their fronds bear numerous 3- to 5-inch pointed leaflets, each about 1 inch wide. The basic species has smooth-edged leaflets; the variety *C. falcatum caryotideum* has sharply toothed leaflets; Rocheford's holly fern, *C. falcatum rochefordianum,* has tough 2-inch-wide leaflets with wavy sawtoothed edges.

HOW TO GROW. Holly ferns do best in the shadowless light of a north window; if only artificial light is available, provide at least 150 foot-candles. The plants prefer night temperatures of 50° to 55° and day temperatures of 68° to 72° but tolerate temperatures as low as 35° without injury. Keep the soil barely moist at all times. Newly purchased or potted plants should not be fed for six months; established plants should be fed every six months with standard house-plant fertilizer diluted to one half the minimum strength recommended on the label. Repot overcrowded plants in early spring, using a mixture of 1 part loam, 1 part peat moss or leaf mold, 1 part finely ground fir bark and 1 part sharp sand; to each gallon pailful of this mixture add 2 tablespoons of bone meal. Or use a mixture of equal parts of a packaged general-purpose potting soil and peat moss or leaf mold. Be especially careful not to set the plants any deeper than the depth at which they had been growing, and firm the soil gently around the roots. Propagate in spring by dividing the roots. New plants can also be started at any time from spores, the dustlike reproductive particles of ferns.

SLENDER UMBRELLA PLANT
Cyperus alternifolius gracilis

HOLLY FERN
Cyrtomium falcatum

FIJI DAVALLIA
Davallia fejeensis

RUDOLPH ROEHRS DIEFFENBACHIA
Dieffenbachia picta 'Rudolph Roehrs'

D

DATE PALM See *Phoenix*

DAVALLIA

D. canariensis (deer's-foot fern), *D. fejeensis* (Fiji davallia), *D. mariesii* (ball fern), *D. trichomanoides* (squirrel's-foot fern). (All also called davallia)

These davallia species are characterized by creeping aboveground stems, or rhizomes, covered with coarse tan or brown hairs that make them look like the feet of animals. Because the rhizomes eventually extend over the edge of the container, the plants are especially suited to hanging baskets. The dark green fronds tend to be feathery, except for those of the deer's-foot fern, which are somewhat leathery and coarse. The deer's-foot fern has ¾-inch-thick rhizomes covered with hairy white-edged brown scales. The Fiji davallia has ½-inch-thick rhizomes covered with hairy brown scales. The ball fern has ¼-inch-thick rhizomes covered with hairless brown scales. The squirrel's-foot fern has ¼-inch-thick rhizomes with white to tan scales. All grow 12 to 18 inches tall except the ball fern, which becomes only 6 to 8 inches tall.

HOW TO GROW. Davallias do best in the shadowless light of a north window; if only artificial light is available, provide at least 150 foot-candles. Night temperatures of 50° to 65° and day temperatures of 65° to 85° are ideal. Keep the growing medium barely moist at all times. Do not feed newly purchased or newly potted plants for six months; established plants should be fed every six months with standard house-plant fertilizer diluted to one half the minimum strength recommended on the label. These ferns will grow on moist bark or osmunda-fern fiber but do best on top of a soil mixture consisting of 1 part loam, 1 part peat moss or leaf mold, 1 part finely ground fir bark and 1 part sharp sand; to each gallon pailful of this mixture add 2 tablespoons of bone meal. Otherwise, use a mixture composed of equal parts of packaged general-purpose potting soil and peat moss or leaf mold. Because the rhizomes lie on the growing material and do not send down deep roots, they do not need deep pots. Propagate at any season by dividing the rhizomes and pinning them to the soil surface with bent wire until they form roots. New plants can also be started at any season from spores, the dustlike reproductive particles of ferns.

DEER'S-FOOT FERN See *Davallia*
DEVIL'S BACKBONE See *Pedilanthus*
DEVIL'S IVY See *Scindapsus*
DICHORISANDRA See *Geogenanthus*

DIEFFENBACHIA

D. amoena (charming dieffenbachia); *D. bausei* (Bause dieffenbachia); *D. exotica,* also called *D. arvida* (exotic dieffenbachia); *D. picta,* also called *D. brasiliensis* (variable dieffenbachia). (All also called dumb cane)

Dieffenbachias have been popular house plants for more than 150 years not only because of their attractive foliage, but because they withstand the many handicaps of the indoor environment better than most other plants. Dieffenbachias are usually less than 2½ feet tall when they are sold by florists, and at this stage in their lives their lower leaves cover the edges of the flowerpots. As the plants get larger, the lower leaves gradually wither, and younger ones at the tops of the stems make the plants look like miniature palm trees. Plants may eventually become 4 to 5 feet tall but usually need to be cut back, as described below, before they reach this size. The leaves and stems are poisonous; they contain calcium oxalate, which can cause temporary speechlessness and painful swelling of the mouth.

The charming dieffenbachia tolerates dim light. Its 18-inch-long blue-green leaves have irregular white blotches along the crosswise veins. The Bause dieffenbachia, a hybrid, has 6- to 18-inch greenish yellow leaves with green edges and green and white spots. The exotic dieffenbachia has 8- to 10-inch firm dull green leaves with white blotches. The variable dieffenbachia is seldom grown, but its varieties are very popular. One of the best is Rudolph Roehrs, whose 10- to 12-inch gold-green leaves have white blotches and dark green edges and central ribs.

HOW TO GROW. Dieffenbachias do best in bright indirect or curtain-filtered sunlight; if only artificial light is available, provide at least 400 foot-candles. Night temperatures of 65° to 70° and day temperatures of 75° to 85° are ideal. Let the soil become moderately dry between thorough waterings. Feed established plants every two or three months with any standard house-plant fertilizer diluted to one half the minimum strength recommended on the label, but wait three or four months before feeding newly purchased or newly potted plants. Repot overcrowded plants at any season, using a mixture of 1 part loam, 1 part peat moss or leaf mold and 1 part sharp sand; to each gallon pailful of this mixture add 1½ teaspoons of 20 per cent superphosphate, 1 tablespoon of ground limestone and 2 teaspoons of 5-10-5 fertilizer. Otherwise, use a packaged general-purpose potting soil. To stimulate new growth, cut the plants back in spring to within 4 to 6 inches of the rim of the pot. Propagate at any season from sections of main stems or by the method known as air layering.

DIZYGOTHECA

D. elegantissima, also called *Aralia elegantissima* (false aralia)

The false aralia is an upright-growing 3- to 5-foot plant. Its leathery leaves are made up of 7 to 10 slender jagged leaflets, each 3 to 5 inches long, arranged like fingers of a hand. They are coppery in color when they unfold, but then become so dark a green they seem nearly black.

HOW TO GROW. False aralias do best in bright indirect or curtain-filtered sunlight; if only artificial light is available, provide at least 400 foot-candles. Night temperatures of 65° to 70° and day temperatures of 75° to 85° are ideal. Keep the soil barely moist at all times. Feed established plants every two weeks from early spring to early fall with standard house-plant fertilizer diluted to half the minimum strength recommended on the label, but do not feed during the balance of the year; wait at least three or four months before feeding newly potted plants. Repot overcrowded plants in very early spring, using a mixture of 1 part loam, 1 part peat moss or leaf mold and 1 part sharp sand; to each gallon pailful of this mixture add 1½ teaspoons of 20 per cent superphosphate, 1 tablespoon of ground limestone and 2 teaspoons of 5-10-5 fertilizer. Otherwise, use a packaged general-purpose potting soil. Propagate in spring or summer from stem cuttings.

DONKEY'S TAIL See *Sedum*

DRACAENA

D. deremensis, D. draco (dragon tree), *D. fragrans* (fragrant dracaena), *D. godseffiana* (gold-dust dracaena), *D. marginata* (red-margined dracaena), *D. sanderiana* (Sander's dracaena). (All also called dracaena)

Dracaenas display such amazing diversity in foliage that it is hard to realize they all belong to one genus. *D. deremensis,* rarely grown in the form of the basic species, comes in several popular varieties, most of which grow 2

FALSE ARALIA
Dizygotheca elegantissima

MASSANGE'S DRACAENA
Dracaena fragrans massangeana

FLORIDA BEAUTY DRACAENA
Dracaena godseffiana 'Florida Beauty'

RED-MARGINED DRACAENA
Dracaena marginata

to 5 feet tall. Two of the best are Janet Craig, which has straplike shiny dark green leaves 12 to 18 inches long and about 2 inches wide, and Warneckei, a variety particularly suited to dim light, which has 8- to 12-inch stiff swordlike gray-green leaves with white stripes.

The dragon tree has thick stiff pointed leaves 18 to 24 inches long and about 1½ inches wide. The leaves are silvery green and grow in a rosette form when the plant is young. As the plant matures, it forms a stubby trunk and may in some cases become 3 to 4 feet tall.

The fragrant dracaena is most famous for its variety *D. fragrans massangeana,* Massange's dracaena, which grows up to 6 feet tall and bears leaves 18 to 30 inches long and 2 to 3 inches wide. The leaves, marked with a yellow stripe down the center, resemble those of corn plants.

The gold-dust dracaena is quite unlike the other dracaena species. It grows 2½ feet tall and has thin wiry stems and flat oval leaves, 3 to 4 inches long, that are held horizontally in tiers or spirals along the stems. The dark green leaves are generously spotted with a creamy yellow that fades to white as the leaves mature. The stunning variety Florida Beauty has so much yellow or white on its leaves that little green is visible.

The red-margined dracaena is sometimes erroneously called Spanish dagger because it looks like *Yucca gloriosa,* the plant that is generally known by that common name. The red-margined dracaena bears clusters of 12- to 15-inch red-edged leaves about ½ inch wide that grow atop ¾-inch-wide main stems, which become as tall as 8 feet.

Sander's dracaena, an extremely durable species that grows well in plain water, has gracefully lax leaves 7 to 10 inches long and about 1 inch wide. They are gray green and have broad white edges. Young plants a few inches tall are frequently used in dish gardens. Mature plants grow 4 to 5 feet tall with stems up to ½ inch thick. In the variety Borinquensis the coloring of the species is reversed: the leaves have a broad milky central stripe flanked by a pair of narrow white stripes and edged with green.

HOW TO GROW. Dracaenas do best in bright indirect or curtain-filtered sunlight; if only artificial light is available, provide at least 400 foot-candles. Night temperatures of 65° to 70° and day temperatures of 75° to 85° are ideal. Keep the soil moist at all times, but do not let the pots stand in water. Newly purchased or potted plants should not be fertilized for six months; established plants should be fed at six-month intervals. Repot overcrowded plants at any season, using a mixture of 1 part loam, 1 part peat moss or leaf mold and 1 part sharp sand; to each gallon pailful of this mixture add 1½ teaspoons of 20 per cent superphosphate, 1 tablespoon of ground limestone and 2 teaspoons of 5-10-5 fertilizer. Otherwise, use a packaged general-purpose potting soil. To stimulate fresh growth and rejuvenate old plants, cut back dracaenas at any season —even as close as 4 to 6 inches to the rim of the pot. Propagate from stem cuttings, from sections of main stems or by the method known as air layering.

DRAGON BONES See *Euphorbia*
DRAGON TREE See *Dracaena*
DUMB CANE See *Dieffenbachia*

E
ECHEVERIA
E. derenbergii (painted lady); *E. elegans,* also called *Cotyledon elegans* (Mexican snowball); *E. peacockii,* also called *E. desmetiana* (peacock echeveria); *E. pulvinata* (plush plant). (All also called echeveria)

Echeverias generally produce symmetrical rosettes of

ground-hugging succulent leaves. The species described here stay small enough—usually 2 to 4 inches across—to be kept on a window sill or in a dish garden indefinitely, occasionally sending up slender stalks topped by clusters of tiny yellow, orange, pink or red flowers. The plush plant forms rosettes of tiny new plants at the tips of its stems.

The painted lady has red-edged pale green leaves. The Mexican snowball's pale green leaves are so covered with a waxy powder called bloom that they appear white. The peacock echeveria has silvery blue leaves with red edges and tips. The plush plant's leaves are densely covered with white hairs that occasionally become reddish at the leaf edges when the plant is grown in a cool location. Old plush plants often develop several irregularly branching stems 12 to 18 inches tall, each tipped with a rosette of its own.

HOW TO GROW. All echeverias except the plush plant do best where they get four or more hours a day of direct sunlight, or where artificial and natural light average 1,000 foot-candles over 12 hours a day, but they grow fairly well in bright indirect light, such as that reflected from light walls. The plush plant does best in curtain-filtered or bright indirect sunlight or at least 400 foot-candles of artificial light. All echeverias prefer night temperatures of 50° to 55° and day temperatures of 68° to 72°. Let the soil become moderately dry between thorough waterings from spring through fall; in winter, water only enough to keep the leaves from shriveling. Do not feed newly potted plants the first year; established plants should be fed once each spring with standard house-plant fertilizer diluted to half the minimum strength recommended on the label. Repot overcrowded or straggly plants at any season. For best results use a mixture of 1 part loam, 1 part leaf mold, 1 part sharp sand and ½ part crushed charcoal, or else use a mixture of equal parts of a packaged general-purpose potting soil and sharp sand; to each gallon pailful of whichever of these mixtures you use, add 1 tablespoon of ground limestone and 1 tablespoon of bone meal. Propagate at any season from leaf or stem cuttings. The plush plant can also be propagated from the rosettes at the tips of straggly stems.

ECHINOCACTUS APRICUS See *Notocactus*
ECHINOCACTUS FAMATIMENSIS See *Lobivia*
ECHINOCACTUS LENINGHAUSII See *Notocactus*
ECHINOCACTUS SCOPA See *Notocactus*

ECHINOPSIS
E. multiplex, also called *Cereus multiplex* (pink Easter lily cactus)

The pink Easter lily cactus in late spring bears fragrant pink lilylike flowers up to 6 inches across that open at night and close the next day. The plant, a 5-inch ribbed globe, has 1-inch black-tipped brown spines. Tiny plants often sprout from the base of young plants.

HOW TO GROW. The pink Easter lily cactus does best where it can get four or more hours a day of direct sunlight, or where artificial and natural light average 1,000 foot-candles over 12 hours a day, but it grows fairly well in bright indirect light, such as that reflected from light walls. In winter, night temperatures of 40° to 45° and day temperatures under 65° are ideal; from spring through fall, night temperatures of 65° to 70° and day temperatures of 75° to 85° are recommended. Keep the soil moderately dry between thorough waterings from spring through fall; in winter, water only enough to keep the plants from shriveling. Do not fertilize newly potted plants for a year; established plants should be fed once each spring. For fast growth repot annually in early spring; otherwise, repot in spring only when the plants become overcrowded. For best

PLUSH PLANT
Echeveria pulvinata

PINK EASTER LILY CACTUS
Echinopsis multiplex

results use a mixture of 1 part loam, 1 part leaf mold, 1 part sharp sand and ½ part crushed charcoal, or else use a mixture of equal parts of a packaged general-purpose potting soil and sharp sand; to each gallon pailful of whichever of these mixtures you use, add 1 tablespoon of ground limestone and 1 tablespoon of bone meal. Propagate from the shoots at the base of the plant or from seeds.

ECHINOPSIS AUREA See *Lobivia*
ELEPHANT-FOOT TREE See *Beaucarnea*
ENGLISH HEDGE FERN See *Polystichum*
EPIPREMNUM AUREUM See *Scindapsus*
ERANTHEMUM See *Hypoestes*

EUONYMUS

E. fortunei, also called *E. radicans* (winter creeper); *E. japonicus* (evergreen euonymus)

Several types of euonymus make fine house plants. The silver-edged winter creeper, *E. fortunei gracilis,* a slow-growing creeping or climbing plant with 18-inch stems and ½-inch dark green white-edged leaves sometimes tinged with pink, is attractive in dish gardens and against a bark-covered slab of wood. The 3-foot evergreen euonymus has 1-inch bright green leaves. The Pearl Edge euonymus, *E. japonicus albo-marginatus,* has whitish green leaves with narrow white edges; Silver Queen euonymus, *E. japonicus argenteo-variegatus,* has green leaves with broad white edges; and Yellow Queen euonymus, *E. japonicus aureo-variegatus,* has green leaves with broad yellow edges.

HOW TO GROW. Euonymuses do best in bright indirect or curtain-filtered sunlight; if only artificial light is available, provide at least 400 foot-candles. The plants prefer night temperatures of 40° to 55° and day temperatures of 65° or lower, but tolerate a span of 35° to 75°. Keep the soil barely moist. Feed established plants every three or four months; wait four to six months before feeding newly purchased or potted plants. Repot overcrowded plants at any season, except when light-colored new growth is tender in spring. For best results use a mixture of 1 part loam, 1 part peat moss or leaf mold and 1 part sharp sand; to each gallon pailful of this mixture add 1½ teaspoons of 20 per cent superphosphate, 1 tablespoon of ground limestone and 2 teaspoons of 5-10-5 fertilizer. Or use a packaged general-purpose potting soil. Prune overgrown plants in spring, cutting just above a leaf joint, where a new branch will grow. Propagate at any season from stem cuttings.

EUPHORBIA

E. lactea (milk-striped euphorbia, dragon bones); *E. mammillaris* (corncob euphorbia); *E. milii splendens,* also called *E. splendens* (crown of thorns); *E. obesa* (basketball euphorbia). (All also called euphorbia)

Of the more than 1,600 species of *Euphorbia,* a genus that includes the familiar Christmas plant poinsettia *(E. pulcherrima),* few would be confused with cacti. But there is one group from Africa and Asia that resembles cacti so closely only an expert can tell the difference. These succulent euphorbias, which usually send out short-lived small leaves, are of special interest because of their strange shapes. Some, however, contain an acrid milky sap that may be harmful; it should be kept out of eyes and cuts.

The milk-striped euphorbia looks like a green candelabra. It grows 3 or more feet tall and has leafless triangular or square stems streaked with white and lined with stout thorns. The corncob euphorbia grows about 8 inches tall and has many leafless spiny stems that look like green corncobs. The crown of thorns is entirely different—it is an extremely thorny branching shrub 2 to 3 feet tall with

SILVER QUEEN EUONYMUS
Euonymus japonicus argenteo-variegatus

½-inch bright green leaves that fall off if the plant does not get enough water. A few ¼-inch red blossoms are almost always in evidence at the tips of the branches. The basketball euphorbia is a globular plant, about 8 inches across and marked by eight spineless ridges, that looks like a basketball. As the plant ages, it stretches upward a bit, becoming an elongated sphere.

HOW TO GROW. Euphorbias do best where they get four or more hours a day of direct sunlight, or where artificial and natural light average 1,000 foot-candles over 12 hours a day, but they will grow fairly well in bright indirect light, such as that reflected from light walls. Night temperatures of 55° to 65° and day temperatures of 70° to 80° are ideal. Allow the soil to become moderately dry between thorough waterings from spring through fall; in winter, water only enough to keep the plants from shriveling. Newly potted plants should not be fertilized for a year; established plants should be fertilized once each spring. When plants become overcrowded, repot them at any season, using heavy gloves to protect your hands from the sharp spines. For best results use a potting mixture of 1 part loam, 1 part leaf mold, 1 part sharp sand and ½ part crushed charcoal, or use a mixture of equal parts of a packaged general-purpose potting soil and sharp sand; to each gallon pailful of whichever of these mixtures you use, add 1 tablespoon of ground limestone and 1 tablespoon of bone meal. Propagate the basketball euphorbia at any season from seeds; new plants of the other species can be started in spring and summer from stem cuttings.

EUPHORBIA CANALICULATA See *Pedilanthus*
EUPHORBIA CARINATA See *Pedilanthus*
EUPHORBIA TITHYMALOIDES See *Pedilanthus*
EUROPEAN FAN PALM See *Chamaerops*

F

FALSE ARALIA See *Dizygotheca*
FALSE HOLLY See *Osmanthus*
FAN PALM, CHINESE See *Livistona*
FAN PALM, EUROPEAN See *Chamaerops*

FATSHEDERA
F. lizei (tree ivy, aralia ivy, botanical wonder)

The tree ivy is a hybrid resulting from an accidental cross that occurred in a nursery in France in the year 1910 between Irish ivy, *Hedera helix hibernica,* and Moser's Japanese fatsia, *Fatsia japonica moserii.* The plant combines the shrubby character of the Japanese fatsia with the five-lobed leaves of the Irish ivy—but increased in size to as much as 10 inches across. The result is a semierect vine-shrub that can be tied to a support or else can be allowed to grow as a bush up to 3 feet tall. The variegated tree ivy, *F. lizei variegata,* has white-marked green leaves.

HOW TO GROW. Tree ivies do best where they get four or more hours a day of direct sunlight, or where artificial and natural light average 800 foot-candles over 12 hours a day, but they will grow fairly well in bright indirect light, such as that reflected from light walls. The plants prefer night temperatures of 40° to 55° and day temperatures of 65° to 72°, but they tolerate temperatures as low as 35° without injury, even when actively growing. Keep the soil barely moist at all times. Feed established plants at three- to four-month intervals with a standard house-plant fertilizer, but wait four to six months before feeding newly purchased or potted plants. Repot overcrowded plants at any season except when new growth is still pale green and tender. For best results use a mixture of 1 part loam, 1 part peat moss or leaf mold and 1 part sharp sand; to each

MILK-STRIPED EUPHORBIA
Euphorbia lactea

TREE IVY
Fatshedera lizei

JAPANESE FATSIA
Fatsia japonica

gallon pailful of this mixture add 1½ teaspoons of 20 per cent superphosphate, 1 tablespoon of ground limestone and 2 teaspoons of 5-10-5 fertilizer. Otherwise, use a packaged general-purpose potting soil. To rejuvenate old plants, cut them back in spring to within 4 to 6 inches from the soil. Propagate at any season from stem cuttings or by the method known as air layering.

FATSIA
F. japonica, also called *Aralia japonica* and *A. sieboldii* (Japanese fatsia, Japanese aralia)

The Japanese fatsia has bold shiny leaves, up to 16 inches across, with up to nine deeply cut lobes. It grows 4 or more feet tall but can be pruned to any desired size. Moser's Japanese fatsia, *F. japonica moserii,* has denser foliage than the basic species. The variegated Japanese fatsia, *F. japonica variegata,* has medium green leaves with irregularly marked creamy white edges.

HOW TO GROW. Fatsias do best where they get four or more hours a day of direct sunlight, or where artificial and natural light average 800 foot-candles over 12 hours a day, but they will grow fairly well in bright indirect light, such as that reflected from light walls. Night temperatures of 40° to 55° and day temperatures of 65° or lower are ideal. Keep the soil barely moist at all times. Newly purchased or potted plants should not be fertilized for four to six months; established plants should be fed twice a year, in early spring and early summer. Repot overcrowded plants in early spring, using a mixture of 1 part loam, 1 part peat moss or leaf mold and 1 part sharp sand; to each gallon pailful of this mixture add 1½ teaspoons of 20 per cent superphosphate, 1 tablespoon of ground limestone and 2 teaspoons of 5-10-5 fertilizer. Otherwise, use a packaged general-purpose potting soil. To encourage large leaves, remove any flower buds that may develop. Prune old plants in spring; they will produce vigorous new growth within a few weeks. Propagate in spring from the young shoots, or suckers, that spring up near the base of the plant.

FATSIA PAPYRIFERA See *Tetrapanax*
FERN, ASPARAGUS See *Asparagus*
FERN, BALL See *Davallia*
FERN, BIRD'S-NEST See *Asplenium*
FERN, BOSTON See *Nephrolepis*
FERN, BRAKE See *Pteris*
FERN, DEER'S-FOOT See *Davallia*
FERN, FIJI See *Davallia*
FERN, GOLDEN POLYPODY See *Polypodium*
FERN, HAWAIIAN TREE See *Cibotium*
FERN, HOLLY See *Cyrtomium*
FERN, MAIDENHAIR See *Adiantum*
FERN, MEXICAN TREE See *Cibotium*
FERN, MOTHER See *Asplenium*
FERN, RABBIT'S-FOOT See *Polypodium*
FERN, SOFT-SHIELD See *Polystichum*
FERN, SQUIRREL'S-FOOT See *Davallia*
FERN, STAGHORN See *Platycerium*
FERN, SWORD See *Nephrolepis*
FERN, TABLE See *Pteris*
FERN, TSUSSIMA HOLLY See *Polystichum*
FERN, VENUS'S MAIDENHAIR See *Adiantum*
FERN, VICTORIA See *Pteris*
FERN, WEST INDIAN TREE See *Cyathea*
FERN PALM See *Cycas*

FICUS
F. benjamina (weeping fig and Benjamin fig); *F. diversifolia,* also called *F. lutescens* (mistletoe fig); *F. elastica*

(India-rubber tree, rubber tree); *F. lyrata,* also called *F. pandurata* (fiddle-leaved fig); *F. retusa nitida,* also called *F. nitida* (Indian laurel)

Ask a gardener to name the two most popular foliage plants and he is apt to say philodendron and rubber tree, for both of these plants have been bringing satisfaction to indoor gardeners for generations. The great popularity of the India-rubber tree led plantsmen to search for other species with equal durability under household conditions. The selections discussed here cover a wide range of sizes, from types that usually grow less than 1 foot tall to others that can touch the ceiling unless they are pruned back occasionally. Under humid conditions many species form roots on their stems; the roots stretch down to the soil, take hold and form auxiliary trunks.

The weeping fig has 2- to 4-inch-long pointed shiny leathery leaves and many-twigged slender branches that arch gracefully. A variety of the weeping fig called the Java fig, *F. benjamina exotica,* grows in a pronounced weeping manner, and each of its leaves has a slight twist that adds to the gracefulness of the plant. Both the basic species and the variety are usually grown as 4- to 6-foot trees.

The mistletoe fig makes a bushy little plant, 8 inches to 2 feet tall, with long-lasting leathery dark green leaves. The leaves, roundish and 1 to 3 inches across, combine with ¼-inch woody inedible yellowish red fruit to give the plant the appearance of mistletoe.

The basic India-rubber tree pleased gardeners for many years with its glistening dark green oval leaves that open from pointed rosy sheaths and become 4 to 10 inches long and 2 to 3 inches wide. But its popularity waned in the late 1940s with the discovery of a type whose dark green leaves were more broadly oval and had a richer texture —the broad-leaved India-rubber tree, *F. elastica decora.* Its leaves emerge bronze-colored from bright red sheaths and grow up to 6 inches wide and 12 inches long; a prominent central rib is white on top and red on the underside. Another handsome variety is Doescher's India-rubber tree, *E. elastica doescherii,* whose leaves are the same size as those of the basic India-rubber tree but are mottled with gray green, creamy yellow and white; its central ribs and leaf stems are pink. All types of the India-rubber tree are usually sold as 2- to 4-foot plants with one or more trunks. The plants eventually reach ceiling height; since by that time they will have lost some of their lower leaves, they should be either pruned or propagated.

The fiddle-leaved fig grows to about the same size as the India-rubber tree. Its 12- to 18-inch leaves are shaped like the body of a violin and have such a gleaming leathery texture that they always seem freshly waxed.

The Indian laurel, an elegant species, is often sold as a 4- to 6-foot tree. Its upright branches are densely clothed with blunt-ended oval dark green leaves, 2 to 4 inches long, that feel waxy to the touch.

HOW TO GROW. *Ficus* species do best in bright indirect or curtain-filtered sunlight; if only artificial light is available, provide at least 400 foot-candles. Night temperatures of 65° to 70° and day temperatures of 75° to 85° are ideal. Keep the soil barely moist at all times. Newly purchased or newly potted plants should not be fertilized for six months; once established, plants should be fed at six-month intervals. Do not be too quick to repot *Ficus* species, for they do very well in relatively small containers even though their roots are crowded. When the plants become too crowded, as evidenced by a general lack of flourishing and new leaves that seem stunted, repot in early spring, using a mixture of 1 part loam, 1 part peat moss or leaf mold and 1 part sharp sand; to each gallon pailful of this

WEEPING FIG
Ficus benjamina

BROAD-LEAVED INDIA-RUBBER TREE
Ficus elastica decora

FIDDLE-LEAVED FIG
Ficus lyrata

mixture add ½ teaspoon of 20 per cent superphosphate, 1 tablespoon of ground limestone and 2 teaspoons of 5-10-5 fertilizer. Otherwise, use a packaged general-purpose potting soil. Plants that become too large for their space can be cut back to within a few inches of the soil in early spring; they will soon make new growth. Propagate at any season by the method known as air layering.

FIG See *Ficus*
FISHTAIL PALM See *Caryota*

FITTONIA
F. argyroneura (silver-nerved fittonia, mosaic plant), *F. verschaffeltii* (red-nerved fittonia)

Fittonias are 8-inch-long creeping plants that require very warm, humid growing conditions, but they are worth the extra care because their 2- to 4-inch oval leaves are so curiously and prominently veined—the patterns branch intricately like a nerve network. Fittonias begin to look straggly after they are about a year old, but new plants are easy to propagate.

HOW TO GROW. Fittonias do best in the shadowless light of a north window; if only artificial light is available, provide at least 150 foot-candles. Fittonias flourish most luxuriantly in the humid atmosphere of a terrarium, but do reasonably well on a tray that has been filled with pebbles and water to increase the humidity around them to 50 per cent or more. Night temperatures of 65° to 70° and day temperatures of 75° to 85° are ideal. Keep the soil moist at all times. Fertilize established plants monthly with any standard house-plant fertilizer diluted to one half the minimum strength recommended on the label, but wait three or four months before feeding newly purchased or potted plants. Repot overcrowded plants at any season. For best results use a mixture of 1 part loam, 1 part peat moss or leaf mold and 1 part sharp sand; to each gallon pailful of this mixture add 1½ teaspoons of 20 per cent superphosphate, 1 tablespoon of ground limestone and 2 teaspoons of 5-10-5 fertilizer. Otherwise, use a packaged general-purpose potting soil. Propagate from stem cuttings in spring or early summer.

FLAT PALM See *Howeia*
FRECKLE FACE See *Hypoestes*

G
GASTERIA
G. liliputana (Lilliput gasteria), *G. maculata* (spotted gasteria), *G. verrucosa* (oxtongue or warty gasteria)

These three gasterias are extremely easy-to-grow succulent plants. Their odd tongue-shaped leaves, marked with white spots called tubercles, rise from the base of each plant, then separate into facing rows. The 2-inch-high Lilliput gasteria has shiny dark green leaves about 2 inches long and 1 inch wide. The spotted gasteria grows 6 inches tall and has dark green leaves, 8 inches long and 2 inches wide, that have horizontal bands of white spots. The popular oxtongue gasteria has 6-inch-long leaves that are almost completely covered with prominent white dots.

HOW TO GROW. These plants do best in bright indirect or curtain-filtered sunlight; if only artificial light is available, provide at least 400 foot-candles. Night temperatures of 50° to 55° and day temperatures of 68° to 72° are ideal. Let the soil become moderately dry between thorough waterings. Do not fertilize newly potted plants for the first year; established plants should be fed once each spring with standard house-plant fertilizer diluted to half the minimum strength recommended on the label. Repot over-

SILVER-NERVED FITTONIA
Fittonia argyroneura

crowded plants at any season. For best results use a mixture of 1 part loam, 1 part leaf mold, 1 part sharp sand and ½ part crushed charcoal, or else use a mixture of equal parts of a packaged general-purpose potting soil and sharp sand; to each gallon pailful of whichever of these mixtures you use, add 1 tablespoon of ground limestone and 1 tablespoon of bone meal. Propagate at any season from seeds, from leaf cuttings or from the young shoots, or suckers, that spring up from the base of the plants.

GEOGENANTHUS

G. undatus, also called *Dichorisandra mosaica undata* (seersucker plant)

The seersucker plant gets its common name because its 2- to 3-inch leaves have a puckered texture like seersucker fabric. The plant forms a clump 6 to 10 inches tall and is relatively easy to grow.

HOW TO GROW. Seersucker plants do best in bright indirect or curtain-filtered sunlight; if only artificial light is available, provide at least 400 foot-candles. Night temperatures of 65° to 70° and day temperatures of 75° to 85° are ideal. Keep the soil barely moist at all times. Feed established plants at two- to three-month intervals, but wait three or four months before feeding newly purchased or newly potted plants. Repot overcrowded plants at any season, using a mixture composed of equal parts of peat moss or leaf mold and perlite or vermiculite; to each gallon pailful of this mixture add 1½ teaspoons of 20 per cent superphosphate, 1 tablespoon of ground limestone and 2 teaspoons of 5-10-5 fertilizer. Otherwise, use a packaged highly organic potting mixture formulated for African violets. Propagate at any season from stem cuttings.

GERMAN IVY See *Senecio*
GOLD-DUST TREE See *Aucuba*
GOLDEN EASTER LILY CACTUS See *Lobivia*
GOLDEN FEATHER PALM See *Chrysalidocarpus*
GOLDEN LACE CACTUS See *Mammillaria*
GOLDEN POLYPODY FERN See *Polypodium*
GOLDEN STAR CACTUS See *Mammillaria*
GRAPE IVY See *Cissus*

GREVILLEA

G. robusta (silk oak)

Seedlings of the silk oak tree perform a special service indoors: their 6- to 18-inch-long leaves provide a lacy fernlike effect in sunny places where ferns—and many other foliage house plants—cannot thrive. However, silk oaks grow rapidly—often a foot or more in their first year.

HOW TO GROW. Silk oaks do best where they get four or more hours of direct sunlight, or where they get artificial and natural light averaging 800 foot-candles over 12 hours a day, but they will grow fairly well in bright indirect light, such as that reflected from light walls. Night temperatures of 50° to 55° and day temperatures of 68° to 72° are ideal. Let the soil become moderately dry between thorough waterings. Fertilize established plants at two- to three-month intervals, but wait three to four months before fertilizing newly purchased or newly potted plants. Repot silk oaks at any season except when light-colored new growth appears. For best results use a mixture of 1 part loam, 1 part peat moss or leaf mold and 1 part sharp sand; to each gallon pailful of this mixture add 1½ teaspoons of 20 per cent superphosphate, 1 tablespoon of ground limestone and 2 teaspoons of 5-10-5 fertilizer. Otherwise, use a packaged general-purpose potting soil. Plants can have as much as half the length of their branches pruned in early spring; fresh new growth will appear quick-

OXTONGUE GASTERIA
Gasteria verrucosa

SEERSUCKER PLANT
Geogenanthus undatus

SILK OAK
Grevillea robusta

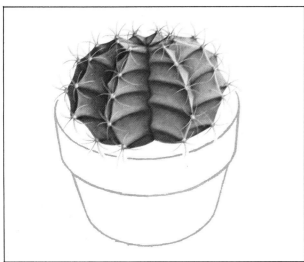

PLAID CACTUS
Gymnocalycium mihanovichii

JAVA VELVET PLANT
Gynura aurantiaca

ly. After two or three years plants lose their shape and should be replaced by new plants, which can be easily grown from seeds at any season.

GYMNOCALYCIUM
G. mihanovichii (plaid cactus, chin cactus)

The ordinary plaid cactus is an interesting plant in its own right—it forms a 2-inch ribbed globe, with faint reddish bands that account for its common name, and 1½-inch pink-tinged green flowers that appear from time to time throughout the year. But there are even more interesting types, formed through a startling mutation that was found in Japan in the 1940s among seedlings of the variety *G. mihanovichii friedrichiae variegata:* this sport was entirely red, its body lacking the green chlorophyll other plants use to manufacture food. It was grafted to another cactus to give it a food supply, and it then started a line that has since produced numerous other mutations in yellow, pink and orange as well as red. They are sold, each grafted to a green cactus for sustenance, as Red Cap, Orange Cap, Pink Cap and Yellow Cap cacti.

HOW TO GROW. Plaid cacti do best where they get four or more hours a day of direct sunlight, or where artificial and natural light average 1,000 foot-candles over 12 hours a day, but they will grow fairly well in bright indirect light, such as that reflected from light walls. Unlike most other cacti, which need cold winter temperatures, these plants do best with night temperatures of 50° to 55° and day temperatures of 68° to 72° throughout the year. Let the soil become moderately dry between thorough waterings from spring through fall; in winter, water only enough to keep the plants from shriveling. Newly potted plants should not be fertilized during their first year; established plants should be fed once each spring. For fast growth repot annually in early spring; otherwise, repot in spring only when the plants become overcrowded. For best results use a mixture of 1 part loam, 1 part leaf mold, 1 part sharp sand and ½ part crushed charcoal, or else use a mixture of equal parts of a packaged general-purpose potting soil and sharp sand; to each gallon pailful of whichever of these mixtures you use, add 1 tablespoon of ground limestone and 1 tablespoon of bone meal. Propagate the basic species at any season from seeds. Propagate colored varieties in early spring by grafting the tiny plantlets that sometimes form at the side of the plants to a green cactus such as myrtillocactus or hylocereus.

GYNURA
G. aurantiaca (Java, purple or royal velvet plant), *G. sarmentosa* (purple passion vine). (Both also called gynura)

No other common foliage plant can duplicate the iridescent leaves of gynuras, which are covered with velvety purple hairs that gleam in the sunshine. The purple is especially noticeable on new leaves; older ones are dark green with purple hairs along the veins and at the leaf edges. The Java velvet plant, with 2½- to 3½-inch-long leaves, becomes a bush as much as 2 feet tall, but most gardeners keep it pruned to a smaller size. The purple passion vine has 3- to 4-inch irregularly lobed lance-shaped leaves. The 2-foot-long stems as well as the undersides of the leaves are wine red and have some tendency to twine. Both species occasionally bear small orange flowers and are particularly attractive in hanging containers.

HOW TO GROW. Gynuras do best where they get four or more hours a day of direct sunlight, but they will grow fairly well in bright indirect light, such as that reflected from light walls; if only artificial light is available, provide at least 800 foot-candles. Night temperatures of 65° to 70°

and day temperatures of 75° to 85° are ideal. Keep the soil barely moist at all times. Feed established plants monthly with standard house-plant fertilizer diluted to one half the minimum strength recommended on the label, but wait two or three months before feeding newly purchased or newly potted plants. Repot overcrowded plants in spring or early summer, using a mixture of 1 part loam, 1 part peat moss or leaf mold and 1 part sharp sand; to each gallon pailful of this mixture add 1½ teaspoons of 20 per cent superphosphate, 1 tablespoon of ground limestone and 2 teaspoons of 5-10-5 fertilizer. Otherwise, use a packaged general-purpose potting soil. To avoid straggliness and to encourage dense, brightly colored new growth, pinch off the tips of branches as they become too long. The tips will root easily to make new plants.

H

HAWAIIAN TREE FERN See *Cibotium*

HAWORTHIA
H. fasciata (zebra haworthia), *H. margaritifera* (pearly haworthia)

The haworthias described here are extremely easy-to-grow succulent plants; they form small rosettes of upward-curving leaves with back surfaces that are marked with various patterns of warty protuberances called tubercles. The zebra haworthia forms a rosette about 3 to 4 inches across and has 2-inch-long leaves with horizontal bands of tubercles. The pearly haworthia grows 3 to 6 inches across and has 1½- to 3-inch-long leaves, which are profusely dotted with tubercles. Both of the haworthias are frequently used in dish gardens.

HOW TO GROW. Haworthias do best in bright indirect or curtain-filtered sunlight; if only artificial light is available, provide at least 400 foot-candles. Night temperatures of 50° to 55° and day temperatures of 68° to 72° are ideal. Let the soil become moderately dry between thorough waterings. Do not fertilize newly potted plants for the first year; established plants should be fed once each spring with a standard house-plant fertilizer diluted to half the minimum strength recommended on the label. Repot overcrowded plants at any season. For best results use a mixture of 1 part loam, 1 part leaf mold, 1 part sharp sand and ½ part crushed charcoal, or else use a mixture of equal parts of a packaged general-purpose potting soil and sharp sand; to each gallon pailful of whichever of these mixtures you use, add 1 tablespoon of ground limestone and 1 tablespoon of bone meal. Haworthias can be propagated most easily from the young shoots, or suckers, that spring up from the base of established plants. New plants can also be started from leaf cuttings or from seeds.

HEARTS ENTANGLED See *Ceropegia*

HEDERA
H. canariensis (Canary Island or Algerian ivy), *H. helix* (English ivy)

The ivies of legend belong to the genus *Hedera*. They are climbing vines that cling to upright surfaces by roots that sprout from their stems and work into any available crevice. Given the support of a thin stake, a single stem can be trained to grow upward and then branch out to make a little "ivy tree." The vines can also be trained to cover fanciful shapes formed of wires stuffed with sphagnum moss. But usually the trailing stems are allowed to cascade over the sides of pots or hanging containers.

The most valuable of the Canary Island ivies is the variegated Canary Island ivy, *H. canariensis variegata,* also

ZEBRA HAWORTHIA
Haworthia fasciata

VARIEGATED CANARY ISLAND IVY
Hedera canariensis variegata

117

called Gloire de Marengo, whose leaves are usually 1½ to 2½ inches across.

The basic English ivy has 2- to 4-inch-long three- or five-lobed dark green leaves, but its varieties exhibit some of the oddest-shaped foliage known. There are round or heart-shaped leaves with no lobes at all, as well as others with three, four, five or seven lobes as small as ½ inch and as big as 6 inches across; still others are wavy, curled, crested, cupped or ruffled. In color they combine green with white, cream, yellow or pink. Typical varieties are Silver King, with green-and-white leaves; Buttercup, whose leaves are yellow; Manda's Crested, whose star-shaped leaves have wavy-edged lobes; and Caenwoodiana, a particularly durable type whose dark green leaves are accented by prominent ivory-white veins. All grow well in water.

HOW TO GROW. Ivies do best where they get four or more hours a day of direct sunlight, but will grow fairly well in bright indirect light, such as that reflected from light walls; if only artificial light is available, provide at least 800 foot-candles. Night temperatures of 50° to 55° and day temperatures of 68° to 72° are ideal, but English ivies tolerate night temperatures as low as 35° without injury, even when actively growing. Keep the soil barely moist. Newly purchased or potted plants should not be fed for three to four months; established plants should be fed every three or four months. Repot overcrowded plants at any season. For best results use a mixture of 1 part loam, 1 part peat moss or leaf mold and 1 part sharp sand; to each gallon pailful of this mixture add 1½ teaspoons of 20 per cent superphosphate, 1 tablespoon of ground limestone and 2 teaspoons of 5-10-5 fertilizer. Or use a packaged general-purpose potting soil. To induce bushiness, pinch off stem tips at any season; they will root easily.

HOLLY, FALSE See *Osmanthus*
HOLLY FERN See *Cyrtomium*
HOLLY FERN, TSUSSIMA See *Polystichum*

HOWEIA
H. belmoreana, also called *Kentia belmoreana* (sentry or curly palm); *H. forsteriana*, also called *Kentia forsteriana* (paradise, flat or thatchleaf palm)

Sentry and paradise palms rank side by side as the best palms for indoor use. They grow slowly (6 to 8 inches a year), last indefinitely and make fine house plants from the time they are a few inches tall until they outgrow the space they occupy. Both have long feathery arching leaves composed of many slender leaflets. The sentry palm has a spreading habit of growth. The paradise palm becomes rather vase-shaped as it grows because the new leaves growing at the top are considerably larger than the older ones below and spread a greater distance. Both species have a single trunk, but three or more seedlings are sometimes potted together to give the effect of multiple trunks.

HOW TO GROW. Sentry and paradise palms do best in bright indirect or curtain-filtered sunlight; if only artificial light is available, provide at least 400 foot-candles. Night temperatures of 60° to 65° and day temperatures of 75° to 85° are ideal. Keep the soil barely moist at all times. Feed established plants monthly from early spring until early fall, but do not feed them during the balance of the year, and wait at least four to six months before feeding newly purchased or newly potted plants. Palms do well in relatively small containers and can go for many years without being repotted. When overcrowding becomes severe, repot in early spring, using a mixture of 1 part loam, 1 part peat moss or leaf mold, 1 part sharp sand and ½ part well-rotted or dried cow manure; to each gallon pailful of this

ENGLISH IVY
IN POT: *Hedera helix* 'Silver King'
LEAF DETAILS (left to right): *H. helix* 'Caenwoodiana,'
H. helix 'Buttercup,' *H. helix* 'Manda's Crested'

mixture add 2 tablespoons of bone meal. Otherwise, use a packaged highly organic potting mixture formulated for African violets. Propagate from seeds at any season.

HURRICANE PLANT See *Monstera*
HYOPHORBE See *Chrysalidocarpus*

HYPOESTES
H. phyllostachya, also called *H. sanguinolenta* and *Eranthemum sanguinolentum* (freckle face, pink polka dot)

As its common names suggest, this plant has leaves spotted with pink. It grows rapidly, usually becoming 6 to 12 inches tall and sometimes equally wide, though it may become as much as 2 feet tall. The 1½- to 2½-inch leaves are hairy and densely set. Two varieties, Pink Brocade and Splash, are even more attractive than the basic species because their leaves have many more spots. The plants tend to become straggly after a year and should be discarded, but new plants are easy to propagate.

HOW TO GROW. Freckle faces do best in bright indirect or curtain-filtered sunlight; if only artificial light is available, provide at least 400 foot-candles. Night temperatures of 65° to 70° and day temperatures of 75° to 85° are ideal. The soil should be barely moist at all times. Do not fertilize. Propagate from stem cuttings at any season. Some gardeners start a few young plants at least once a year as replacements for straggly old ones. For best results pot in a mixture of 1 part peat moss or leaf mold and 1 part perlite or vermiculite; to each gallon pailful of this mixture add 1½ teaspoons of 20 per cent superphosphate, 1 tablespoon of ground limestone and 2 teaspoons of 5-10-5 fertilizer. Otherwise, use a packaged highly organic potting mixture formulated for African violets.

I
INCH PLANT See *Callisia, Tradescantia*
INDIAN LAUREL See *Ficus*
INDIA-RUBBER TREE See *Ficus*
INDOOR OAK See *Nicodemia*
IVY See *Hedera*
IVY, ARALIA See *Fatshedera*
IVY, DEVIL'S See *Scindapsus*
IVY, GERMAN See *Senecio*
IVY, GRAPE See *Cissus*
IVY, KANGAROO See *Cissus*
IVY, PARLOR See *Senecio*
IVY, SWEDISH See *Plectranthus*
IVY, TREE See *Fatshedera*

J
JADE PLANT See *Crassula*
JAPANESE SWEET FLAG See *Acorus*

K
KALANCHOE
K. daigremontiana, also called *Bryophyllum daigremontianum* (Daigremont kalanchoe); *K. marmorata* (penwiper plant); *K. tomentosa* (panda plant and pussy ears). (All also called kalanchoe)

Kalanchoes are extremely easy-to-grow succulent plants popular for their unusually colored foliage. They remain small enough to fit on a window sill or in a dish garden and in winter occasionally bear small white, pink, red or yellow flowers. The Daigremont kalanchoe grows on a slender single stem 10 to 15 inches tall and has 1½- to 3-inch blue-green leaves abundantly blotched with reddish purple. The edges of the leaves have shallow teeth, and between each pair of teeth is borne a tiny replica of the whole plant.

SENTRY PALM
Howeia belmoreana

FRECKLE FACE
Hypoestes phyllostachya

119

PANDA PLANT
Kalanchoe tomentosa

LAUREL
Laurus nobilis

These plantlets drop off easily and soon root and grow, forming a clump around the parent. The penwiper plant also grows 10 to 15 inches tall but bears closely set, nearly round gray-green leaves, 2 to 4 inches across, that are heavily spotted with reddish brown. The panda plant may reach 2 feet, but is more commonly seen as a 6- to 8-inch plant; its 2- to 3-inch leaves are completely covered with silvery white hairs except for a ridge of brown hairs along the tips.

HOW TO GROW. Kalanchoes do best where they get four or more hours of direct sunlight, or where artificial and natural light average 1,000 foot-candles over 12 hours a day, but they will grow fairly well in bright indirect light, such as that reflected from light walls. Night temperatures of 50° to 55° and day temperatures of 68° to 72° are ideal. Let the soil become moderately dry between thorough waterings. Newly purchased or potted plants should not be fed for six months; once established, plants should be fed every six months. Repot overcrowded plants at any season. For best results use a mixture of 1 part loam, 1 part leaf mold, 1 part sharp sand and ½ part crushed charcoal, or else use a mixture of equal parts of a packaged general-purpose potting soil and sharp sand; to each gallon pailful of whichever of these mixtures you use, add 1 tablespoon of ground limestone and 1 tablespoon of bone meal. Propagate at any season from leaf or stem cuttings or from the plantlets that form on the leaves of some species.

KANGAROO IVY See *Cissus*
KENTIA See *Howeia*

L

LADY PALM See *Rhapis*
LAUREL See *Laurus*
LAUREL, INDIAN See *Ficus*

LAURUS
L. nobilis (laurel, sweet bay)

The laurel of ancient Greece and Rome, from whose leaves crowns were once woven for heroes, does double duty as a fine slow-growing house plant and as a seasoning —its leaves are the bay leaves used in cooking. It prefers cool locations and is particularly suited to drafty places where more tender plants would die. The laurel is single-stemmed when young, with leathery leaves 3 to 4 inches long and about 1 inch wide, but it usually develops multiple stems and thick foliage as it matures. It generally is kept at 2 to 4 feet by shearing or pruning.

HOW TO GROW. Laurels do best where they get four or more hours a day of direct sunlight, or where artificial and natural light average 800 foot-candles over 12 hours a day, but they will grow fairly well in bright indirect light, such as that reflected from light walls. Night temperatures of 40° to 55° and day temperatures of 65° or lower are ideal. Keep the soil barely moist at all times. Fertilize established plants at two-month intervals from early spring until midsummer; do not fertilize for the balance of the year, and wait at least four to six months before feeding newly potted plants. Laurels can go for several years without being repotted, but when the roots become extremely overcrowded, the plants should be repotted in early spring before new growth starts. For best results use a potting mixture of 1 part loam, 1 part peat moss or leaf mold and 1 part sharp sand; to each gallon pailful of this mixture add 1½ teaspoons of 20 per cent superphosphate, 1 tablespoon of ground limestone and 2 teaspoons of 5-10-5 fertilizer. Otherwise, use a packaged general-purpose potting soil. Propagate at any season from stem cuttings or by the method known as air layering.

LEOPARD'S SPOTS See *Adromischus*

LIGUSTRUM

L. japonicum (wax-leaved, luster-leaved or Texas privet, or wax-leaved ligustrum)

The tough and handsome wax-leaved privet, long a mainstay in frost-free gardens, has only in recent years been tried out as a house plant—and has proved to be happier indoors than many plants from the tropics. It can be grown as a young 4- to 6-inch plant in a dish garden, as a medium-sized table plant or as a 4- to 6-foot floor plant. It resists chilling and is especially useful in drafty places.

HOW TO GROW. Wax-leaved privets do best where they get four or more hours a day of direct sunlight, or where artificial and natural light average 800 foot-candles over 12 hours a day, but they will grow fairly well in bright indirect light, such as that reflected from light walls. Night temperatures of 40° to 55° and day temperatures of 65° or lower are ideal. Keep the soil barely moist at all times. Feed established plants at two-month intervals from early spring until midsummer; do not feed them during the balance of the year and wait at least four to six months before feeding newly potted plants. Repot overcrowded plants before new growth starts in early spring. For best results use a mixture of 1 part loam, 1 part peat moss or leaf mold and 1 part sharp sand; to each gallon pailful of this mixture add 1½ teaspoons of 20 per cent superphosphate, 1 tablespoon of ground limestone and 2 teaspoons of 5-10-5 fertilizer. Otherwise, use a general-purpose packaged potting soil. Large plants can be pruned as much as desired, even to within a few inches of the ground in very early spring just before new growth starts; they will soon make fresh new growth. Light pruning can be done at any time from early spring until midsummer. Propagate at any season from stem cuttings.

LIVISTONA

L. chinensis (Chinese fan palm)

The Chinese fan palm is a durable species whose leaves form huge semicircles resembling open fans; on young 2- to 3-foot plants the leaves may be 12 to 18 inches across; they become progressively larger as the plants mature. Scarcely visible threadlike fibers hang from between the fingerlike segments of the leaves, and thick 1-inch spines cover the lower half of each leaf stalk.

HOW TO GROW. Chinese fan palms do best in bright indirect or curtain-filtered sunlight; if only artificial light is available, provide at least 400 foot-candles. Night temperatures of 60° to 65° and day temperatures of 70° to 75° are ideal. Keep the soil wet at all times but do not let the pots stand in water. Fertilize established plants monthly from early spring until early fall but do not feed them the rest of the year; wait until the following spring before feeding newly potted plants. Repot overcrowded plants in early spring, using a mixture of 1 part loam, 1 part peat moss or leaf mold, 1 part sharp sand and ½ part well-rotted or dried cow manure; to each gallon pailful of this mixture add 2 tablespoons of bone meal. Otherwise, use a packaged highly organic potting mixture formulated for African violets. Cram the fresh soil between the old soil ball and the sides of the new container with a stick to make it firm. Propagate at any season from seeds.

LOBIVIA

L. aurea, also called *Echinopsis aurea* (golden Easter lily cactus); *L. famatimensis,* also called *Echinocactus famatimensis* (orange cob cactus). (All also called cob cactus)

Cob cacti are easy-to-grow dwarf plants whose cylin-

WAX-LEAVED PRIVET
Ligustrum japonicum

CHINESE FAN PALM
Livistona chinensis

drical stems resemble corncobs. The two species listed here bear showy flowers up to 4 inches across in early summer. The golden Easter lily cactus grows about 4 inches tall and has trumpet-shaped bright yellow flowers. The orange cob cactus has 6-inch-tall purplish green stems divided into about 20 small notched ribs that are lined with masses of flattened tiny yellow spines. Its prolific flowers range in color from yellow to dark red.

HOW TO GROW. Cob cacti do best where they get four or more hours a day of direct sunlight or where they get artificial and natural light averaging 1,000 foot-candles over 12 hours, but they will grow fairly well in bright indirect light, such as that reflected from light walls. In winter, night temperatures of 40° to 45° and day temperatures under 65° are ideal; from spring through fall, night temperatures of 65° to 70° and day temperatures of 75° to 85° are recommended. Let the soil become moderately dry between thorough waterings from spring through fall; in winter, water only enough to keep the plants from shriveling. Do not fertilize newly potted plants for the first year; established plants should be fed once each spring. Repot annually in early spring for fast growth; otherwise, repot overcrowded plants in spring. For best results use a mixture of 1 part loam, 1 part leaf mold, 1 part sharp sand and ½ part crushed charcoal, or else use a mixture of equal parts of a packaged general-purpose potting soil and sharp sand; to each gallon pailful of whichever of these mixtures you use, add 1 tablespoon of ground limestone and 1 tablespoon of bone meal. Propagate at any season from seeds or from the young shoots, or suckers, that spring up from the base of the plants.

M

MADAGASCAR PALM See *Chrysalidocarpus*
MAIDENHAIR FERN See *Adiantum*

MAMMILLARIA

M. bocasana (powder puff cactus), *M. camptotricha* (bird's-nest cactus), *M. candida* (snowball pincushion), *M. elongata* (golden star or golden lace cactus), *M. hahniana* (old lady cactus). (All also called mammillaria cactus)

Mammillaria cacti are especially suited for window sills and dish gardens. They usually produce clumps of young plants at the base of the main stem, and in winter and spring bear flowers in concentric rings at their stem tips.

The powder puff cactus forms a cluster of globular dark green stems about 1½ inches tall. They are covered with ¾-inch-long silky white hairs that hide ½-inch yellow hooked spines. This species has yellowish flowers with pink stripes. The bird's-nest cactus also forms clumps of globular dark green stems, but they grow 2 to 3 inches tall and are covered with a haphazard network of curving 1½-inch pale yellow spines; this species has white flowers. The snowball pincushion usually starts out as a single globular or columnar stem 2 to 3 inches tall, but eventually it too forms small clusters of stems, each woolly looking with small white bristles and short white spines; its flowers are also white. The golden star cactus, a 4- to 6-inch-tall multistemmed plant, is studded with starburstlike clusters of slender curving yellow spines; its flowers are yellow. The old lady cactus first grows as a 3-inch flat-topped globe, then gradually forms a clump of multiple stems and young shoots. A dense covering of long white hairs hides ½-inch white spines. The flowers are crimson.

HOW TO GROW. Mammillaria cacti do best where they get four or more hours a day of direct sunlight, or where artificial and natural light average 1,000 foot-candles over 12 hours a day, but they will grow fairly well in bright in-

GOLDEN EASTER LILY CACTUS
Lobivia aurea

GOLDEN STAR CACTUS
Mammillaria elongata

direct light, such as that reflected from light walls. In winter, night temperatures of 40° to 45° and day temperatures under 65° are ideal; from spring through fall, night temperatures of 65° to 70° and day temperatures of 75° to 85° are recommended. Let the soil become moderately dry between thorough waterings from spring through fall; in winter, water only enough to keep the plants from shriveling. Newly potted plants should not be fertilized for a year; established plants should be fed once each spring. For fast growth repot annually in early spring; otherwise, repot in spring only when the plants become overcrowded. For best results use a mixture of 1 part loam, 1 part leaf mold, 1 part sharp sand and ½ part crushed charcoal, or else use a mixture consisting of equal parts of a packaged general-purpose potting soil and sharp sand; to each gallon pailful of whichever of these mixtures you use, add 1 tablespoon of ground limestone and 1 tablespoon of bone meal. Propagate at any season from the new plants that develop at the base of the plants or from seeds.

MAN-IN-A-BOAT See *Rhoeo*

MARANTA
M. leuconeura (prayer plant, banded arrowroot)

Prayer plants derive their common name from the orientation of their leaves when at rest in darkness, a vertical position that makes them look like hands in prayer. In light the leaves are held horizontally. The plants are especially interesting when grown beneath a table lamp. When the light is turned on after dark, the "sleeping" leaves awaken and spread to their horizontal position in a matter of minutes, then become vertical again after the light is turned off. Two fine varieties grow 6 to 8 inches tall. *M. leuconeura kerchoveana*, called red-spotted arrowroot and sometimes rabbit tracks, has grayish green leaves that, when young, have reddish brown spots resembling animal tracks running parallel to the central ribs. As the leaves age, the tracks become dark green on the topsides of the leaves. *M. leuconeura massangeana*, Massange's or Leige arrowroot, has leaves that are noted for the fishbone pattern of their veins and for their purple undersides.

HOW TO GROW. Prayer plants do best in bright indirect or curtain-filtered sunlight; if only artificial light is available, provide at least 400 foot-candles. Night temperatures of 65° to 70° and day temperatures of 75° to 85° are ideal. Keep the soil moist at all times except in winter, when it should be allowed to dry a bit between light waterings; newly potted plants should be watered lightly until new growth begins, then should be kept moist. Repot annually in early spring, using a mixture of 1 part loam, 1 part peat moss or leaf mold and 1 part sharp sand; to each gallon pailful of this mixture add 1½ teaspoons of 20 per cent superphosphate, 1 tablespoon of ground limestone and 2 teaspoons of 5-10-5 fertilizer. Otherwise, use a packaged general-purpose potting soil. Wait at least three to four months before feeding newly potted plants, then feed them every two months until fall; do not feed the rest of the year. When plants become too large, shake off the soil and propagate new plants by dividing the roots in early spring.

MEXICAN SNOWBALL See *Echeveria*
MEXICAN TREE FERN See *Cibotium*

MONSTERA
M. deliciosa, also called *Philodendron pertusum* (monstera, Swiss cheese plant, cut-leaved or split-leaved philodendron, ceriman, hurricane plant)

Monsteras are jungle vines from Mexico and Guatemala

MASSANGE'S ARROWROOT
Maranta leuconeura massangeana

whose 8- to 12-inch roughly circular leaves are perforated and lobed in a variety of unusual patterns, accounting for one of the plant's many common names, Swiss cheese plant. The leaves feel like soft polished leather; they are light green as they unfold but become deep green as they mature. Because monsteras are vines, they are sometimes grown against bark-covered slabs of wood. Their stems send out roots, some of which penetrate the support, while others hang in mid-air. When the hanging roots become long enough, they push their tips into the soil; when they do this they help bring up nourishment from the soil and also act as props to hold plants erect. Monsteras eventually outgrow their space indoors, becoming ceiling high and straggly. When this happens they should be discarded; however, new plants are easy to propagate.

Monsteras have been confused with philodendrons because the leaves, when young, lack perforations or lobes and resemble philodendron leaves. Even today some commercial growers call the seedlings *Philodendron pertusum,* and the common names cut-leaved and split-leaved philodendron are often used. But whatever the name used, monsteras have long been popular. Praise for the species was summed up in a famous horticultural encyclopedia at the turn of the century: "It is one of the best plants for enduring the varying conditions of temperature in a dwelling-house, as nothing short of a freeze seems to hurt it."

HOW TO GROW. Monsteras do best in bright indirect or curtain-filtered sunlight; if only artificial light is available, provide at least 400 foot-candles. Night temperatures of 65° to 70° and day temperatures of 75° to 85° are ideal; the plants will tolerate temperatures below 60° but will not make new growth. Keep the soil barely moist at all times. Newly purchased or potted plants should not be fed for four to six months; established plants should be fed twice a year, in early spring and early summer. Repot overcrowded plants at any season, using a mixture of 1 part loam, 1 part peat moss or leaf mold and 1 part sharp sand; to each gallon pailful of this mixture add 1½ teaspoons of 20 per cent superphosphate, 1 tablespoon of ground limestone and 2 teaspoons of 5-10-5 fertilizer. Otherwise, use a packaged general-purpose potting soil. Propagate at any season from stem cuttings, sections of main stems, seeds or by the method known as air layering.

MOONSTONES See *Pachyphytum*
MOSAIC PLANT See *Fittonia*
MOSES-IN-THE-BULRUSHES See *Rhoeo*
MOSES-IN-THE-CRADLE See *Rhoeo*
MOTHER FERN See *Asplenium*
MOTHER-IN-LAW TONGUE See *Sansevieria*
MOTHER-OF-THOUSANDS See *Tolmiea*
MYRTLE See *Myrtus*

MYRTUS
M. communis (true, Greek or classic myrtle)

The basic species of true myrtle, long a favorite garden shrub in warm dry climates, grows too large for indoor use, but its dwarf variety *M. communis microphylla* makes a fine house plant. It usually becomes only 2 to 4 feet tall with an equal spread and retains the attractive leaves and tiny fragrant fuzzy white flowers of the basic species.

The leaves, which are aromatic when bruised, are about ½ inch long and ⅛ inch wide and are closely set on slender twiggy branches. The variegated dwarf myrtle, *M. communis microphylla variegata,* has leaves of varying shades of green and creamy white. Both varieties are often sold as 4- to 6-inch plants for dish gardens.

HOW TO GROW. Myrtles do best where they get four or

MONSTERA
Monstera deliciosa

more hours a day of direct sunlight, or where artificial and natural light average 800 foot-candles over 12 hours a day, but they will grow fairly well in bright indirect light, such as that reflected from light walls. Night temperatures of 40° to 55° and day temperatures of 55° to 85° are ideal. Let the soil become moderately dry between thorough waterings. Feed established plants every three to four months from early spring until early fall; do not feed the rest of the year. Wait four to six months before feeding newly potted plants. Repot overcrowded plants in early spring before new growth starts, using a mixture of 1 part loam, 1 part peat moss or leaf mold and 1 part sharp sand; to each gallon pailful of this mixture add 1½ teaspoons of 20 per cent superphosphate, 1 tablespoon of ground limestone and 2 teaspoons of 5-10-5 fertilizer. Otherwise, use a packaged general-purpose potting soil. Prune overlarge plants as much as desired in early spring before new growth starts. Propagate at any season from stem cuttings.

N

NEANTHE See *Chamaedorea*

NEPHROLEPIS
N. exaltata (sword fern)

Styles in foliage plants have come full circle since Victorian days with the present upsurge of interest in the Boston fern, *N. exaltata bostoniensis,* a widely acclaimed mutation of the sword fern that was found near Boston in the 1890s and soon became a fixture of the overstuffed parlors of the time, but has seemed old-fashioned until recently. (The basic species is seldom grown.) The Boston fern has arching fronds up to 3 feet long with flat 3- to 4-inch closely set leaflets. If the plant is grown on a pedestal, the fronds can cascade on all sides. The more commonly available dwarf Boston fern, *N. exaltata bostoniensis compacta,* has 15- to 18-inch fronds. In addition, there are a number of mutations with fronds so finely divided that each resembles a brush, as thick as it is wide. Typical varieties include three 10- to 12-inch types—Childsii, with overlapping curling leaflets; Fluffy Ruffles, with stiff, densely leaved upright fronds; and Verona, with lacy drooping fronds—as well as a smaller type, Mini-Ruffle, similar to Fluffy Ruffles but only 6 to 8 inches tall, and a larger one, Whitmanii, a lacy arching plant 12 to 14 inches tall.

HOW TO GROW. These ferns do best in bright indirect or curtain-filtered sunlight; if only artificial light is available, provide at least 400 foot-candles. Night temperatures of 50° to 55° and day temperatures of 68° to 72° are ideal. Keep the soil barely moist at all times. Newly purchased or potted plants should not be fed for six months; established plants should be fed twice yearly, in early spring and midsummer, with standard house-plant fertilizer diluted to half the minimum strength recommended on the label. Repot overcrowded plants in early spring, using a mixture of 1 part loam, 1 part peat moss or leaf mold, 1 part finely ground fir bark and 1 part sharp sand; to each gallon pailful of this mixture add 2 tablespoons of bone meal. Otherwise, use a mixture composed of equal parts of a packaged general-purpose potting soil and peat moss or leaf mold. All of the ferns described above are sterile—that is, they are incapable of producing spores, the dustlike reproductive particles of ferns. However, in spring they send out shoots, or runners, that root as they creep along the top of the soil and, by early summer, form new plants that can be cut off and potted. You can also propagate Boston ferns by dividing the roots of old plants in early spring.

NEPHTHYTIS See *Syngonium*

VARIEGATED DWARF MYRTLE
Myrtus communis microphylla variegata

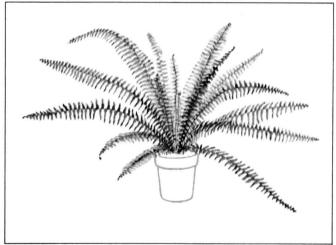

BOSTON FERN
Nephrolepis exaltata bostoniensis

INDOOR OAK
Nicodemia diversifolia

GOLDEN BALL CACTUS
Notocactus leninghausii

NICODEMIA
N. diversifolia (indoor oak)

The indoor oak, a relative newcomer as a house plant, grows 12 to 18 inches tall and has 1- to 2-inch iridescent leaves shaped like oak leaves. The species is naturally bushy but can be made even more so if new growth is pinched off, causing more branches to develop.

HOW TO GROW. Indoor oaks do best where they get four or more hours a day of direct sunlight, but they will grow fairly well in bright indirect light, such as that reflected from light walls; if only artificial light is available, provide at least 800 foot-candles. Night temperatures of 65° to 70° and day temperatures of 75° to 85° are ideal. Keep the soil barely moist at all times. Feed established plants once a week from spring until midsummer with standard house-plant fertilizer diluted to half the minimum strength recommended on the label; do not fertilize the plants the rest of the year and wait at least two to three months before fertilizing newly potted plants. When plants become overcrowded, repot them in early spring, using a mixture of 1 part loam, 1 part peat moss or leaf mold and 1 part sharp sand; to each gallon pailful of this mixture add 1½ teaspoons of 20 per cent superphosphate, 1 tablespoon of ground limestone and 2 teaspoons of 5-10-5 fertilizer. Or else use a packaged general-purpose potting soil. Propagate from stem cuttings in spring or summer.

NOLINA See *Beaucarnea*
NORFOLK ISLAND PINE See *Araucaria*

NOTOCACTUS
N. apricus, also called *Echinocactus apricus* (sun cup); *N. leninghausii*, also called *Echinocactus leninghausii* (golden ball cactus); *N. scopa*, also called *Echinocactus scopa* (silver ball cactus). (All also called ball cactus)

Ball cacti live up to their name when they are young, forming clumps of handsome globular plants 1½ to 2½ inches across. As they become older, however, they stretch upward, becoming cylindrical in shape. All are easy to grow on a window sill. Those listed here have yellow flowers.

The sun cup has pale green stems with 15 to 20 ribs and 1¼-inch reddish yellow spines that curve upward and intertwine; it generally becomes 3 inches tall. The golden ball cactus has about 30 ribs covered with yellow spines; it becomes 6 inches or more tall. The silver ball cactus has pale green stems with 30 to 35 ribs and is covered with soft white hairs that hide ¼-inch white spines; it reaches a height of 4 to 5 inches.

HOW TO GROW. Ball cacti do best where they get four or more hours a day of direct sunlight, or where artificial and natural light average 1,000 foot-candles over 12 hours a day, but they will grow fairly well in bright indirect light, such as that reflected from light walls. In winter, night temperatures of 40° to 45° and day temperatures under 65° are ideal; from spring through fall, night temperatures of 65° to 70° and day temperatures of 75° to 85° are recommended. Let the soil become moderately dry between thorough waterings from spring through fall; in winter, water only enough to keep the plants from shriveling. Newly potted plants should not be fertilized for the first year; established plants should be fed once each spring. Repot annually in early spring for fast growth; otherwise, repot in spring when the plants become overcrowded. For best results use a mixture of 1 part loam, 1 part leaf mold, 1 part sharp sand and ½ part crushed charcoal, or else use a mixture of equal parts of a packaged general-purpose potting soil and sharp sand; to each gallon pailful of whichever of these mixtures you use, add 1 tablespoon of ground limestone and 1 tablespoon of bone meal. Propagate at any season from the young shoots, or suckers, that spring up from the base of the plant. New plants can also be started at any season from seeds.

O

OAK, INDOOR See *Nicodemia*
OAK, SILK See *Grevillea*
OCTOPUS TREE See *Brassaia*
OLD LADY CACTUS See *Mammillaria*
OLD-MAN CACTUS See *Cephalocereus*

OLEA

O. europaea (olive)

The common olive tree, cultivated for its oil and fruit since antiquity, makes a highly durable indoor plant that is attractive even in a small flowerpot. It can grow to the ceiling but can be kept much smaller by being pruned. It is often grown as a standard—that is, with a single trunk topped by a cluster of branches so that it looks like a mature tree in miniature. The plant bears 1½- to 3-inch-long leathery leaves and occasional fragrant tiny white flowers, but does not normally produce fruit indoors because the blossoms are not easily pollinated there.

HOW TO GROW. Olive trees do best where they get four or more hours a day of direct sunlight, or where artificial and natural light average 800 foot-candles over 12 hours a day, but they will grow fairly well in bright indirect light, such as that reflected from light walls. Night temperatures of 40° to 55° and day temperatures of 60° to 75° are ideal, but the plants will endure temperatures as low as 15° when dormant and as high as 100° when actively growing, provided they are not allowed to dry out completely. However, the soil should be allowed to become moderately dry between thorough waterings. Newly purchased or newly potted plants should not be fertilized for at least four to six months; established plants should be fertilized twice a year, in early spring and early summer. Olive trees can grow in relatively small containers; when overcrowding becomes extreme, repot in early spring. For best results use a mixture of 1 part loam, 1 part peat moss or leaf mold and 1 part sharp sand; to each gallon pailful of this mixture add 1½ teaspoons of 20 per cent superphosphate, 1 tablespoon of ground limestone and 2 teaspoons of 5-10-5 fertilizer. Otherwise, use a packaged general-purpose potting soil. Pinch off the tips of overlong stems at any season. Prune as drastically as desired in early spring. Propagate at any season from stem cuttings.

OLIVE See *Olea*

OPUNTIA

O. basilaris (beavertail cactus), *O. glomerata* (paperspine cactus), *O. microdasys* (bunny ears). (All also called opuntia cactus)

The most familiar species of opuntia cacti are those known as prickly pears—a group of odd-looking plants with paddle-shaped sectional stems called pads. Most grow too fast and too tall for indoor use, but two similar species make excellent house plants; they are the beavertail cactus and bunny ears. Both grow relatively slowly, ultimately reaching a height of 3 to 4 feet. They do not have true spines but are dotted with even more prickly growths, clusters of ¹⁄₁₆-inch glochidia. Innocent to look at, glochidia are painful to touch and difficult to find when lodged in a finger. The beavertail cactus has 4- to 8-inch-long purplish green pads with reddish brown glochidia. Bunny ears has 3- to 6-inch green pads with white, yellow or reddish brown

OLIVE
Olea europaea

BUNNY EARS
Opuntia microdasys

glochidia. A third species of opuntia cacti, not resembling prickly pears at all and bearing spines rather than glochidia, is the paperspine cactus. It grows about 4 inches tall and has columnar gray-brown stems divided into 1- to 2-inch-long sections that carry flat whitish papery spines up to 4 inches long.

HOW TO GROW. Opuntia cacti do best where they get four or more hours a day of direct sunlight, or where artificial and natural light average 1,000 foot-candles over 12 hours a day, but they will grow fairly well in bright indirect light, such as that reflected from light walls. In winter, night temperatures of 40° to 45° and day temperatures under 65° are ideal; from spring through fall, night temperatures of 65° to 70° and day temperatures of 75° to 85° are recommended. Let the soil become moderately dry between thorough waterings from spring through fall; in winter, water only enough to keep the plants from shriveling. Newly potted plants should not be fed the first year; established plants should be fed once each spring. Repot annually in early spring for fast growth; otherwise, repot in spring when the plants become overcrowded. For best results use a mixture of 1 part loam, 1 part leaf mold, 1 part sharp sand and ½ part crushed charcoal, or else use a mixture of equal parts of a packaged general-purpose potting soil and sharp sand; to each gallon pailful of whichever of these mixtures you use, add 1 tablespoon of ground limestone and 1 tablespoon of bone meal. Propagate at any season from stem cuttings or from seeds.

OSMANTHUS

O. heterophyllus, also called *O. aquifolium* and *O. illicifolius* (holly osmanthus, false holly)

The holly osmanthus is a slow-growing durable plant that grows 3 or more feet tall; its 1½- to 2-inch spiny-edged, extremely dark green leaves look like those of English holly, even to the point of having a similar gloss. The leaves, borne closely together, cling to the plants for a long time. The variegated holly osmanthus, *O. heterophyllus variegatus,* has green leaves with creamy white edges occasionally tinged with pink. Both tolerate cold temperatures and drafty places. They are often sold as young plants combined with other plants in dish gardens.

HOW TO GROW. The holly osmanthus does best where it gets four or more hours a day of direct sunlight, or where artificial and natural light average 800 foot-candles over 12 hours a day, but it will grow fairly well in bright indirect light, such as that reflected from light walls. Night temperatures of 40° to 55° and day temperatures of 65° to 75° are ideal. Keep the soil barely moist at all times. Newly purchased or potted plants should not be fed for four to six months; established plants should be fed twice a year, in early spring and early summer. Repot overcrowded plants in early spring, using a mixture of 1 part loam, 1 part peat moss or leaf mold and 1 part sharp sand; to each gallon pailful of this mixture add 1½ teaspoons of 20 per cent superphosphate, 1 tablespoon of ground limestone and 2 teaspoons of 5-10-5 fertilizer. Otherwise, use a packaged general-purpose potting soil. Prune overtall plants in early spring. Propagate at any season from stem cuttings or by the method known as air layering.

OYSTER PLANT See *Rhoeo*

P

PACHYPHYTUM

P. bracteosum (silver bract), *P. oviferum* (moonstones, sugared almonds). (Both also called pachyphytum)

Pachyphytums are succulent plants that are easy to grow

VARIEGATED HOLLY OSMANTHUS
Osmanthus heterophyllus variegatus

on sunny window sills. Silver bract grows 6 to 12 inches tall and bears thick tongue-shaped upward-curving grayish white leaves. Moonstones seldom grows more than 6 inches tall and has ½- to ¾-inch leaves that take on pinkish tints in the sun.

HOW TO GROW. Pachyphytums do best where they get four or more hours a day of direct sunlight, or where they get artificial and natural light averaging 1,000 foot-candles over 12 hours a day, but they will grow fairly well in bright indirect light, such as that reflected from light walls. Night temperatures of 50° to 55° and day temperatures of 68° to 72° are ideal. Let the soil become moderately dry between thorough waterings from spring through fall; in winter, water only enough to keep the leaves from shriveling. Do not fertilize newly potted plants during the first year; when the plants become established, feed them once each spring with standard house-plant fertilizer diluted to one half the minimum strength recommended on the label. Repot overcrowded plants at any season. For best results use a mixture of 1 part loam, 1 part leaf mold, 1 part sharp sand and ½ part crushed charcoal, or else use a mixture of equal parts of a packaged general-purpose potting soil and sharp sand; to each gallon pailful of whichever of these mixtures you use, add 1 tablespoon of ground limestone and 1 tablespoon of bone meal. Propagate at any season from leaf or stem cuttings.

PAINTED LADY See *Echeveria*
PALM, ARECA See *Chrysalidocarpus*
PALM, BUTTERFLY See *Chrysalidocarpus*
PALM, CANE See *Chrysalidocarpus*
PALM, CHINESE FAN See *Livistona*
PALM, CURLY See *Howeia*
PALM, DATE See *Phoenix*
PALM, EUROPEAN FAN See *Chamaerops*
PALM, FERN See *Cycas*
PALM, FISHTAIL See *Caryota*
PALM, FLAT See *Howeia*
PALM, GOLDEN FEATHER See *Chrysalidocarpus*
PALM, LADY See *Rhapis*
PALM, MADAGASCAR See *Chrysalidocarpus*
PALM, PARADISE See *Howeia*
PALM, PARLOR See *Chamaedorea*
PALM, SAGO See *Cycas*
PALM, SENTRY See *Howeia*
PALM, THATCHLEAF See *Howeia*
PAN-AMERICAN FRIENDSHIP PLANT See *Pilea*
PANAMIGA See *Pilea*
PANAX See *Polyscias*
PANDA PLANT See *Kalanchoe*

PANDANUS
P. veitchii (Veitch screw pine)

The Veitch screw pine is a durable plant from the South Seas with very sharp spiny-edged leaves about 2 feet long and 1½ to 3 inches wide rising from a rosette in a spiral formation like the threads of a screw. The plant is not a true pine but is probably so named because of the conelike fruit it bears when grown outdoors. The plant grows slowly, eventually becoming 3 to 5 feet tall. As it ages, the rosette generally develops into a main stem. When the plant becomes 2 to 3 feet tall, the stem begins to send out stiff wide-spreading roots below the base of the leaves. The roots can be allowed to hang over the sides of the container or else can be gradually pulled inward until they grow into the soil. On Polynesian beaches, where screw pines are ubiquitous, these stilt roots, as they are called, steady the plants in high winds. The dwarf Veitch screw

MOONSTONES
Pachyphytum oviferum

VEITCH SCREW PINE
Pandanus veitchii

129

VARIEGATED DEVIL'S BACKBONE
Pedilanthus tithymaloides variegatus

EMERALD RIPPLE PEPEROMIA
Peperomia caperata 'Emerald Ripple'

pine, *P. veitchii compacta,* grows as tall as the basic species, but its dark green leaves are only 12 to 18 inches long and 1 to 2 inches wide and have pure white margins.

HOW TO GROW. Veitch screw pines do best in bright indirect or curtain-filtered sunlight; if only artificial light is available, provide at least 400 foot-candles. Night temperatures of 65° to 70° and day temperatures of 75° to 85° are ideal. Let the soil become moderately dry between thorough waterings. Fertilize established plants at three- to four-month intervals, but wait four to six months before feeding newly purchased or potted plants. Veitch screw pines can go for several years without having to be repotted, but when they do become overcrowded, repot them in spring, using a mixture of 1 part loam, 1 part peat moss or leaf mold and 1 part sharp sand; to each gallon pailful of this mixture add 1½ teaspoons of 20 per cent superphosphate, 1 tablespoon of ground limestone and 2 teaspoons of 5-10-5 fertilizer. Or use a packaged general-purpose potting soil. Because of the leaves' sharp spines, wear heavy gloves and wrap newspaper around the leaves when you transfer the plant from one pot to another. Propagate at any season from the young shoots, or suckers, that spring up from the base of the plant.

PAPERSPINE CACTUS See *Opuntia*
PARADISE PALM See *Howeia*
PARLOR IVY See *Senecio*
PARLOR PALM See *Chamaedorea*
PASSION VINE, PURPLE See *Gynura*
PEACOCK PLANT See *Calathea*

PEDILANTHUS
P. tithymaloides variegatus, also called *Euphorbia tithymaloides variegatus, E. canaliculata variegatus* and *E. carinata variegatus* (variegated devil's backbone, redbird slipperflower, redbird cactus)

The common name devil's backbone is apt for this plant, since the stems of each alternate leaf bend left or right, producing a mischievous zigzag effect. The stems also contain an acrid milky sap that can cause skin irritation and is especially harmful to eyes and open cuts. The plant grows from a few inches to 3 feet tall and has 2- to 3-inch-long leaves. The "redbird" part of the other common names refers to the birdlike shape of the small red flowers that occasionally appear at the tips of the stems. But the word cactus is completely misleading: the plant is not in the cactus family and does not even have spines.

HOW TO GROW. Devil's backbones do best in bright indirect or curtain-filtered sunlight; if only artificial light is available, provide at least 400 foot-candles. Night temperatures of 50° to 70° and day temperatures of 70° to 85° are ideal. Keep the soil barely moist at all times. Fertilize established plants at two- to three-month intervals from early spring until late summer; do not fertilize them the rest of the year, and wait at least four to six months before fertilizing newly potted plants. Repot overcrowded plants in spring. For best results use a mixture of 1 part loam, 1 part peat moss or leaf mold and 1 part sharp sand; to each gallon pailful of this mixture add 1½ teaspoons of 20 per cent superphosphate, 1 tablespoon of ground limestone and 2 teaspoons of 5-10-5 fertilizer. Otherwise, use a packaged general-purpose potting soil. Propagate from stem cuttings at any season, allowing the cuttings to dry in a shady place for two days before inserting them in the rooting medium. When making the cuttings, be careful not to touch the milky sap that oozes from the stem.

PENNOCK'S ARALIA See *Polyscias*

130

PENWIPER PLANT See *Kalanchoe*

PEPEROMIA

P. caperata (wrinkled-leaved peperomia); *P. griseo-argentea,* also called *P. hederaefolia* (ivy peperomia); *P. obtusifolia* (blunt-leaved peperomia, pepper face); *P. sandersii,* also called *P. arifolia argyreia* (watermelon peperomia, watermelon begonia)

Indoor gardeners who are looking for low-growing foliage plants for coffee tables and window sills will find several excellent possibilities among peperomias. All have unusually thick leaves, grow less than 12 inches tall and send out flower stalks in spring that look like mouse tails.

The most popular of all peperomias are varieties of the wrinkled-leaved peperomia. Emerald Ripple grows 3 to 4 inches tall with a spread of about 5 inches and has leaves that range from ¾ to 1½ inches across. Little Fantasy is similar in appearance but shorter, 2½ to 3 inches tall. Tricolor grows 3 to 4 inches tall; its leaves are creamy white with a central blotch of milky green and are held by red leaf stems.

The ivy peperomia resembles the wrinkled-leaved peperomia but is taller, usually reaching a height of 6 to 8 inches, and its leaves are larger, 2 to 2½ inches across, and less deeply wrinkled. The leaves are a silvery gray, with dark olive-green "valleys"; the stems are pink. Blackie, a well-known variety, has copper-black leaves.

The blunt-leaved peperomia, an extremely easy-to-grow species if it is not overwatered, has smooth dark green roundish leaves about 2 to 3 inches long. It becomes 8 to 10 inches tall, but by then the thick leaves have begun to weigh the stems into a curve. The variegated blunt-leaved peperomia, *P. obtusifolia variegata,* has light green leaves irregularly edged with creamy white.

The watermelon peperomia grows 8 to 10 inches tall and has 2- to 4-inch leaves striped like some watermelons.

HOW TO GROW. Peperomias do best in bright indirect or curtain-filtered sunlight; if only artificial light is available, provide at least 400 foot-candles. Night temperatures of 65° to 70° and day temperatures of 75° to 85° are ideal. Be careful not to overwater the plants, especially in winter; let the soil become moderately dry between thorough waterings. Feed established plants at three- to four-month intervals with a standard house-plant fertilizer diluted to half the minimum strength recommended on the label, but wait four to six months before feeding newly purchased or potted plants. Peperomias rarely outgrow their pots, but when they do, repot in very early spring just as new growth starts. For best results use a mixture of 1 part loam, 1 part peat moss or leaf mold and 1 part sharp sand; to each gallon pailful of this mixture add 1½ teaspoons of 20 per cent superphosphate, 1 tablespoon of ground limestone and 2 teaspoons of 5-10-5 fertilizer. Otherwise, use a packaged general-purpose potting soil. Propagate at any season from leaf or stem cuttings or by dividing the crowns of old plants in very early spring.

PEPPER See *Piper*
PEPPER FACE See *Peperomia*

PHILODENDRON

P. 'Burgundy' (Burgundy philodendron); *P.* 'Florida' (Florida philodendron); *P. hastatum* (spearhead philodendron); *P. micans* (velvet-leaved philodendron); *P. miduhoi* 'Silver Sheen' (Silver Sheen philodendron); *P. oxycardium,* also called *P. cordatum* (heart-leaved philodendron); *P. panduraeforme,* also called *P. bipennifolium* (fiddle-leaved philodendron); *P. radiatum,* also called

VARIEGATED BLUNT-LEAVED PEPEROMIA
Peperomia obtusifolia variegata

WATERMELON PEPEROMIA
Peperomia sandersii

BURGUNDY PHILODENDRON
Philodendron 'Burgundy'

HEART-LEAVED PHILODENDRON
Philodendron oxycardium

SADDLE-LEAVED PHILODENDRON
Philodendron selloum

P. dubium; P. selloum (saddle-leaved philodendron); *P.* 'Weber's Self-Heading' (Weber's Self-Heading philodendron); *P. wendlandii* (Wendland's philodendron)

From the more than 200 species of philodendrons that have been discovered in Central and South America and the Caribbean islands, thousands of hybrids have been developed, providing a great range of leaf sizes and shapes as well as variations in the form of the plants themselves. (One plant called philodendron is not a philodendron at all: split-leaved philodendron is one of the common names for *Monstera deliciosa,* described on page 123.) Most philodendrons grown indoors are vines, but some types, called self-heading, send out their leaves from a heavy clump of growth at their base. In addition, many climbing philodendrons change leaf size drastically, depending on how they are grown. So long as they are allowed to trail along the ground or cascade from a hanging container, they bear moderate-sized leaves, but as soon as they are given a support upon which to climb, the leaves become gigantic, often several times as large as the ones that developed before a support was provided.

Most climbing philodendrons for indoor decoration are trained and tied to a slab of bark-covered wood. A number of excellent selections are readily available. The Burgundy philodendron is an attractive slow-growing variety with 8- to 12-inch leaves that glisten as though polished. The Florida philodendron has 4- to 8-inch shiny leaves that are divided into five widely spaced lobes; the leaf stalks are covered with a reddish fuzz, and the undersides of the leaves are brownish red. The spearhead philodendron has 8- to 12-inch dark green leaves shaped like spearheads. The velvet-leaved philodendron has 2- to 3-inch heart-shaped leaves; the tops are an iridescent bronze green and the undersides are reddish brown. The Silver Sheen philodendron has 3- to 4-inch heart-shaped silvery green leaves. The most popular member of the genus, the heart-leaved philodendron, has 2- to 4-inch heart-shaped green leaves; it can grow in plain water. The fiddle-leaved philodendron, rather slow growing but durable, has dense overlapping 5- to 8-inch leaves shaped like violins. *P. radiatum,* a handsome vigorous climber, has 4- to 10-inch deeply lobed heart-shaped leaves; young seedlings, however, have leaves with few lobes—a stage of development that confused the plant collectors who first found seedlings of the plant in the jungles of Central America. As a result the plant was called *P. dubium*—that is, doubtful philodendron. The species has since been given the botanical name *P. radiatum,* but the original name stuck and the plants are still often sold as dubium philodendrons.

Among the self-heading philodendrons, three are particularly outstanding. The saddle-leaved philodendron is a fine species for large spaces. It eventually forms a short trunk and becomes 3 to 4 feet tall with a 4- to 6-foot spread. Its handsome leaves grow 12 to 18 inches long and 8 to 12 inches wide. Weber's Self-Heading philodendron has 8- to 12-inch smooth-edged oval leaves that are very shiny and leathery. The leaf stalks and the central ribs on the undersides of the leaves are red. Wendland's philodendron has leathery 12- to 18-inch leaves arising from a central point like those of the bird's-nest fern, *Asplenium nidus (page 91).* Wendland's philodendron is unusual among philodendrons in that it occasionally blossoms indoors. Each of its flowers consists of a single 6- to 8-inch white cupped petallike bract called a spathe that is furled in the manner of a calla lily; the tiny true flowers are borne on the spikelike center, or spadix, within each spathe.

HOW TO GROW. Philodendrons do best in bright indirect or curtain-filtered sunlight; if only artificial light is available, provide at least 400 foot-candles. Night temperatures of 65° to 70° and day temperatures of 75° to 85° are ideal. Keep the soil barely moist at all times. Feed established plants every three or four months, but wait four to six months before feeding newly purchased or potted plants. Repot overcrowded plants at any season, using a mixture of 1 part loam, 1 part peat moss or leaf mold and 1 part sharp sand; to each gallon pailful of this mixture add 1½ teaspoons of 20 per cent superphosphate, 1 tablespoon of ground limestone and 2 teaspoons of 5-10-5 fertilizer. Otherwise, use a packaged general-purpose potting soil. Propagate at any season from stem cuttings, from sections of main stems or by the method known as air layering.

PHILODENDRON PERTUSUM See *Monstera*
PHLEBODIUM See *Polypodium*

PHOENIX
P. roebelenii, also called *P. loureirii* (miniature date palm, pygmy date palm)

Miniature date palms are among the most durable, as well as attractive, palms for indoor use. Even when old they rarely exceed 2 feet in height and have gracefully arching 1- to 2-foot leaves consisting of many 7- to 9-inch leaflets. The plants tend to send up young shoots, or suckers, from their base, but most gardeners remove them so that only one trunk will develop. Because the plants adapt to varying conditions, young miniature date palms are often combined with other types of plants in dish gardens.

HOW TO GROW. Miniature date palms do best in bright indirect or curtain-filtered sunlight; if only artificial light is available, provide at least 400 foot-candles. Night temperatures of 65° to 70° and day temperatures of 75° to 85° are ideal. Keep the soil wet at all times, but do not let the pots stand in water. Feed miniature date palms monthly from early spring through summer, but do not feed them during the balance of the year, and wait until the following spring before feeding newly potted plants. Repot overcrowded plants in early spring, using a mixture of 1 part loam, 1 part peat moss or leaf mold, 1 part sharp sand and ½ part well-rotted or dried cow manure; to each gallon pailful of this mixture add 2 tablespoons of bone meal. Otherwise, use a packaged highly organic potting mixture formulated for African violets. Cram the fresh soil between the old soil ball and the sides of the new pot with a stick to make it firm. Propagate at any season from seeds.

PIGGYBACK PLANT See *Tolmiea*

PILEA
P. cadierei (aluminum plant, watermelon pilea); *P. crassifolia; P. involucrata,* also called *P. spruceana* (panamiga, Pan-American friendship plant); *P. pubescens* (silver panamiga); *P. repens* (black-leaved panamiga); *P.* 'Silver Tree' (Silver Tree panamiga)

The species of *Pilea* listed here are ideally suited for window sills and tables. Most grow no more than 12 inches tall and have peculiarly puffy leaves with depressed veins that make them look quilted.

The aluminum plant grows about 10 inches tall and has 2½- to 3½-inch leaves, each with three conspicuous sunken veins; the quilted sections appear to have been brushed with aluminum paint. The dwarf aluminum plant, *P. cadierei minima,* becomes only 5 to 6 inches tall and has 1½- to 2-inch leaves on pink stems. *P. crassifolia* grows up to 10 inches tall and has shiny bright green quilted leaves generally about 2 inches long. The panamiga is an easy-to-grow 6- to 8-inch plant with 2- to 3-inch hairy

WENDLAND'S PHILODENDRON
Philodendron wendlandii

MINIATURE DATE PALM
Phoenix roebelenii

133

copper-colored leaves; the undersides are reddish but rarely turn upward enough to be visible. The silver panamiga grows 8 to 10 inches tall; its 2- to 3-inch-long scalloped leaves are bluish silver accented with three dark gray veins. The black-leaved panamiga grows 4 to 8 inches tall and has 1½-inch hairy copper-colored leaves with purplish undersides. The 8- to 12-inch Silver Tree panamiga has 2- to 3-inch bronze-green leaves with a wide silver central stripe; the bronzy parts of the leaves are dotted with silver and the undersides are covered with reddish hairs.

HOW TO GROW. *Pilea* species do best in bright indirect or curtain-filtered sunlight; if only artificial light is available, provide at least 400 foot-candles. Night temperatures of 65° to 70° and day temperatures of 75° to 85° are ideal. Keep the soil barely moist at all times. Feed established plants at two-month intervals with standard house-plant fertilizer diluted to half the minimum strength recommended on the label, but wait three or four months before feeding newly purchased or potted plants. Because old plants become straggly, it is best to start new plants—from stem cuttings or by dividing the roots—early each spring. The plants generally grow most satisfactorily in 3- to 4-inch pots, a size that allows space for a good balance between root and top growth. Use a potting soil composed of 2 parts peat moss or leaf mold, 1 part loam and 1 part sharp sand; to each gallon pailful of this mixture add 1½ teaspoons of 20 per cent superphosphate, 1 tablespoon of ground limestone and 2 teaspoons of 5-10-5 fertilizer. Otherwise, use a mixture of equal parts of a packaged general-purpose potting soil and peat moss or leaf mold.

PINE, NORFOLK ISLAND See *Araucaria*
PINE, SCREW See *Pandanus*
PINK EASTER LILY CACTUS See *Echinopsis*
PINK POLKA DOT See *Hypoestes*

PIPER

P. crocatum (saffron pepper); *P. nigrum,* also called *P. aromaticum* (black pepper); *P. ornatum* (Celebes pepper); *P. porphyrophyllum,* also called *Cissus porphyrophyllus* (porphyry-leaved pepper)

The peppers listed here include the plant that provides the common condiment; they are not related to bell or chili peppers of the genus *Capsicum.* All are vines that usually become 3 to 5 feet tall if given a stake upon which to climb. They also do well in hanging containers, with their stems cascading over the edges. Although easy to grow and handsome, they are still relatively hard to find. They do not bear fruit indoors.

Most of the species have leaves that are 4 to 6 inches long. The leaves of the saffron pepper have pink veins and purple undersides. The leaves of the black pepper are oval and look like shiny black-green leather. The Celebes pepper has 2½- to 5-inch heart-shaped deep green leaves with an intricate lacy pattern of silvery pink veins; they have pale green undersides and red stems. The porphyry-leaved pepper has broad heart-shaped bronze-green leaves with yellow veins bordered by clusters of pink spots; the leaves have dull purple undersides and red stems that are accented with stiff white hairs.

HOW TO GROW. Peppers do best in curtain-filtered or bright indirect sunlight; if only artificial light is available, provide at least 400 foot-candles. Night temperatures of 65° to 70° and day temperatures of 75° to 85° are ideal. Keep the soil barely moist at all times. Fertilize established plants at two-month intervals, but wait three to four months before fertilizing newly purchased or newly potted plants. Repot overcrowded plants in early spring, using a

ALUMINUM PLANT
Pilea cadierei

PANAMIGA
Pilea involucrata

mixture of 1 part loam, 1 part peat moss or leaf mold and 1 part sharp sand; to each gallon pailful of this mixture add 1½ teaspoons of 20 per cent superphosphate, 1 tablespoon of ground limestone and 2 teaspoons of 5-10-5 fertilizer. Otherwise, use a packaged general-purpose potting soil. Propagate at any season from stem cuttings.

PITTOSPORUM
P. tobira (Japanese pittosporum)

Japanese pittosporums are extremely accommodating house plants, surviving for years with relatively little care. They tolerate chills and are especially valuable in drafty locations where many other plants would not do well. They grow 3 or more feet tall with an equal spread unless pruned back and have 2- to 4-inch leaves. In spring, it is not uncommon for them to bear tiny cream-colored flowers with an orange-blossom fragrance. The variegated Japanese pittosporum, *P. tobira variegata,* has milky green leaves irregularly outlined in creamy white.

HOW TO GROW. Pittosporums do best where they get four or more hours of direct sunlight, or where artificial and natural light average 800 foot-candles over 12 hours a day, but they will grow fairly well in bright indirect light, such as that reflected from light walls. Night temperatures of 40° to 55° and day temperatures of 65° to 80° are ideal. Let the soil become moderately dry between thorough waterings. Feed established plants twice a year, in very early spring and early summer, but wait at least four to six months before feeding newly purchased or potted plants. A plant can remain in the same pot for a long time, but when it becomes overcrowded, repot in very early spring, using a mixture of 1 part loam, 1 part peat moss or leaf mold and 1 part sharp sand; to each gallon pailful of this mixture add 1½ teaspoons of 20 per cent superphosphate, 1 tablespoon of ground limestone and 2 teaspoons of 5-10-5 fertilizer. Otherwise, use a packaged general-purpose potting soil. If plants become too large, prune them in very early spring just before new growth starts. Propagate from stem cuttings in late summer or by the method known as air layering at any season.

PLAID CACTUS See *Gymnocalycium*

PLATYCERIUM
P. bifurcatum (staghorn fern)

The staghorn fern is an air-growing, or epiphytic, plant—that is, it grows naturally on the rough bark of a tree rather than in soil, sending its roots into the tree bark until they make a tight bond. As a house plant, it is generally grown in a wall container or hanging basket on moisture-retaining organic matter such as a bark-covered slab of wood, a piece of cork bark, a section of the trunk of a tree fern or a clump of osmunda-fern root—all materials generally available at garden-supply centers—or on a mixture of equal parts of coarse peat moss and long-fibered sphagnum moss. The plant has two distinct kinds of gray-green fronds. The most conspicuous are antler-shaped and hang down from the support material to a length of 2 or more feet. At the base of the plant are overlapping kidney-shaped fronds, which are generally used to tie the plant to its support. Growing from between these basal fronds are little plants called "pups."

HOW TO GROW. Staghorn ferns do best in bright indirect or curtain-filtered sunlight; if only artificial light is available, provide at least 400 foot-candles. Night temperatures of 50° to 55° and day temperatures of 68° to 72° are ideal. Keep the organic material on which the plant grows moist at all times by soaking the material thoroughly in a sink or pail about once a week; at the same time, wash the foliage

SAFFRON PEPPER
Piper crocatum

JAPANESE PITTOSPORUM
Pittosporum tobira

135

STAGHORN FERN
Platycerium bifurcatum

WHITE-EDGED SWEDISH IVY
Plectranthus coleoides marginatus

SONG OF INDIA PLEOMELE
Pleomele reflexa 'Song of India'

with a spray of tepid water. Do not fertilize. Propagate at any season either from the small plants that grow among the basal fronds or from spores, the dustlike reproductive particles of ferns.

PLECTRANTHUS
P. australis (Swedish ivy), *P. coleoides marginatus* (white-edged Swedish ivy), *P. oertendahlii* (candle plant), *P. purpuratus* (purple-leaved Swedish ivy). (All also called Swedish ivy)

Plectranthus species come from Africa and Australia but are called Swedish ivy because they were first grown as house plants in Sweden. Most are fast-growing trailing soft-stemmed plants with roundish thick-textured leaves shallowly scalloped along the edges. All are easy to grow, even in plain water, and the trailing ones are especially attractive in hanging containers.

Swedish ivy has 1½- to 2-foot-long trailing stems that bear waxy dark green leaves about 1 inch across. The white-edged Swedish ivy, a bushy plant 8 to 12 inches tall, has 2- to 3-inch hairy green leaves with creamy white edges. The candle plant, one of the most attractive trailing types with stems up to 2 feet long, has 1-inch bronze-green leaves accented by a network of bright silvery veins; the leaf stalks and undersides of old leaves are purplish. The variegated candle plant, *P. oertendahlii variegatus,* has dark green foliage with broad, irregular white blotches. The purple-leaved Swedish ivy has trailing stems up to 2 feet long; its ¾-inch purplish green leaves are covered with tiny velvety hairs and have dull purple undersides.

HOW TO GROW. Swedish ivies do best in bright indirect or curtain-filtered sunlight; if only artificial light is available, provide at least 400 foot-candles. Night temperatures of 55° to 65° and day temperatures of 65° to 75° are ideal. Keep the soil barely moist at all times. Feed established plants at two-month intervals with a standard house-plant fertilizer diluted to half the minimum strength recommended on the label, but wait three to four months before feeding newly purchased or potted plants. Repot overcrowded plants at any season, using a mixture of 1 part loam, 1 part peat moss or leaf mold and 1 part sharp sand; to each gallon pailful of this mixture add 1½ teaspoons of 20 per cent superphosphate, 1 tablespoon of ground limestone and 2 teaspoons of 5-10-5 fertilizer. Otherwise, use a packaged general-purpose potting soil. Pinch off long stems at any season to encourage dense branching; these tips can then be rooted to make new plants.

PLEOMELE
P. angustifolia honoriae (narrow-leaved pleomele), *P. reflexa* 'Song of India' (Song of India pleomele)

The pleomeles listed here are usually sold at less than 2 feet but eventually grow to 4 feet or more. The bases of their 6- to 10-inch closely set leaves clasp around supple slender stems. Under the weight of the leaves, the stems gradually bend to a nearly horizontal position. The narrow-leaved pleomele has green leathery leaves with cream-yellow edges. Song of India has broader cream-yellow edges and needs very high humidity.

HOW TO GROW. Pleomeles do best in bright indirect or curtain-filtered sunlight; if only artificial light is available, provide at least 400 foot-candles. Night temperatures of 65° to 70° and day temperatures of 75° to 85° are ideal. Song of India should be placed on a tray that has been filled with pebbles and water to increase the humidity around the plant to 50 per cent or more. Keep the soil barely moist at all times for both species. Feed established plants at three- to four-month intervals, but wait four to six months before feeding newly purchased or potted plants. Repot overcrowded plants in early spring, using a mixture of 1 part loam, 1 part peat moss or leaf mold and 1 part sharp sand; to each gallon pailful of this mixture add 1½ teaspoons of 20 per cent superphosphate, 1 tablespoon of ground limestone and 2 teaspoons of 5-10-5 fertilizer. Otherwise, use a packaged general-purpose potting soil. Propagate at any season from stem cuttings.

PLOVER EGGS See *Adromischus*
PLUSH PLANT See *Echeveria*

PODOCARPUS
P. macrophyllus maki (Chinese or shrubby podocarpus)
The Chinese podocarpus lives indefinitely indoors, even tolerating cold drafts except when actively growing. It grows 6 feet or more but may be pruned to any size. Its dense soft-textured dark green needles, 1½ to 3 inches long and ¼ to ½ inch wide, are bright green when young.

HOW TO GROW. Chinese podocarpuses do best where they get four or more hours a day of direct sunlight, or where artificial and natural light average 800 foot-candles over 12 hours a day, but will grow fairly well in bright indirect light, such as that reflected from light walls. Night temperatures of 40° to 55° and day temperatures of 65° to 85° are ideal. Keep the soil barely moist. Feed established plants twice a year, in early spring and in early summer; wait at least four to six months before feeding newly purchased or potted plants. Chinese podocarpuses can go for years without being repotted, but when the roots become overcrowded, repot in early spring before new growth starts, using a mixture of 1 part loam, 1 part peat moss or leaf mold and 1 part sharp sand; to each gallon pailful of this mixture add 1½ teaspoons of 20 per cent superphosphate, 1 tablespoon of ground limestone and 2 teaspoons of 5-10-5 fertilizer. Or else use a packaged general-purpose potting soil. Prune to the desired size before new growth starts in spring; cut ends are quickly covered by new growth. Propagate from stem cuttings in fall.

POLYPODIUM
P. aureum, also called *Phlebodium aureum* (rabbit's-foot fern, golden polypody fern)
The rabbit's-foot fern, an easy-to-grow plant, has durable leathery fronds, 2 or more feet long, composed of many wavy-edged leaflets. Manda's rabbit's-foot fern, *P. aureum mandaianum,* has bluish-green fronds with twisted and toothed edges. Both grow from thick, hairy brown stems, or rhizomes, that creep along the top of the soil.

HOW TO GROW. Rabbit's-foot ferns do best in bright indirect or curtain-filtered sunlight; if only artificial light is available, provide at least 400 foot-candles. Night temperatures of 50° to 55° and day temperatures of 68° to 72° are ideal. Keep the growing medium barely moist. Do not feed newly purchased or potted plants for six months; established plants should be fed twice a year with standard house-plant fertilizer diluted to half the minimum strength recommended on the label. Because the rhizomes creep along the top of the soil and do not penetrate deeply, the plants do not need deep pots. Do not bury the rhizomes; instead, pin them to the soil with pieces of bent wire until they form new roots. For best results when repotting, use a mixture of 1 part loam, 1 part peat moss or leaf mold, 1 part finely ground fir bark and 1 part sharp sand; to each gallon pailful of this mixture add 2 tablespoons of bone meal. Otherwise, use a mixture composed of equal parts of a packaged general-purpose potting soil and either peat moss or leaf mold. Rabbit's-foot ferns will also grow on pieces

CHINESE PODOCARPUS
Podocarpus macrophyllus maki

RABBIT'S-FOOT FERN
Polypodium aureum

BALFOUR ARALIA
Polyscias balfouriana marginata

TSUSSIMA HOLLY FERN
Polystichum tsus-simense

of bark or osmunda-fern fiber. Propagate at any season by dividing the rhizomes. New plants can also be started from spores, the dustlike reproductive particles of ferns.

POLYSCIAS

P. balfouriana, also called *Aralia balfouriana* and *Panax balfourii* (Balfour aralia); *P. guilfoylei victoriae* (Victoria aralia)

Aralias grow 1½ to 3 feet tall on one or more erect stems; they prefer high humidity. The Balfour aralia bears shiny dark green leaves, each with three roundish leaflets 2 to 4 inches across. Two fine varieties are more widely grown than the basic species: *P. balfouriana marginata,* with white-edged leaves, and Pennock's aralia, *P. balfouriana pennockii,* with slightly cupped, milky green leaves edged in dark green. The Victoria aralia has white-edged dark green leaves 12 to 16 inches or more long, with three to seven sawtoothed leaflets; the end leaflet may be 6 inches long, the side leaflets 2 to 3 inches long.

HOW TO GROW. Balfour aralias do best where they get four or more hours a day of direct sunlight, but will grow fairly well in bright indirect light, such as that reflected from light walls; Victoria aralias do best in bright indirect light or curtain-filtered sunlight. Both do fairly well where artificial and natural light average 800 foot-candles over 12 hours a day. Night temperatures of 65° to 70° and day temperatures of 75° to 85° are ideal. Increase the humidity to 50 per cent or more by placing the plants on a tray filled with pebbles and water. Keep the soil barely moist. Feed established plants every three to four months; wait four to six months before feeding newly purchased or potted plants. Repot overcrowded plants in early spring, using a mixture of 1 part loam, 1 part peat moss or leaf mold and 1 part sharp sand; to each gallon pailful of this mixture add 1½ teaspoons of 20 per cent superphosphate, 1 tablespoon of ground limestone and 2 teaspoons of 5-10-5 fertilizer. Otherwise, use a packaged general-purpose potting soil. Propagate at any season from stem cuttings.

POLYSTICHUM

P. setiferum, also called *P. angulare* (soft-shield fern); *P. proliferum, P. tsus-simense,* also called *Aspidium tsus-simense* (Tsussima holly fern)

These ferns will tolerate cold drafts except when they are actively growing. The 12- to 18-inch soft-shield fern has dark green arching fronds, which are finely divided; *P. proliferum* forms tiny replicas of itself on its fronds. The Tsussima holly fern grows up to 12 inches tall and is an excellent choice for a terrarium.

HOW TO GROW. Soft-shield ferns and Tsussima holly ferns do best in the shadowless light of a north window; if only artificial light is available, provide a minimum of 150 foot-candles. Temperatures of 50° to 55° at night and day temperatures of 68° to 72° are ideal. Keep the soil barely moist. Feed every two weeks from early spring until midsummer with any standard house-plant fertilizer diluted to one half the minimum strength recommended on the label; do not feed the rest of the year, and do not feed newly potted plants until the next spring. Repot overcrowded plants in early spring, using a mixture of 1 part loam, 1 part peat moss or leaf mold and 1 part sharp sand. Otherwise, use a packaged general-purpose potting soil. Do not add fertilizer. Propagate at any season from the plantlets on the fronds or from spores, the dustlike reproductive particles of ferns, or by dividing the roots in early spring.

PONY TAIL See *Beaucarnea*
POTHOS See *Scindapsus*

POWDER PUFF CACTUS See *Mammillaria*
PRAYER PLANT See *Maranta*
PRETTY PEBBLES See *Adromischus*
PRIVET See *Ligustrum*

PTERIS
P. cretica (Cretan brake fern); *P. ensiformis,* also called
P. chinensis (sword brake fern); *P. multifida,* also called
P. serrulata (spider brake fern); *P. tremula* (trembling or
Australian brake fern). (All also called table fern)

Table ferns are handsome easy-to-grow plants bearing
fronds generally 6 to 12 inches long. Three fine varieties
of the Cretan brake fern are *P. cretica albo-lineata,* an attractive low-growing type with a cream-white stripe down
the center of each of its dark green leaflets; *P. cretica childs-
sii,* whose light green leaflets are frilled along the edges;
and *P. cretica wilsonii,* a low-growing bright green type
with finely divided fan-shaped frond tips. The sword brake
fern is noted for its dwarf variety *P. ensiformis victoriae,*
the Victoria fern, whose silvery white fronds are edged in
dark green. The crested spider brake fern, *P. multifida cristata,* the most unusual of the spider brake ferns, has dense
dark green fronds with long slender leaflets that end in
frilly crestlike clusters. The trembling brake fern, with finely divided light green fronds 3 feet long and 2 feet wide,
makes a fine plant to set on the floor, but when only a foot
tall is superb as a centerpiece.

HOW TO GROW. Table ferns do best in the shadowless
light of a north window; if only artificial light is available,
provide at least 150 foot-candles. Night temperatures of
50° to 55° and day temperatures of 68° to 72° are ideal.
Keep the soil barely moist. Newly purchased or newly potted plants should not be fertilized for six months; feed established plants every six months with any standard house-
plant fertilizer diluted to one half the strength recommended on the label. Repot overgrown plants at any season,
using a mixture of 1 part loam, 1 part peat moss or leaf
mold, 1 part finely ground fir bark and 1 part sharp sand;
to each gallon pailful of this mixture add 2 tablespoons of
bone meal. Otherwise, use a mixture composed of equal
parts of a packaged general-purpose potting soil and peat
moss or leaf mold. Propagate at any season from spores,
the dustlike reproductive particles of ferns, or by dividing
the base, or crown, of the plant from which the stems rise.

PURPLE HEART See *Setcreasea*
PURPLE PASSION VINE See *Gynura*
PUSSY EARS See *Kalanchoe*
PYGMY PAPYRUS See *Cyperus*

Q
QUEENSLAND UMBRELLA TREE See *Brassaia*

R
RABBIT TRACKS See *Maranta*
RABBIT'S-FOOT FERN See *Polypodium*
RAPHIDOPHORA See *Scindapsus*
RATTAIL CACTUS See *Aporocactus*
REDBIRD CACTUS See *Pedilanthus*
REDBIRD SLIPPERFLOWER See *Pedilanthus*

RHAPIS
R. excelsa, also called *R. aspera* and *R. flabelliformis* (large
lady palm, broad-leaved lady palm); *R. humilis* (slender
lady palm)

Lady palms bear clusters of 6- to 12-inch-wide fan-
shaped shiny leaves at various levels on several slender 5-
foot bamboolike main stems covered with hairy brown

CHILD'S CRETAN BRAKE FERN
Pteris cretica childsii

VICTORIA FERN
Pteris ensiformis victoriae

CRESTED SPIDER BRAKE FERN
Pteris multifida cristata

LARGE LADY PALM
Rhapis excelsa

fiber. The leaves of the large lady palm have 3 to 10 leathery segments. The more graceful slender lady palm has slightly thinner stems and deeper green leaves with 9 to 20 narrow segments.

HOW TO GROW. Lady palms do best in bright indirect or curtain-filtered sunlight; if only artificial light is available, provide at least 400 foot-candles. Night temperatures of 50° to 55° and day temperatures of 68° to 72° are ideal. Keep the soil wet, but do not let pots stand in water. Feed lady palms monthly from early spring through summer; do not feed the rest of the year, and wait until the next spring before feeding newly potted plants. Repot overcrowded plants in early spring, using a mixture of 1 part loam, 1 part peat moss or leaf mold, 1 part sharp sand and ½ part well-rotted or dried cow manure; to each gallon pailful of this mixture add 2 tablespoons of bone meal. Or use a packaged highly organic potting mixture formulated for African violets. Propagate at any season from the young shoots, or suckers, that spring up near the main stem or from seeds.

RHOEO
R. spathacea, also called *R. discolor* and *Tradescantia discolor* (Moses-in-the-cradle, Moses-in-the-bulrushes, man-in-a-boat, boat-lily, oyster plant)

Moses-in-the-cradle derives its name from its tiny white flowers, which lie deep within boat-shaped petallike leaves, or bracts, like a baby in a cradle. The showy parts of the plant, however, are the 8- to 15-inch stiff swordlike leaves, which have purple-and-green topsides and purple undersides. In the variety *R. spathacea vittata,* the variegated Moses-in-the-cradle, the leaves are striped with yellow.

HOW TO GROW. Moses-in-the-cradle does best in bright indirect or curtain-filtered sunlight; if only artificial light is available, provide at least 400 foot-candles. Night temperatures of 50° to 55° and day temperatures of 68° to 72° are ideal. Keep the soil barely moist. Feed established plants every three or four months, but wait four to six months before feeding newly purchased or potted plants. Repotting is not generally needed. Propagate old and straggly plants at any season by dividing the roots. New plants can also be started from seeds or from the young shoots, or suckers, that spring up from the base of the plant. For best results pot in a mixture of 1 part loam, 1 part peat moss or leaf mold and 1 part sharp sand; to each gallon pailful of this mixture add 1½ teaspoons of 20 per cent superphosphate, 1 tablespoon of ground limestone and 2 teaspoons of 5-10-5 fertilizer. Otherwise, use a packaged general-purpose potting soil.

RIBBON PLANT See *Chlorophytum*
RICE-PAPER PLANT See *Tetrapanax*
ROSARY VINE See *Ceropegia*
RUBBER PLANT, CHINESE See *Crassula*
RUBBER TREE See *Ficus*

S
SAGO PALM See *Cycas*

SANSEVIERIA
S. trifasciata, also called *S. zebrina* (sansevieria, bowstring hemp, mother-in-law tongue, snake plant)

Sansevierias, with thick, almost succulentlike leaves, are among the toughest house plants in the world, surviving dim light and little moisture. The basic species has upright sword-shaped leaves, 18 to 30 inches tall and 2 to 3 inches wide, that rise in rosettes from thick underground stems, or rhizomes. The leaves have snakelike, horizontally zigzagging grayish white or pale green stripes. The variety

Laurentii has leaves with broad yellow edges. Hahnii, colored like the basic species, has 4-inch-tall leaves, with a 6- to 8-inch spread like the foliage on top of a pineapple. Two similar varieties are Golden Hahnii, grayish green leaves with broad lengthwise yellow stripes and crosswise bands of light gray; and Silver Hahnii, silvery green leaves with scattered dark green horizontal bands.

HOW TO GROW. Sansevierias grow well in a wide range of light conditions, varying from full sun to the shadowless light of a north window. If only artificial light is available, provide at least 150 foot-candles. Night temperatures of 65° to 70° and day temperatures of 75° to 85° are ideal. From early spring until late fall, let the soil become moderately dry between thorough waterings; in winter, water just enough to keep the leaves from shriveling. Feed established plants every three or four months from early spring until late fall; do not feed the rest of the year, and wait at least four or six months before feeding newly potted plants. Sansevierias can often go for three to five years without being repotted. When plants finally become overcrowded, repot at any season, using a mixture of 1 part loam, 1 part peat moss or leaf mold and 1 part sharp sand; to each gallon pailful of this mixture add 1½ teaspoons of 20 per cent superphosphate, 1 tablespoon of ground limestone and 2 teaspoons of 5-10-5 fertilizer. Otherwise, use a packaged general-purpose potting soil. Propagate at any season by dividing the rhizomes. All except Laurentii can also be propagated at any season from leaf cuttings rooted in sand; each cutting will send out a new rhizome and a cluster of foliage. Laurentii is the exception to this propagation method because if leaf cuttings are made of it, the leaves of the resulting plants lose their distinctive yellow stripes, reverting to the species form.

SCHEFFLERA See *Brassaia*
SCHISMATOGLOTTIS See *Aglaonema*

SCINDAPSUS

S. aureus, also called *Epipremnum aureum, Pothos aureus* and *Raphidophora aurea* (devil's ivy and golden pothos); *S. pictus argyraeus,* also called *Pothos argyraeus* (silver pothos)

Gardeners who have visited subtropical gardens have undoubtedly noticed vines with waxy green-and-yellow leaves sometimes as much as 2 feet across clinging to the trunks of tall trees. These vines are the adult version of the popular house plant called devil's ivy. As an indoor plant, with its climbing tendencies restricted and its roots confined, devil's ivy never reaches maturity, regardless of its age. Instead, it comes in two forms: the so-called juvenile type, with leaves only 2 to 4 inches long, and the intermediate type, with 6- to 10-inch leaves. Both forms are extremely versatile. They grow well in simple flowerpots on a table, the vines eventually arching over and crawling along the table's surface. The plants are also attractive in hanging containers, with their stems cascading over the edges. And they make handsome climbers if given a support—usually an upright slab of bark-covered wood or a section of the trunk of a tree fern. They also grow remarkably well in plain water. The stems grow indefinitely but can be pinched back to any desired size. Two of the best varieties are Marble Queen, whose green leaves are extensively marked with white as they first unfold, becoming increasingly green as they age; and Tricolor, with medium green leaves blotched with cream, yellow and pale green.

Although silver pothos belongs to the same genus as devil's ivy, it looks considerably different. It has 2- to 3-inch heart-shaped leaves with irregularly shaped silver blotches

VARIEGATED MOSES-IN-THE-CRADLE
Rhoeo spathacea vittata

SANSEVIERIA
Sansevieria trifasciata

MARBLE QUEEN DEVIL'S IVY
Scindapsus aureus 'Marble Queen'

BURRO'S TAIL
Sedum morganianum

and a silver pencil-line around the edge, and it is not as rampant a vine. It is rarely grown as a climber, but it makes a stunning hanging plant or pot plant for a table. It, too, grows to any length but can be pinched back.

HOW TO GROW. Devil's ivy and silver pothos do best in bright indirect or curtain-filtered sunlight; if only artificial light is available, provide at least 400 foot-candles. At lower light levels the leaves tend to lose their colorful markings and revert to solid green. Night temperatures of 65° to 70° and day temperatures of 75° to 85° are ideal. The soil for devil's ivy should be allowed to become moderately dry between thorough waterings; the soil for silver pothos should be barely moist at all times. Feed established plants at three- to four-month intervals, but wait four to six months before feeding newly purchased or potted plants. Propagate at any season from stem cuttings.

SCREW PINE See *Pandanus*
SEA SHELLS See *Adromischus*

SEDUM
S. morganianum (burro's or donkey's tail)

The burro's tail is a fascinating plant: its strange 1-inch-long tear-shaped leaves overlap so closely on pendant stems they seem to form 1- to 1½-inch-thick braids as much as 1½ feet long. The green succulent leaves are covered with a powdery blue dust, called bloom, like that found on blueberries and plums. The plants should be placed where they will be undisturbed because the leaves are attached flimsily and fall easily.

HOW TO GROW. Burro's tails do best where they get four or more hours a day of direct sunlight, or where artificial and natural light average 1,000 foot-candles over 12 hours a day, but they will grow fairly well in bright indirect light, such as that reflected from light walls. Night temperatures of 50° to 55° and day temperatures of 68° to 72° are ideal. Let the soil become moderately dry between thorough waterings from spring through fall; in winter, water only enough to keep the leaves from shriveling. Feed established plants three times a year, in very early spring, late spring and late summer; do not feed them the rest of the year and wait four to six months before feeding newly potted plants. Burro's tails rarely need repotting. Because the leaves are brittle, feed and water old, overcrowded plants more often than usual rather than repot them. If repotting is necessary, use a mixture consisting of 1 part loam, 1 part leaf mold, 1 part sharp sand and ½ part crushed charcoal, or else use a mixture of equal parts of a packaged general-purpose potting soil and sharp sand; to each gallon pailful of whichever of these mixtures you use, add 1 tablespoon of ground limestone and 1 tablespoon of bone meal. Propagate at any season by inserting the bottom of an entire leaf into sand.

SEERSUCKER PLANT See *Geogenanthus*

SENECIO
S. mikanioides (parlor ivy, German ivy)

Parlor ivy is an exceedingly easy-to-grow plant—it even grows in plain water—with 2- to 4-inch multilobed leaves resembling those of English ivy. It is generally pruned to grow as a compact, thickly foliaged plant for pots or hanging baskets; allowed to twine around a vertical support, it tends to lose its lower leaves.

HOW TO GROW. Parlor ivies do best in bright indirect or curtain-filtered sunlight; if only artificial light is available, provide at least 400 foot-candles. Night temperatures of 50° to 55° and day temperatures of 68° to 72° are ideal.

Keep the soil barely moist. Feed established plants every two months with standard house-plant fertilizer diluted to half the strength recommended on the label; wait three to four months before feeding newly purchased or potted plants. Repot overcrowded plants at any season, using a mixture of 1 part loam, 1 part peat moss or leaf mold and 1 part sharp sand; to each gallon pailful of this mixture add 1½ teaspoons of 20 per cent superphosphate, 1 tablespoon of ground limestone and 2 teaspoons of 5-10-5 fertilizer. Or use a packaged general-purpose potting soil. For bushy growth pinch off the tips of overlong stems at any season. Propagate from these tips or from tips of old plants about to be discarded.

SENTRY PALM See *Howeia*

SETCREASEA

S. purpurea (purple heart)

Purple hearts derive their name from the color of their leaves. The purple tones on the top surfaces are highlighted by barely visible, extremely fine hairs that glisten in the sun. The 5- to 7-inch leaves are borne on slender 6- to 8-inch stems. Purple hearts are effective as ordinary pot plants but are even more showy in hanging containers where their stems can dip gracefully over the edges.

HOW TO GROW. Purple hearts do best where they get four or more hours a day of direct sunlight, but will grow fairly well in bright indirect light, such as that reflected from light walls; if only artificial light is available, provide at least 800 foot-candles. Night temperatures of 60° to 65° and day temperatures of 70° to 75° are ideal. Let the soil become moderately dry between thorough waterings. Feed established plants every two months; wait three to four months before feeding newly purchased or potted plants. Repot overcrowded plants at any season, using a mixture of 1 part loam, 1 part peat moss or leaf mold and 1 part sharp sand; to each gallon pailful of this mixture add 1½ teaspoons of 20 per cent superphosphate, 1 tablespoon of ground limestone and 2 teaspoons of 5-10-5 fertilizer. Or use a packaged general-purpose potting soil. Propagate at any season from stem cuttings.

SETCREASEA STRIATA See *Callisia*
SILK OAK See *Grevillea*
SILVER BRACT See *Pachyphytum*
SILVER DOLLAR PLANT See *Crassula*
SNAKE PLANT See *Sansevieria*
SNOWBALL, MEXICAN See *Echeveria*
SNOWBALL PINCUSHION See *Mammillaria*
SPIDER PLANT See *Chlorophytum*
SPIRAL FLAG See *Costus*
SPLEENWORT See *Asplenium*
SPLIT-LEAVED PHILODENDRON See *Monstera*
SQUIRREL'S-FOOT FERN See *Davallia*
STAGHORN FERN See *Platycerium*
STEPLADDER PLANT See *Costus*
SUGARED ALMONDS See *Pachyphytum*
SUN CUP See *Notocactus*
SWEDISH IVY See *Plectranthus*
SWEET BAY See *Laurus*
SWEET FLAG, JAPANESE See *Acorus*
SWISS CHEESE PLANT See *Monstera*
SWORD FERN See *Nephrolepis*

SYNGONIUM

S. albolineatum, also called *S. podophyllum albolineatum* and *Nephthytis triphylla* (white-veined arrowhead vine, variegated nephthytis)

PARLOR IVY
Senecio mikanioides

PURPLE HEART
Setcreasea purpurea

143

The white-veined arrowhead vine, one of the most attractive and undemanding foliage plants, is also one of the strangest because its leaves change dramatically as it ages. Young plants have simple 3-inch-long arrowhead-shaped dark green leaves with silvery white markings along the major veins. As the plants mature, the leaves become increasingly complex. For a while they consist of three leaflets—a large central one with a pair of smaller ones at its base—but eventually leaves with up to 11 leaflets appear in the shape of an open fan 9 to 11 inches across. Many plants carry all stages simultaneously. As the leaves develop, they gradually become entirely green. However, if the plant is kept small by pruning and not allowed to climb, the leaves retain their silvery markings and either remain arrowhead-shaped or develop only up to five leaflets. A number of varieties have leaves whose colors and markings differ from those of the basic species. Green Gold has leaves flushed with yellow rather than silver, and Imperial White has greenish white leaves with dark green edges; both remain arrowhead-shaped. All grow well in pots and hanging baskets or against bark-covered slabs of wood or sections of the trunk of a tree fern.

HOW TO GROW. Arrowhead vines do best in bright indirect or curtain-filtered sunlight; if only artificial light is available, provide at least 400 foot-candles. Night temperatures of 65° to 70° and day temperatures of 75° to 85° are ideal. Keep the soil barely moist. Feed established plants every two months with standard house-plant fertilizer diluted to half the minimum strength recommended on the label; wait three or four months before feeding newly purchased or potted plants. Repot overcrowded plants at any season, using a mixture of 1 part loam, 1 part peat moss or leaf mold and 1 part sharp sand; to each gallon pailful of this mixture add 1½ teaspoons of 20 per cent superphosphate, 1 tablespoon of ground limestone and 2 teaspoons of 5-10-5 fertilizer. Or use a packaged general-purpose potting soil. Pinch off long stems at any season to increase branching and foliage markings. Propagate at any season from stem cuttings.

T

TABLE FERN See *Pteris*

TETRAPANAX

T. papyriferus, also called *Aralia papyrifera* and *Fatsia papyrifera* (rice-paper plant)

The rice-paper plant—so named because the white tissue, or pith, in its stems is used to make rice paper—is a 3- to 5-foot plant with fan-shaped green leaves 12 or more inches across. The undersides of the leaves are covered with a white feltlike substance, as are the young stems. The plant sometimes forms a multistemmed clump.

HOW TO GROW. The rice-paper plant does best where it gets four or more hours a day of direct sunlight, or where artificial and natural light average 800 foot-candles over 12 hours a day, but it will grow fairly well in bright indirect light, such as that reflected from light walls. Night temperatures of 50° to 55° and day temperatures of 68° to 72° are ideal. Keep the soil barely moist at all times. Fertilize established plants twice a year, in early spring and early summer; do not feed the rest of the year, and wait until the following spring before fertilizing newly potted plants. Repot overgrown plants in early spring, using a mixture of 1 part loam, 1 part peat moss or leaf mold and 1 part sharp sand; to each gallon pailful of this mixture add 1½ teaspoons of 20 per cent superphosphate, 1 tablespoon of ground limestone and 2 teaspoons of 5-10-5 fertilizer. Otherwise, use a packaged general-purpose pot-

WHITE-VEINED ARROWHEAD VINE
Syngonium albolineatum

ting soil. Propagate at any season from seeds or from the young shoots, or suckers, at the base of the plant.

THATCHLEAF PALM See *Howeia*
TI See *Cordyline*
TIARELLA See *Tolmiea*

TOLMIEA
T. menziesii, also called *Tiarella menziesii* (piggyback plant, mother-of-thousands)

The piggyback plant, 6 to 8 inches tall and 10 to 15 inches wide, has long-stemmed hairy leaves that produce at their base a miniature version of the plant itself.

HOW TO GROW. Piggyback plants do best in bright indirect or curtain-filtered sunlight; if only artificial light is available, provide at least 400 foot-candles. Night temperatures of 40° to 55° and day temperatures of 55° to 70° are ideal. Keep the soil moist. Feed established plants every two months; wait three or four months before feeding newly purchased or potted plants. Repot at any season, using a mixture of 1 part loam, 1 part peat moss or leaf mold and 1 part sharp sand; to each gallon pailful of this mixture add 1½ teaspoons of 20 per cent superphosphate, 1 tablespoon of ground limestone and 2 teaspoons of 5-10-5 fertilizer. Or use a packaged general-purpose potting soil. Propagate at any season from leaves on which a plantlet has formed; insert about 2 inches of the leaf stem into sand, with the base of the leaf resting on the sand.

TRADESCANTIA
T. albiflora albo-vittata (giant white inch plant), *T. blossfeldiana variegata* (Blossfeld's variegated inch plant), *T. fluminensis variegata* (variegated wandering Jew), *T. sillamontana* (white velvet wandering Jew)

Inch plants and wandering Jews are easy-to-grow creeping plants—called inch plants because they inch along the ground, and wandering Jews because their cuttings have been passed along, like wanderers, from gardener to gardener. Natives of Brazil, they are closely related to the Mexican *Zebrina pendula*—also known as wandering Jew *(page 146)*—differing only in minor botanical details. The choices listed here have 1- to 3-inch leaves and are fine for hanging baskets because their stems cascade gracefully. The variegated wandering Jew grows in plain water.

The giant white inch plant has narrow 2-inch-long dark green leaves with lengthwise white stripes and white edges. Blossfeld's variegated inch plant has 1½-inch-long leaves with yellow and white stripes. Their central ribs and undersides are purple. The variegated wandering Jew has 1-inch-long green leaves with cream or white stripes of varying widths; some leaves are nearly all green, others almost entirely white or cream. The white velvet wandering Jew has leaves whose deep green tops are covered with a dense woolly white fluff and whose undersides and stems are purplish green. As the plant matures, larger leaves develop, eventually becoming 3 inches long and 1 inch wide.

HOW TO GROW. Inch plants and wandering Jews do best in bright indirect or curtain-filtered sunlight; if only artificial light is available, provide at least 400 foot-candles. In less light the plants survive, but the leaves of variegated types turn almost all green. Night temperatures of 50° to 55° and day temperatures of 68° to 72° are ideal. Let the soil become moderately dry between thorough waterings. Feed established plants every two months with standard house-plant fertilizer diluted to half the minimum strength recommended on the label; wait three or four months before feeding newly purchased or potted plants. If the variegated wandering Jew is grown in plain water,

RICE-PAPER PLANT
Tetrapanax papyriferus

PIGGYBACK PLANT
Tolmiea menziesii

145

add a few drops of liquid fertilizer every month or so. Repot overcrowded plants at any season, using a mixture of 1 part loam, 1 part peat moss or leaf mold and 1 part sharp sand; to each gallon pailful of this mixture add 1½ teaspoons of 20 per cent superphosphate, 1 tablespoon of ground limestone and 2 teaspoons of 5-10-5 fertilizer. Or use a packaged general-purpose potting soil. Propagate at any season from stem cuttings.

TRADESCANTIA DISCOLOR See *Rhoeo*
TRADESCANTIA TRICOLOR See *Zebrina*
TRADESCANTIA ZEBRINA See *Zebrina*
TREE FERN See *Cyathea*
TREE FERN, HAWAIIAN See *Cibotium*
TREE FERN, MEXICAN See *Cibotium*
TREE FERN, WEST INDIAN See *Cyathea*
TREE IVY See *Fatshedera*
TREEBINE, BEGONIA See *Cissus*
TSUSSIMA HOLLY FERN See *Polystichum*

U

UMBRELLA PLANT See *Cyperus*
UMBRELLA TREE See *Brassaia*

V

VELVET PLANT See *Gynura*
VENUS'S MAIDENHAIR FERN See *Adiantum*
VICTORIA ARALIA See *Polyscias*
VICTORIA FERN See *Pteris*
VITIS See *Cissus*

W

WANDERING JEW See *Tradescantia, Zebrina*
WATERMELON BEGONIA See *Peperomia*
WINTER CREEPER See *Euonymus*

Z

ZEBRINA

Z. pendula, also called *Cyanotis vittata*, *Tradescantia tricolor* and *T. zebrina* (wandering Jew)

This wandering Jew is a creeping plant with drooping stems and 3-inch-long, 1½-inch-wide leaves; the silvery white top surfaces have a broad green central stripe and narrow green edges; the undersides are purplish red. The two-colored wandering Jew, *Z. pendula discolor*, has a bronze-green central stripe with a purplish tinge. The four-colored wandering Jew, *Z. pendula quadricolor*, has leaves irregularly striped with shades of green, purple, red, pink and white; the edges and undersides are purplish red. All types are excellent in both pots and hanging baskets. They are similar to plants often called by the same name in the genus *Tradescantia* (page 145).

HOW TO GROW. Wandering Jews do best in bright indirect or curtain-filtered sunlight; if only artificial light is available provide at least 400 foot-candles. Night temperatures of 65° to 70° and day temperatures of 75° to 85° are ideal. Keep the soil barely moist at all times. Fertilize established plants every two months with any standard house-plant fertilizer diluted to half the minimum strength recommended on the label, but wait three to four months before fertilizing newly purchased or newly potted plants. Repot overcrowded plants at any season, using a mixture of 1 part loam, 1 part peat moss or leaf mold and 1 part sharp sand; to each gallon pailful of this mixture add 1½ teaspoons of 20 per cent superphosphate, 1 tablespoon of ground limestone and 2 teaspoons of 5-10-5 fertilizer. Or use a packaged general-purpose potting soil. Propagate plants at any season from stem cuttings.

VARIEGATED WANDERING JEW
Tradescantia fluminensis variegata

FOUR-COLORED WANDERING JEW
Zebrina pendula quadricolor

Appendix
Characteristics of 239 foliage house plants

Unless varietal names are given, the chart includes the characteristics of all of the recommended varieties of the species listed.

	SPECIAL TYPE OF PLANT					PLANT HEIGHT*			FOLIAGE COLOR			SPECIAL USES						LIGHT			NIGHT TEMP.		
Plant	Vine	Cactus	Succulent	Palm	Fern	Under 1 foot	1 to 2 feet	Over 2 feet	All green	White or yellow markings	Brightly colored	Hanging container	Terrarium	Dish garden	Stake or trellis	Floor container	Water-filled container	Bright	Medium	Dim	40° to 55°	55° to 65°	65° to 70°
ACALYPHA GODSEFFIANA (acalypha)							●		●							●		●				●	
ACALYPHA WILKESIANA (copperleaf)							●		●							●		●				●	
ACALYPHA WILKESIANA MACAFEANA (copperleaf)							●				●					●		●				●	
ACORUS GRAMINEUS PUSILLUS (dwarf Japanese sweet flag)						●			●								●		●			●	
ACORUS GRAMINEUS VARIEGATUS (white-striped Japanese sweet flag)						●				●				●			●		●			●	
ADIANTUM CAPILLUS-VENERIS (southern maidenhair fern)					●	●	●		●				●						●	●		●	
ADIANTUM RADDIANUM (delta maidenhair fern)					●	●	●		●				●						●	●		●	
ADIANTUM TENERUM 'FARLEYENSE' (Farleyense delicate maidenhair fern)					●		●		●				●						●	●		●	
ADIANTUM TENERUM WRIGHTII (fan maidenhair fern)					●		●		●				●						●	●		●	
ADROMISCHUS CLAVIFOLIUS (pretty pebbles)			●			●			●							●		●			●		
ADROMISCHUS COOPERII (Cooper's adromischus)			●			●					●					●		●			●		
ADROMISCHUS CRISTATUS (sea shells)			●			●			●							●		●			●		
ADROMISCHUS FESTIVUS (plover eggs)			●			●					●					●		●			●		
ADROMISCHUS MACULATUS (calico hearts)			●			●					●					●		●			●		
AGAVE FILIFERA (thread-bearing century plant)			●			●					●					●		●			●		
AGAVE PICTA (painted century plant)			●					●	●							●		●			●		
AGAVE VICTORIAE-REGINAE (Queen Victoria century plant)			●			●			●							●		●			●		
AGLAONEMA COMMUTATUM (Chinese evergreen)						●	●		●	●				●				●					●
AGLAONEMA COMMUTATUM 'WHITE RAJAH' (White Rajah Chinese evergreen)							●			●				●				●					●
AGLAONEMA COSTATUM (spotted Chinese evergreen)						●				●				●				●					●
AGLAONEMA CRISPUM (aglaonema)							●	●		●				●				●					●
AGLAONEMA MODESTUM (Chinese evergreen)							●	●	●				●	●				●					●
ALOE ARISTATA (lace aloe)			●			●			●							●		●			●		
ALOE BREVIFOLIA (short-leaved aloe)			●			●			●							●		●			●		
ALOE NOBILIS (gold-toothed aloe)			●			●			●							●		●			●		
ALOE VARIEGATA (tiger aloe)			●			●					●					●		●			●		
ALOE VERA (true aloe)			●				●		●							●		●			●		
APOROCACTUS FLAGELLIFORMIS (rattail cactus)		●					●	●				●						●				●	
ARAUCARIA HETEROPHYLLA (Norfolk Island pine)							●	●	●							●		●	●			●	
ASPARAGUS DENSIFLORUS SPRENGERII (Sprenger asparagus fern)					●		●		●		●							●	●			●	
ASPARAGUS MYERSII (foxtail asparagus fern)					●		●		●									●	●			●	
ASPARAGUS MYRIOCLADUS (many-branched asparagus fern)							●	●										●	●			●	
ASPARAGUS PLUMOSUS (asparagus fern)	●						●	●						●				●	●			●	
ASPARAGUS RETROFRACTUS (twisted asparagus fern)							●	●										●	●			●	
ASPIDISTRA ELATIOR (cast-iron plant)							●	●	●										●	●		●	
ASPLENIUM BULBIFERUM (mother fern)					●		●		●				●						●	●		●	
ASPLENIUM NIDUS (bird's-nest fern)					●		●		●				●						●	●		●	
ASPLENIUM VIVIPARUM (Mauritius mother fern)					●		●		●				●						●	●		●	
AUCUBA JAPONICA (Japanese aucuba)							●	●	●					●				●	●		●		
AUCUBA JAPONICA VARIEGATA (gold-dust tree)							●			●				●				●	●		●		
BEAUCARNEA RECURVATA (elephant-foot tree)							●	●						●		●		●					●
BEGONIA, BASKET (basket begonia)								●	●	●	●	●						●				●	
BEGONIA, RHIZOMATOUS (rhizamatous begonia)						●					●	●						●				●	
BEGONIA MASONIANA (Iron Cross begonia)						●					●	●						●	●			●	
BEGONIA 'MERRY CHRISTMAS' (Merry Christmas begonia)						●	●				●	●						●	●			●	
BEGONIA REX (rex begonia)						●	●			●	●	●						●	●			●	
BRASSAIA ACTINOPHYLLA (schefflera)							●	●							●	●		●					●
BUXUS MICROPHYLLA (little-leaf boxwood)						●	●		●							●		●			●		
BUXUS SEMPERVIRENS (common boxwood)						●	●	●	●							●		●			●		

* In the case of trailing plants, figures given apply to length of stems.

147

CHARACTERISTICS OF FOLIAGE
HOUSE PLANTS: CONTINUED

Column groups: SPECIAL TYPE OF PLANT (Vine–Fern) · PLANT HEIGHT* (Under 1 foot–Over 2 feet) · FOLIAGE COLOR (All green–Brightly colored) · SPECIAL USES (Hanging container–Water-filled container) · LIGHT (Bright–Dim) · NIGHT TEMP (40° to 55°–65° to 70°)

	Vine	Cactus	Succulent	Palm	Fern	Under 1 foot	1 to 2 feet	Over 2 feet	All green	White or yellow markings	Brightly colored	Hanging container	Terrarium	Dish garden	Stake or trellis	Floor container	Water-filled container	Bright	Medium	Dim	40° to 55°	55° to 65°	65° to 70°
BUXUS SEMPERVIRENS SUFFRUTICOSA (edging boxwood)						●	●		●							●		●			●		
CALADIUM HORTULANUM (fancy-leaved caladium)							●				●							●					●
CALATHEA MAKOYANA (peacock plant)							●			●	●							●					●
CALLISIA ELEGANS (striped inch plant)						●	●		●	●		●						●				●	
CARYOTA MITIS (tufted fishtail palm)				●			●	●	●							●		●					●
CEPHALOCEREUS CHRYSACANTHUS (golden old-man cactus)		●				●			●							●		●					●
CEPHALOCEREUS SENILIS (old-man cactus)		●				●			●							●		●					●
CEROPEGIA WOODII (rosary vine)	●		●			●				●		●						●					●
CHAMAEDOREA ELEGANS (parlor palm)				●		●	●		●				●	●					●				●
CHAMAEROPS HUMILIS (European fan palm)				●			●	●	●							●		●				●	
CHLOROPHYTUM COMOSUM (spider plant)							●		●			●						●					●
CHLOROPHYTUM COMOSUM VITTATUM (common spider plant)							●			●		●						●					●
CHRYSALIDOCARPUS LUTESCENS (butterfly palm)				●			●	●	●							●		●					●
CIBOTIUM CHAMISSOI (Hawaiian tree fern)					●			●	●							●	●	●					●
CIBOTIUM MENZIESII (Hawaiian tree fern)					●			●	●							●	●	●					●
CIBOTIUM SCHIEDEI (Mexican tree fern)					●			●	●							●		●					●
CISSUS ANTARCTICA (kangaroo ivy)	●						●		●						●			●				●	
CISSUS DISCOLOR (begonia treebine)	●						●				●				●			●					●
CISSUS RHOMBIFOLIA (grape ivy)	●						●		●						●			●				●	
CODIAEUM VARIEGATUM PICTUM (croton)							●				●			●		●		●					●
COLEUS BLUMEI (common coleus)							●				●					●	●	●					●
COLEUS REHNELTIANUS (Rehnelt coleus)							●				●					●	●	●					●
CORDYLINE TERMINALIS (Hawaiian ti)						●	●				●					●	●	●					●
CORDYLINE TERMINALIS BICOLOR (Hawaiian ti)						●	●				●					●	●	●					●
COSTUS MALORTIEANUS (stepladder plant)							●	●	●									●					●
COSTUS SANGUINEUS (spiral flag)							●		●									●					●
CRASSULA ARBORESCENS (silver dollar plant)			●				●	●	●							●		●				●	
CRASSULA ARGENTEA (jade plant)			●				●	●	●							●		●				●	
CYATHEA ARBOREA (tree fern)					●			●	●							●		●					●
CYCAS CIRCINNALIS (fern palm)								●	●									●					●
CYCAS REVOLUTA (sago palm)								●	●									●					●
CYPERUS ALTERNIFOLIUS (umbrella plant)							●	●	●							●	●	●					●
CYPERUS ALTERNIFOLIUS GRACILIS (slender umbrella plant)							●		●								●	●					●
CYPERUS DIFFUSUS (dwarf umbrella plant)						●			●								●	●					●
CYPERUS HASPAN VIVIPARUS (pygmy papyrus)							●		●								●	●					●
CYRTOMIUM FALCATUM (holly fern)					●		●		●											●	●		
DAVALLIA CANARIENSIS (deer's-foot fern)					●		●		●			●							●			●	
DAVALLIA FEJEENSIS (Fiji davallia)					●		●		●			●							●			●	
DAVALLIA MARIESII (ball fern)					●	●	●		●			●							●			●	
DAVALLIA TRICHOMANOIDES (squirrel's-foot fern)					●		●		●			●							●			●	
DIEFFENBACHIA AMOENA (charming dieffenbachia)							●	●		●						●		●					●
DIEFFENBACHIA BAUSEI (Bause dieffenbachia)							●	●		●						●		●					●
DIEFFENBACHIA EXOTICA (exotic dieffenbachia)							●	●		●						●		●					●
DIEFFENBACHIA PICTA 'RUDOLPH ROEHRS' (Rudolph Roehrs dieffenbachia)							●			●						●		●					●
DIZYGOTHECA ELEGANTISSIMA (false aralia)							●	●	●							●		●					●
DRACAENA DEREMENSIS (dracaena)							●	●	●							●		●					●
DRACAENA DRACO (dragon tree)								●	●							●		●					●
DRACAENA FRAGRANS MASSANGEANA (Massange's dracaena)								●		●						●		●					●
DRACAENA GODSEFFIANA (gold-dust dracaena)							●			●						●		●					●

In the case of trailing plants, figures given apply to length of stems.

Plant care reference chart.

Plant	Vine	Cactus	Succulent	Palm	Fern	Under 1 foot	1 to 2 feet	Over 2 feet	All green	White or yellow markings	Brightly colored	Hanging container	Terrarium	Dish garden	Stake or trellis	Floor container	Water-filled container	Bright	Medium	Dim	40° to 55°	55° to 65°	65° to 70°
	SPECIAL TYPE OF PLANT					PLANT HEIGHT*			FOLIAGE COLOR			SPECIAL USES						LIGHT			NIGHT TEMP.		
DRACAENA GODSEFFIANA 'FLORIDA BEAUTY' (Florida Beauty dracaena)							•			•				•				•					•
DRACAENA MARGINATA (red-margined dracaena)							•	•						•				•					•
DRACAENA SANDERIANA (Sander's dracaena)							•			•			•	•	•			•					•
ECHEVERIA DERENBERGII (painted lady)			•			•			•					•				•				•	
ECHEVERIA ELEGANS (Mexican snowball)			•			•			•					•				•				•	
ECHEVERIA PEACOCKII (peacock echeveria)			•			•				•				•				•				•	
ECHEVERIA PULVINATA (plush plant)			•			•			•					•				•				•	
ECHINOPSIS MULTIPLEX (pink Easter lily cactus)		•				•			•					•				•				•	
EUONYMUS FORTUNEI (winter creeper)						•			•			•	•					•				•	
EUONYMUS JAPONICUS (evergreen euonymus)						•	•		•									•				•	
EUONYMUS JAPONICUS ARGENTEO-VARIEGATUS (Silver Queen euonymus)							•			•								•				•	
EUPHORBIA LACTEA (milk-striped euphorbia)			•			•			•					•				•			•		
EUPHORBIA MAMMILLARIS (corncob euphorbia)			•			•			•					•				•			•		
EUPHORBIA MILII SPLENDENS (crown of thorns)			•				•	•						•				•			•		
EUPHORBIA OBESA (basketball euphorbia)			•			•			•				•	•				•			•		
FATSHEDERA LIZEI (tree ivy)	•					•		•	•				•		•			•				•	
FATSIA JAPONICA (Japanese fatsia)						•	•	•							•	•		•				•	
FICUS BENJAMINA (weeping fig)						•	•								•			•					•
FICUS DIVERSIFOLIA (mistletoe fig)						•	•		•									•					•
FICUS ELASTICA (India-rubber tree)						•	•								•			•					•
FICUS ELASTICA DECORA (broad-leaved India-rubber tree)						•	•								•			•					•
FICUS LYRATA (fiddle-leaved fig)						•	•								•			•					•
FICUS RETUSA NITIDA (Indian laurel)						•	•											•					•
FITTONIA ARGYRONEURA (silver-nerved fittonia)						•				•		•							•			•	
FITTONIA VERSCHAFFELTII (red-nerved fittonia)						•					•	•							•			•	
GASTERIA LILIPUTANA (Lilliput gasteria)			•			•			•									•	•			•	
GASTERIA MACULATA (spotted gasteria)			•			•			•									•	•			•	
GASTERIA VERRUCOSA (oxtongue gasteria)			•			•			•									•	•			•	
GEOGENANTHUS UNDATUS (seersucker plant)						•			•									•					•
GREVILLEA ROBUSTA (silk oak)						•	•								•	•		•				•	
GYMNOCALYCIUM MIHANOVICHII (plaid cactus)		•				•			•		•							•				•	
GYNURA AURANTIACA (Java velvet plant)					•					•	•	•						•					•
GYNURA SARMENTOSA (purple passion vine)					•					•	•	•						•					•
HAWORTHIA FASCIATA (zebra haworthia)			•			•			•									•	•			•	
HAWORTHIA MARGARITIFERA (pearly haworthia)			•			•			•									•	•			•	
HEDERA CANARIENSIS VARIEGATA (variegated Canary Island ivy)	•					•	•	•		•		•			•			•				•	
HEDERA HELIX (English ivy)	•					•	•	•	•	•	•	•		•	•			•				•	
HOWEIA BELMOREANA (sentry palm)				•			•	•							•	•		•			•		
HOWEIA FORSTERIANA (paradise palm)				•			•	•							•	•		•			•		
HYPOESTES PHYLLOSTACHYA (freckle face)					•	•				•								•					•
KALANCHOE DAIGREMONTIANA (Daigremont kalanchoe)			•			•	•			•								•				•	
KALANCHOE MARMORATA (penwiper plant)			•			•	•			•								•				•	
KALANCHOE TOMENTOSA (panda plant)			•			•	•	•	•									•				•	
LAURUS NOBILIS (laurel)							•	•							•	•		•			•		
LIGUSTRUM JAPONICUM (wax-leaved privet)						•	•	•	•					•	•	•		•			•		
LIVISTONA CHINENSIS (Chinese fan palm)				•			•	•							•		•	•			•		
LOBIVIA AUREA (golden Easter lily cactus)		•				•			•					•				•			•	•	•
LOBIVIA FAMATIMENSIS (orange cob cactus)		•				•				•				•				•			•	•	•
MAMMILLARIA BOCASANA (powder puff cactus)		•				•			•					•				•			•		•

149

CHARACTERISTICS OF FOLIAGE HOUSE PLANTS: CONTINUED

Column groups: **SPECIAL TYPE OF PLANT** (Vine, Cactus, Succulent, Palm, Fern); **PLANT HEIGHT*** (Under 1 foot, 1 to 2 feet, Over 2 feet); **FOLIAGE COLOR** (All green, White or yellow markings, Brightly colored); **SPECIAL USES** (Hanging container, Terrarium, Dish garden, Stake or trellis, Floor container, Water-filled container); **LIGHT** (Bright, Medium, Dim); **NIGHT TEMP** (40° to 55°, 55° to 65°, 65° to 70°)

Plant	Vine	Cactus	Succulent	Palm	Fern	Under 1 foot	1 to 2 feet	Over 2 feet	All green	White or yellow markings	Brightly colored	Hanging container	Terrarium	Dish garden	Stake or trellis	Floor container	Water-filled container	Bright	Medium	Dim	40° to 55°	55° to 65°	65° to 70°
MAMMILLARIA CAMPTOTRICHA (bird's-nest cactus)		●				●			●					●				●			●	●	
MAMMILLARIA CANDIDA (snowball pincushion)		●				●			●					●				●			●	●	
MAMMILLARIA ELONGATA (golden star cactus)		●				●			●					●				●			●	●	
MAMMILLARIA HAHNIANA (old lady cactus)		●				●			●					●				●			●	●	
MARANTA LEUCONEURA (prayer plant)						●					●								●				●
MARANTA LEUCONEURA MASSANGEANA (Massange's arrowroot)						●					●								●				●
MONSTERA DELICIOSA (monstera)	●						●	●							●			●					●
MYRTUS COMMUNIS MICROPHYLLA (dwarf myrtle)						●	●		●				●	●				●	●			●	
MYRTUS COMMUNIS MICROPHYLLA VARIEGATA (variegated dwarf myrtle)						●	●			●			●	●				●	●			●	
NEPHROLEPIS EXALTATA BOSTONIENSIS (Boston fern)					●	●	●		●			●						●	●			●	
NICODEMIA DIVERSIFOLIA (indoor oak)							●		●									●				●	
NOTOCACTUS APRICUS (sun cup)		●				●			●					●				●			●		
NOTOCACTUS LENINGHAUSII (golden ball cactus)		●				●			●					●				●			●	●	
NOTOCACTUS SCOPA (silver ball cactus)		●				●			●					●				●			●	●	
OLEA EUROPAEA (olive)							●	●							●			●				●	
OPUNTIA BASILARIS (beavertail cactus)		●				●					●							●					●
OPUNTIA GLOMERATA (paperspine cactus)		●				●			●									●					●
OPUNTIA MICRODASYS (bunny ears)		●				●			●									●					●
OSMANTHUS HETEROPHYLLUS (holly osmanthus)							●	●	●					●				●				●	
OSMANTHUS HETEROPHYLLUS VARIEGATUS (variegated holly osmanthus)							●	●		●				●				●				●	
PACHYPHYTUM BRACTEOSUM (silver bract)			●			●			●									●				●	
PACHYPHYTUM OVIFERUM (moonstones)			●			●			●									●				●	
PANDANUS VEITCHII (Veitch screw pine)							●	●		●						●		●					●
PEDILANTHUS TITHYMALOIDES VARIEGATUS (variegated devil's backbone)						●	●	●		●								●				●	●
PEPEROMIA CAPERATA (wrinkled-leaved peperomia)						●			●		●							●					●
PEPEROMIA CAPERATA 'EMERALD RIPPLE' (Emerald Ripple peperomia)						●												●					●
PEPEROMIA GRISEO-ARGENTEA (ivy peperomia)						●			●	●								●					●
PEPEROMIA OBTUSIFOLIA (blunt-leaved peperomia)						●			●									●					●
PEPEROMIA OBTUSIFOLIA VARIEGATA (variegated blunt-leaved peperomia)						●				●								●					●
PEPEROMIA SANDERSII (watermelon peperomia)						●				●								●					●
PHILODENDRON 'BURGUNDY' (Burgundy philodendron)	●					●	●	●			●				●			●					●
PHILODENDRON 'FLORIDA' (Florida philodendron)	●					●	●	●	●						●			●					●
PHILODENDRON HASTATUM (spearhead philodendron)	●					●	●	●	●						●			●					●
PHILODENDRON MICANS (velvet-leaved philodendron)	●					●	●	●	●						●			●					●
PHILODENDRON MIDUHOI 'SILVER SHEEN' (Silver Sheen philodendron)	●					●	●			●					●			●					●
PHILODENDRON OXYCARDIUM (heart-leaved philodendron)	●					●	●	●	●						●		●	●					●
PHILODENDRON PANDURAEFORME (fiddle-leaved philodendron)	●					●	●	●	●						●			●					●
PHILODENDRON RADIATUM (philodendron)	●					●	●		●						●			●					●
PHILODENDRON SELLOUM (saddle-leaved philodendron)							●	●											●				●
PHILODENDRON 'WEBER'S SELF-HEADING' (Weber's Self-Heading philodendron)							●	●											●				●
PHILODENDRON WENDLANDII (Wendland's philodendron)							●	●											●				●
PHOENIX ROEBELENII (miniature date palm)				●			●		●				●					●					●
PILEA CADIEREI (aluminum plant)						●				●								●					●
PILEA CRASSIFOLIA						●			●									●					●
PILEA INVOLUCRATA (panamiga)						●					●							●					●
PILEA PUBESCENS (silver panamiga)						●				●								●					●
PILEA REPENS (black-leaved panamiga)						●					●							●					●
PILEA 'SILVER TREE' (Silver Tree panamiga)						●				●								●					●
PIPER CROCATUM (saffron pepper)	●							●		●	●			●				●					●

* In the case of trailing plants, figures given apply to length of stems.

	SPECIAL TYPE OF PLANT					PLANT HEIGHT*			FOLIAGE COLOR			SPECIAL USES						LIGHT			NIGHT TEMP.		
	Vine	Cactus	Succulent	Palm	Fern	Under 1 foot	1 to 2 feet	Over 2 feet	All green	White or yellow markings	Brightly colored	Hanging container	Terrarium	Dish garden	Stake or trellis	Floor container	Water-filled container	Bright	Medium	Dim	40° to 55°	55° to 65°	65° to 70°
PIPER NIGRUM (black pepper)	●						●	●	●						●			●					●
PIPER ORNATUM (Celebes pepper)	●						●			●					●			●					●
PIPER PORPHYROPHYLLUM (porphyry-leaved pepper)	●						●			●	●				●			●					●
PITTOSPORUM TOBIRA (Japanese pittosporum)							●	●	●							●		●				●	
PLATYCERIUM BIFURCATUM (staghorn fern)					●		●	●	●			●		●				●				●	
PLECTRANTHUS AUSTRALIS (Swedish ivy)	●					●		●	●			●						●			●		
PLECTRANTHUS COLEOIDES MARGINATUS (white-edged Swedish ivy)	●					●			●			●						●			●		
PLECTRANTHUS OERTENDAHLII (candle plant)	●					●			●	●	●	●						●			●		
PLECTRANTHUS PURPURATUS (purple-leaved Swedish ivy)	●					●				●	●	●						●			●		
PLEOMELE ANGUSTIFOLIA HONORIAE (narrow-leaved pleomele)							●		●									●					●
PLEOMELE REFLEXA 'SONG OF INDIA' (Song of India pleomele)							●			●								●					●
PODOCARPUS MACROPHYLLUS MAKI (Chinese podocarpus)							●	●						●		●		●			●		
POLYPODIUM AUREUM (rabbit's-foot fern)					●		●	●	●		●							●			●		
POLYSCIAS BALFOURIANA (Balfour aralia)						●	●	●								●		●					●
POLYSCIAS BALFOURIANA MARGINATA (Balfour aralia)						●	●			●						●		●					●
POLYSCIAS GUILFOYLEI VICTORIAE (Victoria aralia)						●	●			●						●		●					●
POLYSTICHUM SETIFERUM (soft-shield fern)					●	●		●	●										●	●			
POLYSTICHUM TSUS-SIMENSE (Tsussima holly fern)					●	●	●		●				●						●	●			
PTERIS CRETICA (Cretan brake fern)					●	●	●		●	●			●						●	●			
PTERIS CRETICA CHILDSII (Child's Cretan brake fern)					●	●	●		●				●						●	●			
PTERIS ENSIFORMIS VICTORIAE (Victoria fern)					●	●	●			●			●						●	●			
PTERIS MULTIFIDA CRISTATA (crested spider brake fern)					●	●	●		●				●						●	●			
PTERIS TREMULA (trembling brake fern)					●	●		●	●						●				●	●			
RHAPIS EXCELSA (large lady palm)				●			●	●							●			●	●				
RHAPIS HUMILIS (slender lady palm)				●			●	●							●			●	●				
RHOEO SPATHACEA (Moses-in-the-cradle)						●				●								●		●			
RHOEO SPATHACEA VITTATA (variegated Moses-in-the-cradle)						●				●								●		●			
SANSEVIERIA TRIFASCIATA (sansevieria)						●		●		●							●	●	●	●			●
SCINDAPSUS AUREUS (devil's ivy)	●					●	●	●		●		●		●		●		●					●
SCINDAPSUS AUREUS 'MARBLE QUEEN' (Marble Queen devil's ivy)	●					●	●	●		●		●		●		●		●					●
SCINDAPSUS PICTUS ARGYRAEUS (silver pothos)	●					●	●	●		●		●		●				●					●
SEDUM MORGANIANUM (burro's tail)						●			●			●				●		●					
SENECIO MIKANIOIDES (parlor ivy)	●					●			●			●					●	●			●	●	
SETCREASEA PURPUREA (purple heart)						●				●	●					●		●				●	
SYNGONIUM ALBOLINEATUM (white-veined arrowhead vine)							●	●	●	●				●				●					●
TETRAPANAX PAPYRIFERUS (rice-paper plant)							●	●							●	●		●					
TOLMIEA MENZIESII (piggyback plant)						●			●									●		●			
TRADESCANTIA ALBIFLORA ALBO-VITTATA (giant white inch plant)						●	●	●		●		●						●		●			
TRADESCANTIA BLOSSFELDIANA VARIEGATA (Blossfeld's variegated inch plant)						●	●	●		●	●							●		●			
TRADESCANTIA FLUMINENSIS VARIEGATA (variegated wandering Jew)						●	●	●	●			●				●		●		●			
TRADESCANTIA SILLAMONTANA (white velvet wandering Jew)						●	●		●			●						●		●			
ZEBRINA PENDULA (wandering Jew)						●	●	●		●		●						●					●
ZEBRINA PENDULA QUADRICOLOR (four-colored wandering Jew)						●	●	●		●	●							●					●

First aid for ailing house plants

Promptness is the key to curing the various ailments that afflict house plants. If you recognize the symptoms shown below soon enough, most problems will be easy to correct. Even insects, such as those illustrated on page 154, are readily dealt with if you discover them be-fore they begin to multiply and spread out of control, attacking one plant after another.

To forestall trouble, set up a regular inspection schedule. The twice-a-month washing prescribed for plants provides a good opportunity to scrutinize them. Begin

SYMPTOM		CAUSE	WHAT TO DO
	Lower leaves of most afflicted plants turn yellow, and stems become soft and dark in color; cacti become mushy. Soil stays soggy and green scum forms on clay pots.	Too much water.	Make sure the pot's drainage hole is not clogged and do not let the plant stand in water in its saucer for over half an hour. If the soil has become compacted, roots may decay for lack of oxygen; repot the plant. Water only if necessary (check the encyclopedia for each plant's requirements).
	Leaf edges of most afflicted plants dry and curl under, or lower leaves turn yellow with brown spots and fall; cacti and succulents become yellowed.	Too little water or too much heat.	Water until the excess runs out of the drainage hole in the bottom of the pot; thereafter water as specified for the plant. If the condition persists, move the plant to a cooler location.
	Yellow or brown patches develop on the leaves of most afflicted plants, or leaves on one side of the plant turn brown; cacti become yellow.	Too much light; sunscorch.	Move the plant farther from the window so that it will not be subject to so much direct heat, or shield it with a curtain. If the plant is growing under incandescent lamps, move it farther from the bulbs or use lower-wattage bulbs that generate less heat.
	Stems of most afflicted plants stretch toward the light source and grow very long; leaves on new stems are pale-colored and small. On cacti, the new growth looks weak.	Too little light.	Move the plant closer to a window or to a brighter exposure to get more sunlight. If it is growing under artificial light, shift the plant nearer to the center of the bulbs, or increase the wattage or number of bulbs used and keep them on longer.
	Leaf edges turn brown, and eventually leaves die and fall off.	Too little humidity.	Place the pot on a bed of moist pebbles in a tray or in a larger container with moist peat moss around it or in an enclosed terrarium. Mist the leaves regularly. If the house is equipped with a hot-air furnace, install a humidifier in the system; otherwise use a room-type humidifier.

with the foliage, especially the light-colored new growth, which quickly shows signs of damage or weakness. Look as closely as you can: the brown spots that come from too low a humidity level or too much heat generally start out as very tiny specks. Remember to check the undersides of the leaves where insects are most likely to congregate. And do not overlook the condition of the soil and of the pot itself, for there you can find the discoloration, salty crusts or protruding roots that warn of overcrowding or faulty care.

	SYMPTOM	CAUSE	WHAT TO DO
	Leaf tips turn brown, especially on ferns; leaves or stems appear to be crushed or broken.	Bruising.	For appearance' sake, use scissors to cut off the damaged sections of foliage, keeping as much of each leaf or stem intact as possible. Move the plant to a more protected location where people are less likely to brush against it.
	New growth is rapid but weak and the plant wilts. A white crust of built-up salts develops on the surface of the soil or on the outside of clay pots.	Too much fertilizer.	Give plant more light. Fertilize less frequently or at half the suggested concentration. If salts have formed, water the plant thoroughly to dissolve them; then water again in half an hour to wash the dissolved salts through the pot's drainage hole. Scrape salts off the pot's rim and sides.
	Leaves fade to a pale green and lower leaves turn yellow and drop off. New leaves are small or growth stops.	Too little fertilizer.	Fertilize more often, especially during the plant's growing season.
	Leaves turn yellow and fall off suddenly; the plant tissues appear glassy and translucent.	Sudden rise or fall in temperature.	Move the plant away from drafts, air conditioners or radiators. When the damage is severe, remove the plant from the pot. If the roots have rotted, discard the plant; if the roots are healthy, prune them back to keep them in balance with the surviving top growth and repot the plant.
	Plant appears crowded; roots protrude from the drainage hole in the bottom of the pot or crop out on top of the soil. Plant wilts between waterings or produces only a few small leaves.	Plant is too big for its pot.	Repot the plant in a larger container as illustrated in the drawings on page 46; for repotting overcrowded cacti refer to the drawings on page 73.

Pests that afflict house plants

Insects are not as great a problem to plants indoors as they are outdoors, but they can be brought into the house on new plants. For this reason, keep new plants isolated for a week or two before adding them to a group, especially one in a terrarium. If insects appear on established plants, place the plants in quarantine to keep pests from spreading. Most insects can be washed off with soapy water or swabbed away with alcohol. Serious infestations require chemicals, but be careful to follow the directions on the labels.

PEST	DESCRIPTION	METHODS OF CONTROL
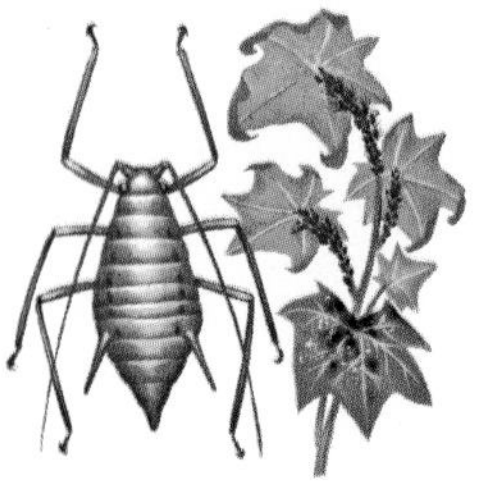	**APHIDS** These common plant lice are about ⅛ inch long and may be green, red, pink, yellow, brown or black. They congregate on soft young tips or the undersides of leaves. Aphids suck out a plant's juices, stunt new growth and cause foliage to pale, curl and die. They also secrete a shiny sticky substance, honeydew, that becomes a host to unattractive sooty black mold. SUSCEPTIBLE PLANTS: DIEFFENBACHIA, FATSHEDERA, FERNS, IVIES, PITTOSPORUM	Pick off and crush any visible aphids, then wash the plant—either dunk it upside down into warm soapy water or swab leaves and stems with a soft soapy cloth. Rinse the foliage with clear tepid water. For serious infestations apply rotenone or pyrethrum, or take the plant outdoors or to a well-ventilated area and spray with malathion. When the spray dries, rinse leaves with clear water.
	**WHITEFLIES** Adult whiteflies, shown here on a red-and-yellow coleus, are exceedingly tiny sucking insects that flutter off the leaves when a plant is disturbed. The eggs they lay on the undersides of leaves hatch into almost invisible transparent green larvae that feed on plant sap and do most of the damage. Green leaves turn yellow and drop. If whiteflies are left unchecked, they can kill the plant. Like aphids, they deposit honeydew. SUSCEPTIBLE PLANTS: BEGONIA, COLEUS, FERNS, PRIVET	For mild cases, wash the leaves with a strong spray of tepid water, making sure to cleanse the undersides thoroughly. Treat serious attacks with rotenone or pyrethrum, or take the plant outdoors or to a well-ventilated area and spray with malathion. Spray from a distance of about 18 inches, let dry, then rinse the leaves with clear tepid water.
	**TWO-SPOTTED SPIDER MITES** These microscopic pests are also called red spider mites, although some types are green. The first sign of attack may be yellow or brown speckles on the foliage. When they attack cacti the whole plant may become mottled and gray. Spider mites usually live under leaves, spinning fine white webs that may cover the plant. In time, the plants become stunted and die. SUSCEPTIBLE PLANTS: ASPARAGUS FERN, CACTI, FALSE ARALIA, IVIES, SCHEFFLERA	Wash small plants at the sink with a strong spray of tepid water to dislodge mites; large plants should be wiped with a soft soapy cloth, then rinsed with tepid clear water. For serious infestations, use difocol or tetradifon, or take the plant outdoors or to a well-ventilated area and spray with malathion. When the spray dries, rinse the leaves with clear water. If the mites persist, destroy the plant.
	**SCALES** Scales, which congregate on the undersides of leaves along the main veins, look like oval spots about ⅛ inch long, but their yellowish or greenish brown color makes them hard to see until the infestation is severe. At that stage the scales encrust stems and leaves like lumpy blisters, and plants may yellow and die. Scales also deposit honeydew, which attracts black mold. SUSCEPTIBLE PLANTS: ALOE, ARALIA, CROTON, DRACAENA, FERNS, INDIA-RUBBER TREE, IVIES, PALMS, PITTOSPORUM	Gently scrub the scales off the leaves, using warm soapy water and a small brush, then rinse the foliage with clear tepid water. Treat severely infested plants with rotenone or pyrethrum, or take the plant outdoors or to a well-ventilated area and spray with malathion. After the spray dries, rinse the foliage thoroughly with clear tepid water.
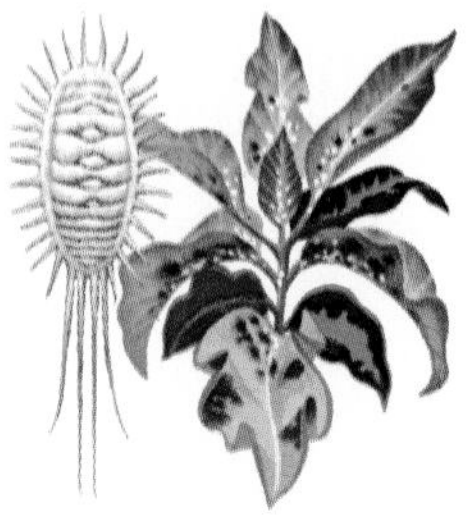	**MEALY BUGS** The soft ¼-inch-long bodies of mealy bugs, shown here on a multicolored croton, are coated with white powdery wax; they look like bits of cotton clustered under leaves and in crevices on the tops of leaves that are in shade. The long-tailed kind shown bears living young; short-tailed mealy bugs lay up to 600 eggs. By sucking sap, both kinds stunt and kill plants. SUSCEPTIBLE PLANTS: CACTI, CISSUS, COLEUS, CROTON, DRACAENA, FERNS, PALMS	Dab the mealy bugs with a cotton swab dipped in rubbing alcohol; they will die and fall off. Then wash the plant with warm soapy water and rinse it with clear water. Take severely infested plants outdoors or to a well-ventilated area and spray with a solution of ½ teaspoon malathion liquid concentrate and a few drops of liquid detergent in 1 quart of water; let the spray dry, then rinse the foliage thoroughly with clear tepid water.

Picture credits

The sources for the illustrations that appear in this book are listed below. Credits for pictures from left to right are separated by semicolons, from top to bottom by dashes. Cover —Richard Jeffery. 4—Keith Martin courtesy James Underwood Crockett. 6—Richard Jeffery. 11,12—Drawings by Vincent Lewis. 15 through 23—Ken Kay. 24—Richard Jeffery. 29 through 32—Richard Jeffery. 34,35—Drawings by Vincent Lewis, data courtesy of General Electric Large Lamp Division. 36,38,42,46—Drawings by Vincent Lewis. 49—Richard Jeffery. 50—Leonard Wolfe. 51—Drawings by Harry McNaught. 52,53—Leonard Wolfe; drawings by Harry McNaught. 54—Richard Jeffery. 55—Drawings by Harry McNaught. 56,57—Drawings by Harry McNaught; Richard Jeffery. 58—Richard Jeffery. 60,63,66,67—Drawings by Vincent Lewis. 70—Richard Jeffery. 73—Drawings by Vincent Lewis. 75 through 78—Richard Jeffery. 80 —Drawings by Vincent Lewis. 82 through 146—Illustrations by artists listed in alphabetical order: Roy Coombs, Leslie Greenwood, Mary Kellner, Harry McNaught, John Murphy, Norman Weaver, John Wilson. 152,153,154—Illustrations by Davis Meltzer.

Acknowledgments

For their help in the preparation of this book, the editors wish to thank the following: J. A. Buck, General Electric, Cleveland, Ohio; Verne H. Buck, John's, Inc., Apopka, Fla.; Richard Champion, Terrestris, New York City; Everett Conklin, Montvale, N.J.; Mrs. Edith Crockett, Librarian, The Horticultural Society of New York, New York City; Miss Marie Giasi, Librarian, Brooklyn Botanic Garden, Brooklyn, N.Y.; Barbara Haines, Abington, Pa.; Dr. Robert Helgesen, Assistant Professor of Entomology, Cornell University, Ithaca, N.Y.; Doyle Jones, Walt Disney World, Orlando, Fla.; Robert H. McColley, Bamboo Nurseries, Inc., Apopka, Fla.; Mrs. Joy Logee Martin, Logee's Greenhouses, Danielson, Conn.; Meadowbrook Farms Greenhouse, Meadowbrook, Pa.; J. L. Merkel, Alberts and Merkel Brothers, Inc., Boynton Beach, Fla.; John K. Michel, Duro-Test Corp., North Bergen, N.J.; The New York Botanical Garden Library, Bronx Park, N.Y.; George W. Park Seed Company, Inc., Greenwood, S.C.; Allen Poole, Apopka, Fla.; Jules V. Powell, U.S. Department of Agriculture, Washington, D.C.; Steve Raleigh, U.S. Department of Agriculture, Washington, D.C.; David Remnek, Farm and Garden Nursery, Inc., New York City; Cinda Siler, New York City; Cecil N. Smith, Department of Agricultural Economics, University of Florida, Gainesville, Fla.; Society of American Florists, Washington, D.C.; Robert C. Steinmetz, Wilton, Conn.; S. J. Thomas, Lord and Burnham, Irvington, N.Y.; Jo Ubogy, Greenwich, Conn.; Dorr Watkins, Jacob O'Hara and Company, Piscataway, N.J. Quote on page 8 is from *The Plant in My Window* by Ross Parmenter, © 1949 by Ross Parmenter, Apollo edition 1962, reprinted with permission of the publisher.

Bibliography

Bailey, L. H., *The Standard Cyclopedia of Horticulture*. The Macmillan Company, 1942.

Brooklyn Botanic Garden Handbook, *Handbook on Ferns*. Brooklyn Botanic Garden, 1969.

Brooklyn Botanic Garden Handbook, *Handbook on Succulent Plants*. Brooklyn Botanic Garden, 1963.

Brooklyn Botanic Garden Handbook, *House Plants*. Brooklyn Botanic Garden, 1965.

Chittenden, Fred J., *The Royal Horticultural Society Dictionary of Gardening*. Clarendon Press, 1956.

Crockett, James Underwood, *Foliage Plants for Indoor Gardening*. Doubleday and Company, Inc., 1967.

Cruso, Thalassa, *Making Things Grow*. Alfred A. Knopf, 1969.

Free, Montague, *Plant Pruning in Pictures*. Doubleday and Company, Inc., 1961.

Graf, Alfred Byrd, *Exotica 3*. Roehrs Company, 1970.

Graf, Alfred Byrd, *Exotica Plant Manual*. Roehrs Company, 1970.

Haage, Walther, *Cacti and Succulents*. E. P. Dutton and Company, Inc., 1963.

Kramer, Jack, *Hanging Gardens*. Charles Scribner's Sons, 1971.

Kramer, Jack, *Miniature Plants Indoors and Out*. Charles Scribner's Sons, 1971.

Kromdijk, G., *200 House Plants in Color*. Lutterworth Press, 1967.

Lamb, Edgar and Brian, *Pocket Encyclopedia of Cacti*. The Macmillan Company, 1969.

McDonald, Elvin, *The World Book of House Plants*. The World Publishing Company, 1963.

Noble, Mary and J. L. Merkel, *Plants Indoors*. D. Van Nostrand Company, Inc., 1954.

Perper, Hazel, *The Avocado Pit Grower's Indoor How-To Book*. Walker and Company, 1965.

Sunset Books, *How to Grow House Plants*. Lane Books, 1968.

Taylor, Norman, *Norman Taylor's Encyclopedia of Gardening*. Houghton Mifflin Company, 1961.

Westcott, Cynthia, *The Gardener's Bug Book*. Doubleday and Company, Inc., 1964.

Index

PRINTED IN U.S.A.